First Hundred Million

How To Sky rocket
Your book Sales
With Slam Dunk titles

E. Haldeman-Julius

Angelican Press
Vancouver

FIRST HUNDRED MILLION:
HOW TO SKY ROCKET YOUR BOOK SALES WITH SLAM DUNK TITLES
AN ANGELICAN PRESS BOOK:
978-0-9783883-7-9

PRINTING HISTORY
Angelican Press edition published 2008
1 3 5 7 9 10 8 6 4 2

TABLE OF CONTENTS

PREFACE

In November, 1927, in the course of a business trip to Chicago I met Emanuel Haldeman-Julius at the Palmer House. No sooner had we ordered our orange juice (at breakfast) or chicken gumbo soup (at dinner) than we began talking shop. In the publishing business this is inevitable. I have talked shop to book publishers, magazine and newspaper publishers, but have never heard anything quite as unusual – to me – as the stories Haldeman-Julius told of his career among the Little Blue Books.

From the mass-production, big-business point of view I was intensely interested to hear how it was possible to manufacture and market a book (even a little blue one) for five cents. From the advertiser's standpoint I was charmed with his candor in giving the exact figures of his results in advertising in the New York Times, Liberty and the Nation. I was as astonished with the results some of these publications produced as I was amused at the magazines refusing to run his advertising – a list that has now dwindled down to three.

But most interesting of all was the psychology of Haldeman-Julius's customers, the American people. In a country where The Saturday Evening Post has the greatest mass appeal, I was surprised to hear that sex seems to interest the public more than any other one subject. Secondly, the public wanted self help: how to order chicken à la King, how to learn Spanish, how to play the saxophone, how to spell correctly. I learned that in California books on the occult have a tremendous vogue, that love interest in literature is most profitable in the solid south.

Here, then, was a man who has sold a hundred million five cent books – not via wholesalers and retailers but direct to the American public. He has corresponded directly with his customers, manufactured their books, accepted their nickels, shipped them packages. He has heard their complaints and knows what they want and how they want it. It seemed to me that if any one man had conducted a laboratory of American intellectual taste, Haldeman-Julius was it.

At our fourth luncheon, therefore, I said to Haldeman-Julius: "Why not tell the story of these first hundred million?" He agreed to the suggestion, but wondered whether a story that would necessarily be extremely personal and commercial – in the sense that it would be the story of building up a business enterprise – might not be regarded as propaganda rather than a book on the anatomy of American taste such as I had in mind. To which I replied: "Tell the whole story anyway. Tell how you edit the books, change their titles to appeal to the public, manufacture them, ship them, advertise them, and even why you say: 'No more copies sold after Midnight May 31!'"

So here is the story. To me it is as enthralling an account as it was in Chicago. If it seems commercial, remember, reader, that his publishers asked him to tell the whole story, to omit no details. And to answer Mr. Haldeman-Julius's query about whether this book might be regarded as an ad for the Little Blue Books: if, after considering that this is a $2.50 book *advertising a five cent one*, the impression still exists that this book is an ad, then so be it, another phenomenon of public psychology!

R.L. S.
New York, June

CHAPTER I
WHAT AMERICA
WANTS TO READ

Why the Little Blue Books Tell a Vital Story

M Y nine years of publishing the series known throughout the world as the Little Blue Books would be, perhaps, interesting as a publishing achievement – but to a limited group, assuredly. It is, after all, more marvelous to manufacture a watch than it is to print a five-cent book; it is even more marvelous to make a fine watch than it is to print and bind an expensive book. It is not that I have produced books in mass quantities at a standardized low price that makes my Little Blue Books of vital significance. That is business, and mechanics, and salesmanship – but the world is full of more spectacular business, more complicated mechanics, and more dynamic salesmanship.

The business side of my Little Blue Book experience and the mechanical and selling side are interesting because the Little Blue Books are really of vital meaning. They tell a story that no other series of books, or no other books published anywhere, can tell. They tell what America wants to read.

There would be no reason for my telling the story of the Little Blue Books if it were not because of this realization of the idea that brought the series into existence. I thought that it might be possible to put books within the reach of everyone, rich or poor, though mostly poor and grading

1

up to those not as poor but by no means wealthy – books that they would want, and that they could choose for the sake of the books alone. By that I mean I dreamed of publishing books in such quantities I could sell them at a price that would put all books on the same level. No book would be chosen instead of another, that is to say, because of any difference in the price. And the price would be so low that no books besides mine would be chosen because of any lower price.

To be more explicit, the Little Blue Books, as they now exist, represent a democracy of literature. All Little Blue Books are born equal, and all have an equal chance to succeed and remain permanently in the series. No single Little Blue Book is given more advertising than any other book. Every endeavor is made to sell each Little Blue Book, if it is at all possible, to make its title attractive or to classify it where the title may catch the eye of a reader. There can never be any favoritism shown any Little Blue Book because of more attractive binding or more desirable size – all are uniformly bound, and all are exactly the same size (31/2 x 5 inches). One Little Blue Book fits as easily into the pocket as any other. The type in all is the same (eight point), with the exception of such special text as dictionaries.

No Little Blue Book can be said to have any special advantage, then. No Little Blue Book suffers any handicap peculiar to itself – unless it is the reading matter in it, which is what I am getting to in my statement that the Little Blue Books tell a vital and astonishingly important story about American readers and their tastes. To be sure, Little Blue Books do vary in length – from 32 up to 128 pages, with most of them running to 64 pages – but the number of pages is not given for any Little Blue Book in any advertisement or catalogue, so even this cannot prejudice any bargain buyer for or against any book in the list. This length is governed entirely by the nature of the text – one of Shakespeare's plays may require 128 pages, while a collection of Poe's tales may take only 64 pages.

My contention is that Little Blue Books are bought for one reason only, and this reason is what makes the story of the Little Blue Books a commentary on the psychology of American readers in general. The reason is that the book is wanted because the buyer wishes to read it. You may see nothing startling or revolutionary in this assertion, and you may even insist that all books are bought to be read. I cannot agree, however, to as sweeping a generalization as this last. All books are not bought to be read, though possibly most of them are. Some – and you will have to admit it – are bought because it is considered elite to own them, or because they match the parlor decoration scheme, or as gifts for friends or relatives, especially at Christmas. All publishers play heavily for Christmas business – when there is no satisfactory assurance that books bought for gifts ever will be read. No one buys Little Blue Books for Christmas gifts – or perhaps I had better say few do – because they are.

But people have no objection to buying five-cent books for themselves, since they want them for only one thing – to read. I can reasonably state that more than 99% of the Little Blue Books sold direct to the purchaser are sold to him because he wants to read them. There cannot be any fraction of error worth considering in my statistics of what American readers buy when they have a wide range of choice with no inducement except the titles and authors of the books.

But, some may object, is there not a thrill, or an inner sense of satisfaction, in being able to buy books at such a low price as five cents each? Perhaps, but this is in addition to the desire to read the books bought. Of course, it is an important part of Little Blue Book advertising to stress the five-cent price, and to indicate that a Little Blue Book is a fat nickel's worth – average 64 pages, 15,000 words of accurate, authentic text, and so on. It sounds compelling to say that you can have your pick of 1,260 different titles – any twenty books for a dollar, sent postpaid to any address in the world. But this serves to attract attention to the advertisement – to the books themselves. If the reader whose attention was attracted in this way found no titles listed that interested him – he would not buy any books, even at five cents apiece, simply to get a thrill or to satisfy an inner craving for taking advantage of a bargain offer.

People do not buy books because they are bargains – unless they have some hope that they will find time to read them. On the contrary, booklovers and collectors with spare funds often buy books because they are expensive – and not necessarily because they want to read them.

There is far less inducement for people to buy Little Blue Books to preserve them, in fact, than there is for them to buy them to read. In this respect Little Blue Books are like newspapers and magazines. A man does not mind losing or mislaying a Little Blue Book, because it is readily replaceable at almost no expense. Or I'll put the matter another way – since there is no need, and no special inducement, to be very careful of a Little Blue Book, the man who buys one reads it almost at once – before it is, indeed, mislaid or lost.

On January 1, 1928, which is the date on which the facts in this book are based, there were 1,260 different titles in the Little Blue Books – all offered, irrespective of their nature or length, at the same price. A purchaser's choice is limited only to twenty books, the minimum he must order at one time. He can order as many more than twenty as he may care to, all at the same price.

From 1,260 books anyone could select twenty or more that he would like to read. This series comprises probably the most representative literary assembly ever published at a standardized price in a uniform format. Not only works of literature, not only standard classics, not only the recognized forms of literary stock in trade such as biography, history, and the like – but the Bible and books against the Bible, books of self-education, love and passion, medical works – in short, something of everything. If there is any craving the American reader has for a particular kind of book, he is practically certain to find a way to express it in making his selection of Little Blue Books.

There is nothing that can compare with the Little Blue Books as a test of reading tastes and desires. I use *desires* deliberately in this discussion, because it is evident that some readers of certain Little Blue Book are not satisfied by them. Their purchase of them indicates a desire, a craving, even perhaps a need. Some of the Little Blue Books, probably most of them, will satisfy the desire that brings about their purchase. Some – such as Modern Aspects of Birth Control – cannot satisfy all of the desire, or the need, that makes the buyer order them. Obviously, the large sale of books with *birth control* in the title indicates both a desire and a need for *birth control information*, something that is not included in the title and that most certainly is not in the books, for it is, unfortunately, against the law to mail such information. I am of the opinion that this widespread interest in contraception – even in discussions of it pro and con, as the sales of the Debate on Birth Control indicate – will eventually bring about a revision of the law in this matter. For it is a healthy sign – and that the sign is expressed by orders for Little Blue Books shows once more the vital significance of this series as an epitome of public taste.

The Little Blue Books are a weathercock that shows which way the breezes of public taste are blowing; or they are a thermometer that registers the temperature of the American reader's blood – a virile and healthy temperature. I know. To a large extent the titles that are now in the Little Blue Book series are representative and indicative of American reading tastes – otherwise they would not be there; other titles would have replaced them ere this. If readers – as, for example, those of *Liberty*, as pointed out under "A Comparison of Advertising Mediums" (Chapter XVI) – express a decided interest in Passion, and buy all books listed under this classification almost regardless of title, that is not my fault. I publish both books that survey human passions artistically and present them in the world's best literature, and scientific books that discuss human passions calmly and sanely – because readers want them. I stop only at printing anything that misrepresents or falsifies human emotions – I do not tolerate *literature* that sensationalizes or sugar-coats passions for the sake of intoxicating gullible readers with inflamed imaginations. I do call passion by passion's name, and for that seeming offense I am sometimes accused of pandering to *low* desires. I scorn the accusation. If the world's best artists are wrong, then I am content to be wrong with them. But I stand by them – I believe they are nearer right than lesser men can be.

Whatever readers have expressed a desire for, I have given them – saving only what I consider trash. Perhaps there are readers who prefer such a palpably false and grossly exaggerated concoction as Three Weeks to a love story that is truly representative of human nature, such as one of the tales of Guy de Maupassant. Elinor Glyn, at any rate, has won a reputation as an authority on love.

But I hardly think that Madame Glyn or even Beatrice Fairfax, their popularity notwithstanding, can come so near telling the truth about love – not, indeed, what many people would like to believe about love, but what love is – as, for example, Montaigne, or Stendhal, or Balzac, or even Emerson.

It cannot be said that the Little Blue Books do not represent American reading tastes and desires on any supposed ground that they are filled with *propaganda*. Such accusations have been aimed at the free-thought books I have included in the series. People say I include such books because I am a hopelessly *lost* atheist, and that I want to make everyone else an atheist too. But I give my honest word that I would not publish such books if I could not sell them – as you will see by the statistics in Chapter VI, "Religion Versus Free-thought." More than this, if I publish a book called *The Truth About William Jennings Bryan*, I also publish Bryan's Prince of Peace, with critical modification or comment, in the same series and at the same price. People may have their choice; if they prefer skepticism and rationalism to sugary idealism or hypocritical superstition, I repeat that it is not my fault – though I am glad of it!

I have named only one example. It may be worth while to settle the question with two or three more. Take, then, Joseph McCabe's scathing arraignment of the Jesuits in his *The Jesuits: Religious Rogues*. Joseph Mc-Cabe is an apostate, I am reminded, and full of the rancor of rebellion. I disagree that this is a just objection to his work, but suppose the viewpoint is that of a man free of religious influence? I give you the chance to compare McCabe's view of Loyola, who founded the Jesuits, with the view of a religionist, Henry C. Vedder, whose book entitled *Loyola: Founder of the Jesuits* is available to all Little Blue Book readers – at the same price as McCabe's book, and on the same terms. One need only take his choice; the statistics tell the story of this choice in Chapter V. Take even the Bible – I have the *Essence of the Bible*, Little Blue Book editions of *Mark* and of *Luke*, even the *Sermon on the Mount*. Here are four religious books entirely free from criticism – you can buy them if you want them. If you object to Joseph McCabe's *Did Jesus Ever Live?* – why, my friend, you can instead Kenan's *Life of Jesus*, in the same form and at the same price.

It is the readers of America who make the final choice, not I. Though the Little Blue Books contained only 1,260 different titles on the first of January, 1928, the actual number of different titles that have at one time or other been in print far exceeds this. Nearly 2,000 different books have been offered in this pocket series to the American reading public during the past nine years. If nearly forty percent of these failed to find a sufficiently large audience, it is because people did not want to read them. The story of many of these failures is told in "The Morgue" (Chapter X). In fact, I have frequently not been content to let a book fail. I have done everything possible to make people want to read it – I have conducted a literary and editorial hospital expressly for the purpose of making the American public want to read something they showed no signs of wanting to read. The story of this is in "The Hospital" (Chapter VIII).

You might liken a Little Blue Book order form – one of those large forms with all the numbers printed, so buyers can circle the numbers of the books they want – to a voting sheet, a literary ballot. These ballots have been sent out from Girard by the million; thousands of them come back every week. On these ballots the people America indicate with painstaking exactness the books they want most from the large list offered them. The ballots also show that the readers take the trouble to examine the catalogues and lists from beginning to end. I have never issued a catalogue containing any book that did not sell some copies. There never was a Little Blue Book completely overlooked. Every candidate gets at least a few votes.

There is no possibility that these ballots have been falsified. If I had sent out an actual ballot, with lists of 1,000 different books, and had said: "Here is a list of 1,000 books. I am curious to know the books you'd like most to read if you had the time and could afford to buy them. I want this information to put in a book about the reading tastes of the American public. Please check off the titles that appeal to you – select from twenty to fifty out of the 1,000 – and mail the ballot back to me at once." If I had done this, and if readers of books had voted, as I asked them to, for the books they would like most to read, the results might be questioned. One could wonder, then, whether people – as they often do – voted for the Bible merely because it was expected of them, whether they avoided *sex* because they did not wish to seem too naughty, whether they showed a profound interest in philosophy in order to make America stand high scholastically, and so on. One could wonder, indeed, if the figures had been obtained in such a way.

But nothing of this kind was done. Instead of offering a voting list, I offered the books themselves. I offered them for sale. The people have had to examine the list with care, and they have had to pay for every vote they made. No man could vote for a book just because he wanted to appear righteous and pure and all that – unless he was willing to buy the book. He knew, furthermore, that if he bought it, it would be of no use to him if he did not want to read it. Still further, no buyer of Little Blue Books knew that he was voting – he had no idea whatever that he was contributing to a set of statistics and even if he had, it would probably have made no difference. There is a vast gulf between having statistics drawn from voluntary acts, and compiling the statistics by securing them as such. Every Little Blue Book buyer has been uninfluenced by anything except his wish to read. He has not bothered about selecting books for appearance's sake, but has picked them out to satisfy his own curiosity and his own peculiar craving.

That is why the statistics of the sales of Little Blue Books are vital; that is why the Little Blue Books tell a story that no other publisher's list can tell. These figures, with all the meaning that they hold, are the backbone of my story of the First Hundred Million. Without these figures there would be no Little Blue Books, and no story. But this analysis of the First Hundred Million shows some astonishing things about the American reading public – things that some people will want to shut their eyes to, perhaps, but facts that others will welcome gladly – and this analysis, which has cost me nine years of experimentation and constant endeavor, I am giving here freely and honestly, without evasion and without any concealment whatever. The actual figures that tell the story of what Americans want to read will follow in the next five chapters. First it was necessary for me to show why these figures tell such a story, why it is a story that strikes deep down into the roots of American character and why all of the hope for a future American culture depends upon it. The story gives me new zest – it is a story that is most encouraging to any progressively-minded person, and it is a story so optimistic in its general trend that I am convinced none of our literary and critical sages has ever suspected the unquestionable truth of its conclusions.

First Hundred Million

CHAPTER II
ARE AMERICANS AFRAID OF
SEX

How the Little Blue Books Answer This Important Question

I t is not new to ask the question that is the title of this chapter. We are told, on the one hand, by self-righteous guardians of the public morals, that sex is a fearsome – even a loathsome – thing. We are given to understand, if we are to believe what we are told, that sex is something to be afraid of, that it should be shrouded in obscurity and carefully rendered harmless by being kept locked in secrecy. We are told, on the other hand, by progressively-minded leaders, that sex needs more light thrown upon it, and that it is desirable for people not to be afraid to learn the truth about sex.

Are Americans afraid of sex? I have definite evidence that they are not afraid of it as a subject to read about in books, for the Little Blue Books contain authentic information on sexual hygiene, written by the best authorities, and they are sold far and wide in quantities ranging from 50,000 to 100,000 copies *per year*. This will hardly permit me to believe that American readers as a whole are afraid of the subject of sex.

In support of my contention that American readers are strongly interested in sex, I am going to give actual sales figures. But first I must explain what these figures represent, so that there will be a clear understanding as to their meaning. I know exactly how many copies of each of the 1,260 different Little Blue Books were sold during 1927, but I cannot use these figures, just as they are, for purposes of comparison. I cannot use them because some of these books were not on sale during all twelve months of 1927 – their sales figures, then, would perhaps be less than those for some of the books on sale throughout the year. Further, it would not be right to increase this figure by the right proportion to put it on a par with other figures, for the total would not indicate how the book compared with others when the entire list was advertised and how it may have been influenced by other similar titles placed in competition with it.

To be more specific, if I advertised a list of 100 selected books on sexual hygiene and pushed these 100 books ahead of all others, there would be a natural reason for these 100 titles to be excellent sellers. I could not contend, in such case, that the 100 sex books so advertised indicate a *preference* on the part of American readers. My data are of value only when I can show that *if given his choice* the average reader will pick out a book dealing with sex or love sooner than one on any other subject whatever. And my data become more significant than ever when I point out that the figures are based on an average choice of from twenty to twenty-five books selected by each person from an assortment of 1,260 different titles. If a person picks out only twenty books from over 1,000 possible choices, it is fairly safe to assume that he picks out the twenty books he wants most. That is what Little Blue Book readers have done. The figures given in this and the immediately following four chapters are based only on returns from advertising or catalogues listing the complete series of 1,260 Little Blue Books as they were on January 1, 1928. These figures are 1927 sales totals. They were obtained from an analysis of 1,156 orders aggregating 25,000 books. These orders were selected at random, averaging about thirty percent women and seventy percent men, and were presumably from readers of all ages, from the teens to the eighties, with the majority in the twenties and thirties. Of the 1,156 orders analyzed, slightly over half were from readers of newspapers – readers, probably, who are only infrequently readers of *books*. The other half was orders from the complete catalogue of Little Blue Books used during 1927.

For these reasons, the figures I give represent accurately what American readers want to read if they have the chance. To make the figures more expressive, as well as impressive, and to make it unnecessary for the reader of this book to perform mental calculations in order to understand their significance, the totals have been converted into the corresponding *annual* sales figures the distribution of the orders for 25,000 books would represent. By this I mean that book sales are usually thought of in terms of the number of copies sold annually. I base the success of a Little Blue Book on an annual sale of 10,000 copies or more. By converting these figures into round thousands per year, I make them more understandable, and make the comparison no less arithmetical, if more idealistic.

The following example may help you to understand exactly how it has been done. Mrs. Margaret Sanger's *What Every Girl Should Know* sold 83 copies in the 1,156 orders for 25,000 books. This is very good, but it might not appear so to the average person unless I convert this figure into something intelligible. I know, from careful investigation, that if I had increased the orders analyzed to twice the number, or aggregating 50,000 books, this book of Mrs. Sanger's would have sold approximately twice as many in orders for 50,000 books as it did in orders for 25,000, or about 165 copies. The percentage of error is extremely small and the percentage of variability is too slight to bother with, I have found. In orders for 100,000 books the number of copies of Mrs. Sanger's book would have been about four times as many, or 330. In orders for a million Little Blue Books, 3,300 copies of *What Every Girl Should Know* would be sold, if the orders were received from advertisements of the *complete* list, so that this book would maintain its ratio or relative popularity with regard to other titles advertised at the same time.

Since I sold 20,700,000 Little Blue Books during 1927, the annual figure for Mrs. Sanger's book, on the basis 83 copies in every 25,000 books sold, is 66,000 copies. This annual figure would have been the actual sales total for this book for 1927 if my advertising had been confined to complete lists only. But I frequently advertise selected lists of from 300 to 600 or 800 best sellers. That is why I am keeping these figures uniform by basing them on sales from the complete list only. Idealistically, the figures I give in this chapter and the four immediately following represent the annual popularity of these books when the readers are given their choice and pick freely from 1,260 different titles on a wide variety of subjects.

I have eight books of the *what you should know* class. By referring to sex information as what one should know, I am guilty of euphemism. I am well aware of this, but I recognize that there is still some embarrassment for many people when this subject touches them in any way. They are not to be blamed for it. If a young lady would rather buy *What Every Young Woman Should Know,* instead of a title like *Sex Facts for Girls,* I am content that she should. The facts are in the book, no matter what the title, and as long as the title indicates the nature of the book accurately, though it is a euphemism, it is all right. We can speak in riddles if the riddles are universally understood.

That these *what you should know* titles are thoroughly understood is shown by the sales of the books. Here are the eight titles with their annual figures:

Book Title	Copies Sold
What Married Women Should Know	112,000
What Married Men Should Know	97,500
What Every Young Man Should Know	95,000
What Every Young Woman Should Know	90,500
What Every Girl Should Know	66,000
What Every Boy Should Know	37,500
What Women Past Forty Should Know	34,000
What Expectant Mothers Should Know	25,000

This indicates, certainly, that there are over 100,000 potential readers, per year, of a book of authentic sex information available in the American public of today, for 112,000 readers were found for William J. Fielding's *What Married Women Should Know.* All of these were not women, however, and certainly not all of them were married women. That does not matter, however, though it seems to indicate that the usual purchaser of these books wants all the facts, and not only those that might be doled out to boys. The books, as a matter of record, contain almost the same information, if one is compared with another. The difference lies in their approach to the reader, based upon the supposed preference of the reader for information suited to him or her.

To express myself succinctly, I see no reason why a woman should wait until she is married to discover what a married woman should know about the facts of life. Apparently, the women who read the Little Blue Books agree with me, and the men, also. Similarly, there is ample justification for every healthy young man or woman to understand the facts that every expectant mother should know, long before the young man expects to be a father or the young woman looks forward to being a mother. This phase of sexual hygiene is not nearly as popular as the others, just because it is so particular or specialized, but many of those 25,500 books went to people who sought the information because of a healthy and justifiable wish to know.

So much for the euphemistic titles. Let us see what the more specific – what some people would call bolder – titles show:

Book Title	Copies Sold
Woman's Sexual Life	97,000
Man's Sexual Life	78,500
The physiology of Sex Life	65,500
The Common Sense of Sex	63,000
Freud on Sleep and Sexual Dreams	61,000
Homosexual Life	54,500
Womanhood: Facts of Life for Women	52,500
Manhood: Facts of Life for Men	52,000
Confidential Chats with Wives	47,000
Confidential Chats with Husbands	29,500
The Determination of Sex	27,500
The Child's Sexual Life	21,500

I think that the sales record for James Oppenheim's *Common Sense of Sex* (63,000) is clear evidence of the healthy attitude people are taking toward this subject. Surely no one would expect anything in a book of *common sense* except the facts! If it is sound information these people are after – and I am sure my figures indicate this – it is immensely encouraging. The outlook for future Americans, and for the much belied younger generation, looms considerably brighter in the light of these totals. The distribution of the list demonstrates beyond question a desire to have all the facts, and to understand the subject as a whole. American readers have reached the point where they are not interested in halfway measures. They want all the facts, and they will get them if they are put within their reach.

Havelock Ellis has done more than any other single investigator to purge the modern atmosphere of the fog and mist that once hovered over sex. He is generously represented in the Little Blue Books, and the popularity of his work is gratifying, both to him and to me. Here are the figures:

Book Title	Copies Sold
Plain Talks with the Married	60,500
The Love Rights of Women	39,000
Four Essays on Sex	31,000
Eugenics Explained	29,500
Ellis and His Plea for Sane Sex Living	29,500
Woman and the New Race	16,000

The interest in eugenics is surprising, and encouraging. Half of these readers, remember, are the sometimes despised readers of daily newspapers. Yet they show a strong desire to find out about eugenics. This America of ours is not nearly as hopeless as some pessimists would have us believe.

Modern discussions of sexual problems are incomplete without the arguments for and against birth control. It is illegal to publish or distribute contraceptive information, so, generally speaking, the popularity of books that discuss birth control indicates not only a desire for the information, could it be obtained, but also a desire to know the why and wherefore, to know why birth control is or is not desirable. Here are the figures that tell the story:

Book Title	Copies Sold
Modern Aspects of Birth Control	73,000
Debate on Birth Control	27,000

There is three times as much interest in a practical, unbiased discussion of the subject as there is in a debate on its morality. And yet the interest in a dispassionate debate is really amazing. It shows, at least, that there is a strong leaning toward threshing out the truth through open discussion pro and con.

The next phase of the question to be considered is the class of books that do not have the word *sex* in their titles, but which have to do with love. The word *love* may or may not be in the title, but the title implies that the book contains information about the subject. We are still in the realm of facts, remember; the books of fiction and poetry, which deal with sex and love in an imaginative way, are to be considered later.

Here are some of the more general titles that belong under the *love* classification, with their annual figures:

Book Title	Copies Sold
The Art of Kissing	60,500
How to Love	52,500
Psychology of Love and Hate	52,000
What Is Love? (Montaigne)	28,500
Hindu Book of Love (Kama Sutra)	28,000
Psychology of the Affections	22,500
The Art of Courtship	17,500

It is to be observed that, with the exception of the last title listed above, the figures are still quite large, and compare favorably with the books in which the word *sex* is dominant in the titles. As long as the subject keeps to broad and universal lines, which is to say as long as it has wide appeal, it is in demand. Though it does seem that fewer people are interested in intelligent courtship than one would expect; possibly the lower figure for this book is due to the fact that *courtship* is a word belonging largely to a bygone day, and it may suggest old-fashioned Victorian ideas. It might be a good idea to change that title to "*How to Choose a Mate.*"

For purposes of comparison, and for the sake of making this discussion of sex books as complete and revealing as possible, I want to put in here the figures for the more specialized sex books. These are along more particular or more abstract lines than those already listed. These are figures:

Book Title	Copies Sold
Catholicism and Sex	65,000
Sex Crimes and American Law	39,000
Facts about Sex Rejuvenation	37,500
Phallic (Sex) Elements in Religion	36,000
Sex Obsessions of Saints and Mystics	35,000
Modern Sex Morality	34,500
America and the Sex Impulse	28,000
The Evolution of Sex	25,000
Sex Symbolism	24,000
Sex in Psycho-Analysis	21,500
Genetics for Beginners	21,000

There is clear evidence of a desire to survey the subject from all angles. But it is noticeable that the figures are becoming more uniform; the only sensational seller in this group is *Catholicism and Sex*, and that is undoubtedly because of the linking of Catholicism and sex. It becomes more and more evident that it will be difficult to find a poor seller if the book tells anything about love or sex. Yet must point out that these books are thoroughly reliable, and state the facts as facts. There is no fringe of sensationalism in the books, and the readers know it. All of these books were not sold to one reader at one time; he bought some, read them, and came back for more. Readers like publishers to print facts, without glamour and also without evasion.

For a moment, now, I want to turn to the historical aspect of sex. I refer particularly to the series of Little Blue Books giving the history of prostitution. This subject is frequently avoided by the avowedly moral, because they seem to think that to mention it will increase its existence. But I am convinced that the subject, important as it unquestionably is, deserves as honest treatment as any other phase of the human or social scheme. It is a social problem, and has been for centuries, and it needs elucidation and discussion as much as religion, or prohibition, or capitalism. These figures tell their own story:

Book Title	Copies Sold
Prostitution in the Modern World	129,500
Prostitution in the Ancient World	84,500
Prostitution in the Medieval World	73,000
Sex Life in Greece and Rome	56,000
Mistresses of Today	52,000
Women Who Have Lived for Love	24,000
The Evolution of Marriage	20,000

It is not surprising that more interest is shown in ancient times and in modern times than in medieval days. I am a little amused, because I think the interest in antiquity is due to the fact that people fancy the ancients were very wicked – much wickeder, indeed, than humanity ever was before or has been since. It will do them no harm, these readers of Little Blue Books, to find out the truth of the matter. As Joseph McCabe relates, he was one asked to write a book called *The Empresses of Rome*, and the publisher was much disappointed to find that it contained so little real wickedness and such a small amount of flagrant immorality. The book discussing prostitution, from the modern standpoint, is one of the most popular titles in the list. It has some close competitors, so it is not quite permissible to say that it is *the* best.

What about marriage? Marriage is the social sanction the law gives to the existence of sex in human affairs. It is interesting to see how the people of America buy books that discuss the various aspects of marriage. The figures are significant:

Book Title	Copies Sold
Why I Believe in Companionate Marriage. (Marcet Haldeman-Julius)	64,000
Judge Ben B. Lindsey on Companionate Marriage	60,500
Beginning Married Life Right	52,000
Marriage and Morals in Soviet Russia (Anna Louise Strong)	36,000
How to Be Happy Though Married	35,000
How to Avoid Marital Discords	27,000
U. S. Marriage and Divorce Laws	18,500
Marriage vs. Divorce (Debate)	9,000

The emphasis is decidedly on finding out how to improve existing conditions. The interest in divorce as opposed to marriage is very slight. Note the strong desire to find out how to better the *status quo*, however, as shown by the wish to avoid marital discords and the desire to be happy even if married. There is no sound evidence that these people wish to abandon marriage or have any inclination to seek divorce. They want to find out how to make marriage a more livable institution, if I may put it that way. The powerful attraction of the subject of companionate marriage bears this out. It is not a wish to enter a loose and uncertain relationship, but a sincere urge to discover, if possible, ways to support and bolster up the existing institution by making it more conducive to happiness than it now is. A large number of people, indeed a gratifying number, want to know the laws; not, I am sure, so they may circumvent them, but so they may understand them and learn how they may make towards general happiness and goodwill.

So far the question has been considered from a mutual point of view – men and women being the principals in the drama of love and sex. Tradition has always emphasized, however, that woman is the main attraction in matters of the heart, and, as I have already said, men are by about three-fourths the greater buyers of Little Blue Books. The titles that have to do with women, then, ought to be good sellers, approaching the figures for the books on sex and love in general. We shall soon see.

First, I want to mention that old stage property the novelists of an older day always had ready and waiting for suitable scenes – the mystery that used to be a woman. This *mystery* has been stereotyped and filed away for reference long enough. The men of the world – of America, anyhow – want to unveil the mystery of woman. Certainly they are strongly interested in finding out all they can learn about her, and they seem to believe that facts are available and worth investigating. Again this shows not an idle curiosity, but a wish to know the facts of human psychology – of feminine psychology because it so strongly influences the happiness of the male – in order the better to understand and appreciate life as it is. I continually stress this point, because I believe and shall always contend that a universal interest in sex is natural, and far more healthy than morbid. I cannot accept for a moment the notion that anyone who wants to find out about sex and love, as they really are, is anything but normal.

Women are well represented among the Little Blue Books. Here are some of the more popular titles, with their annual totals:

Book Title	Copies Sold
How to Know Women (Maeterlinck)	49,000
Mental Differences Between Men and Women (Leo Markun)	36,000
The Degradation of Woman (Joseph McCabe)	27,000
Woman, the Eternal Primitive (William J. Fielding)	20,000
The Subjection of Women (John Stuart Mill)	18,500
Great Women of Antiquity (Clement Wood)	13,500

Go back a few paragraphs and compare the figures of *Women Who Have Lived for Love* and *Mistresses of Today*, also, with the discussion of Havelock Ellis, the figures for *Love Rights of Women* and *Women and the New Race*. There is a wide fluctuation in the figures, partly because the subjects, though all concerning women, are of a widely varying nature. There is an anxiety, still, about the mental differences between men and women, and there is beyond a doubt a strong desire to know women as they are. The interest is at its lowest ebb, you will notice, when particular women of antiquity, are discussed. The preference is for the general, the quest being for a key to human psychology as a whole. This hardly supports the old idea that no two women are like.

There is, too, an influential trend toward health and hygiene in matters of sex. American readers assuredly are not flinching before the pathological phases of the subject. They want to know the facts about sexual disorders, even though those facts may be unpleasant. The older custom of blinding one's self to the evils of the world is passing away. The newer attitude is to find out the truth and face it. Note these figures:

Book Title	Copies Sold
Facts About Venereal Diseases	41,500
Facts About Syphilis	36,000

These books were written by physicians who have the endorsement of the American Medical Association. As a matter of fact, Dr. William Allen Pusey, who wrote the book on syphilis, is recognized as a national authority on the disease. These are facts. There is no mincing of words here. Some editors would contend, however, that the public is not interested in disease – they would call it morbid, pessimistic, and all that. I know they would and readers of this book know they would. But here is evidence that cannot be disputed. American readers do not evade these facts because they are not pretty. They would, I am sure, resent any attempt to make the facts any less unpleasant than they are. They much prefer to know the whole truth.

The interest in sexual hygiene is further evidence of a strong desire to get more happiness out of life. There is an earnest endeavor to avoid disease and pain. Look back and notice, too, the interest in *Facts About Sex Rejuvenation*, a book in which Dr. Morris Fishbein has no hesitancy in branding charlatanism for what it is and in which no false lure is held out where there are no facts to support a method or a treatment that claims to prolong youth. Even *Genetics for Beginners* is much in demand, supporting my general assertion that readers are interested in the betterment of conditions, whatever may help them to bring it about.

So much for the phases of sex and love discussed as matters of fact. As we turn more to the imaginative treatment of love as an emotion and sex as a passion, perhaps the interval may be bridged by glancing for a moment at books of love letters that represent man's endeavor always to win the love of the woman he has chosen for his attentions. Here again, the perpetual quest for happiness shows itself. Always and forever, it is a growing enthusiasm for finding out how to win love – how to realize felicity, fleeting though it may be. These figures are full of meaning:

Book Title	Copies Sold
Love Letters of a Portuguese Nun	46,000
How to Write Love Letters	23,000
Love Letters of a Parisian Actress (Sarah Bernhardt)	21,500
Love Letters of People of Genius	12,000
Love Letters of Abelard and Heloise	10,000

The interest in Abelard and Heloise is slight, I fancy, because people do not know who they were. Mere names mean little to the great mass of readers. They respond to subjects far more than to personalities behind the subject every time.

There are books, too, of comment on love – books of epigrams and maxims, and sententious remarks of one kind or other. These have their place, and they compel an interest because they deal with love:

Book Title	Copies Sold
Jokes About Married Life	45,000
What Men Have Learned About Women	36,000
Best Jokes About Lovers	35,000
Jokes About Kissing	33,000
What French Women Have Learned About Love	29,000
What Women Have Learned About Men	21,500
Love Code of a Parisian Actress (Bernhardt)	17,500

Book Title	Copies Sold
Love from Many Angles	15,000
Maxims of Love (Stendhal)	10,000

Astonishing though it is, in some ways, the popularity of jokes about love, and especially about married life, is a good sign. A sense of humor will save many a serious situation from disaster. Then, too, the desire to laugh at ourselves is healthy – it will keep us sane, and at the same time promote the sum total of human happiness.

Before passing to the great love stories of the world's literature, I want to submit the totals for the books giving biographies of famous lovers:

Book Title	Copies Sold
Secret Memoirs of a French Royal Mistress (Pompadour)	37,500
Cleopatra and Her Loves	35,000
Casanova: History's Greatest Lover	31,000
Pope Alexander VI and His Loves	25,500
Madame du Barry: A King's Mistress	25,000
Love-Life of a Frenchwoman (George Sand)	22,500
Catherine the Great and Her Lovers	20,000
Wagner's Great Love Affair	18,500
Cellini: Swordsman, Lover, etc	18,000
Eleonora Duse and D'Annunzio	17,000
Lord Nelson and Lady Hamilton	16,000
Shelley and His Loves	16,000
Lord Byron and His Loves	15,500
Aucassin and Nicolette, Lovers	13,000
Romance That Balzac Lived	10,500

The interest varies in direct proportion to the degree of notoriety, as is, after all, only natural. Though the superficial impulse is to read something racy – which is a sublimation of a wish to live fully – the result of reading about the world's great lovers must indirectly contribute to human welfare and contentment. It is conceivable that people subconsciously recognize that great loves resulted either in tragedy or a limited and transient bliss. They yearn to find out how it all happened. It is the same sort of lesson that Shakespeare gives in *Romeo and Juliet*, where he shows us the tragedy of two young people who loved not wisely but too well.

Great love stories have an appeal from which nothing – no scruples of morality – can detract. I make no apology for including in the Little Blue Books the greatest stories by the masters of fiction whose work will stand the test of time. I would not mention even the word *apology* here, if it were not for the fact that people still, in some degree, feel somewhat secretive and whisper in hushed tones about the wicked French stories and the *daring tales of that Italian writer, Boccaccio*, and so on. I cannot regard these masterpieces of the world's literature otherwise than as true pictures of life as these geniuses saw it. As such, they are incomparable. They deserve wide popularity, and these Little Blue Book figures show that they are getting it:

Book Title	Copies Sold
Illicit Love, and so forth (Boccaccio)	81,500
One of Cleopatra's Nights (Cautier)	60,000
Tales from Boccaccio's Decameron	57,000
26 Men and a Girl (Gorki)	57,000
A French Prostitute's Sacrifice (Maupassant)	56,000
French Tales of Passion and Cruelty	56,000
Tales of Love and Life (Boccaccio)	47,000
Amorous Tales of the Monks	45,000
Quest for a Blonde Mistress (Gautier)	44,000
A Bath, and so forth (Zola)	42,500
Lustful King Enjoys Himself (Hugo)	42,000
Passion Stories of Many Hues (Gourmont)	41,500
None Beneath the King Shall Enjoy This Woman (Zorrilla)	38,000
Forbidden Love (Barry Pain)	34,500
Queer Night in Paris (Maupassant)	34,500

Book Title	Copies Sold
A Wife's Confession (Maupassant)	34,000
Mme. Tellier's Establishment (Maupassant)	33,500
Night in Whitechapel (Maupassant)	33,500
Night Flirtation (Chekhov)	33,000
Love's Redemption (Tolstoy)	32,000
Love and Other Tales (Maupassant)	29,000
Mlle. Fifi, etc. (Maupassant)	25,500
A Study of a Woman (Balzac)	25,000
Artist's Wife, etc. (Maupassant)	25,000
The Falcon, etc. (Boccaccio)	17,500
Romeo and Juliet (Shakespeare)	14,500
Hedda Gabler (Ibsen)	12,000

The general conclusions to be drawn from this rather abbreviated list are that the tales of Guy de Maupassant are consistently popular; those of Emile Zola are about on a par, the one listed being the best of the Little Blue Books of Zola's work; Honoré de Balzac is less popular than other French writers, though his books all sell well, The sale of Shakespeare's *Romeo and Juliet*, and the popularity of Ibsen's *Hedda Gabler*, are both gratifying; they do not come up to the others, but they are quite popular nevertheless. All of Boccaccio sells well. *The Falcon and Other Tales* being carried along on the crest of the popularity of the more sensational titles. Allow me to insist once more, right here, that the titles may sound sensational, but the text is the best that the world's literature affords. I do not consider the titles misleading, either. I hasten to defend the labeling of a story by what is really its right name. In Chapter VII, "Rejuvenating the Classics," I discuss titles more at length, but here I find it necessary to repeat that these books are of the very best work the greatest writers have been able to do.

What of poetry? Poetry in general is difficult to sell to American readers. This is one literary commodity that comes pretty close to being a drug on the market. But those books of poems that deal with love and passion are fairly good sellers. American readers want their poetry, as well as their other reading, to have the full pulse of life:

Book Title	Copies Sold
The Harlot's House and Other Poems (Wilde)	41,000
A Nun's Desire and Other Poems (John Davidson)	14,500
Passionate Poems (Swinburne)	14,500
The Vampire and Other Poems (Kipling)	14,000
Love Poems of John Keats	12,000
Courtship of Miles Standish (Longfellow)	9,000

When it is remembered that these books were bought in these proportionate quantities when they were advertised, each in competition with 1,259 other books, the showing is not a bad one at all. Of general anthologies, the poems of Walt Whitman, Robert Burns, and Edgar Allan Poe are the only ones that approach the best of these in popularity. Kipling's *Mandalay* and *Gunga Din*, being so famous, are the only poems that surpass them.

American readers, it seems, are not afraid of sex. They recognize it as a fact, and they want to know more facts about it. The Little Blue Books have been a medium to impart facts – I have had numerous letters from readers who tell me that one of their greatest debts will always be to the books of sexual information they selected from the series of Little Blue Books – for it is information that can be depended upon as authentic, and thoroughly matter of fact in its intimate accord with life.

A Note on Censorship

There is one thing that the *sex titles* in the Little Blue Book series have always done – they have inspired censorship and taboo in the advertising offices of some of the country's leading periodicals. All Little Blue Books, it must be remembered, are entirely within the United States Postal Laws. They have to be – otherwise they could not be printed and sold. Entirely aside from whether these laws and regulations are just, the Little Blue Books conform to them. I can send them through the mails to anyone who cares to buy them – if I can reach that purchaser with a list of what I have to sell. But some censorship boards, advising the advertising departments of periodicals like *Collier's*, the *N. Y. Times Book Review*, *Popular Science*, and so forth, do not wish me to tell their readers — not, at least through their columns — that I have certain *sex books* for sale.

Censorship would be less irksome if it were consistent — or, indeed, if it were logical and sensible. But one righteous censorship board will ban a certain half dozen or so Little Blue Books; another board, supposed to be looking at the thing from the same angle and supposed to be working toward the same general end, will censor a totally different dozen titles. Where is there logic or consistency in this?

A censorship board is not even consistent or fair with itself. It sees bug-bears where there are none, and, in the hope of avoiding offense to the magazine's readers, it lets what someone else might regard as far more sensational-appearing titles slip by. Take, for example, Mr. Fielding's *What Every Boy Should Know*, *What Every Young Woman Should Know*, and so forth. These titles are euphemisms in themselves; they avoid the direct ut-terance and the bold phrase. Yet they are censored by one magazine. Why? Is it because they convey information that cannot do anything except aid morality? Is it because they combat nothing except ignorance? This same magazine, however, has no objection to *Confidential Chats With Wives* and *Confidential Chats with Husbands*, which are near-euphemisms of a similar kind. This is inconsistency beyond my understanding. This same maga-zine, further, lists quite complacently all the books with prostitution in the titles. Now why is *What Every Boy, Girl, Young Woman, etc., Should Know* more objectionable than *Prostitution in the Modern World*?

Please understand that I am not pleading the cause of the censors. I do not want those censors to read this note of mine and decide they have been lax and blue-pencil a score more or so of my Little Blue Books from my next advertisement. I do not want that to happen at all. But I do think censorship would be more intelligible if it were consistent. If the censors said, "All sex must be banned" — but they don't say any such thing. They hem and haw, and equivocate, and justify, and hesitate. They want to cen-sor, and yet — they don't do it.

Censorship is always that way. It is subject to the fallibility of the human beings that sit on the boards. I put forth as my guess that censorship of this kind often comes about because some reader – perhaps only one, out of many thousand – writes to the editor protesting against a certain book or against a group of five or six books that have aroused his antagonism and his pious indignation. Without any regard for the rights of thousands of other readers, the censors listen to the lone voice in the wilderness and thenceforth see to it that this one reader, magnified out of all proportion to his real importance, shall no more be offended.

First Hundred Million

CHAPTER III

THE QUEST FOR

SELF-IMPROVEMENT

The Great Demand for Little Blue Books of Self-Education

I
t is not hard to understand why many people object to the so-called *sex-titles* in the Little Blue books, and why they will deplore the great interest that American readers show in such titles. I do not agree with this attitude, but I understand it. I contend that the interest in sex is but one aspect of a widespread desire to find happiness. It is but another phase of that eternal pursuit of elusive happiness that the fathers of the United States regarded as an inalienable right. I heartily agree that it is an inalienable and thoroughly natural right, and I am glad that the Little Blue Books can help in any way whatever. But the fact remains that many people will not look at the matter in this way. They will always hold that it is an unfortunate circumstance, and many of them would even go as far as to prohibit providing such reading if they could.

If the interest in Little Blue Books of sex and love was so paramount as to eclipse everything else, there might be some doubt as to my contention that it is part of a quest for self-improvement, though that self-betterment is along emotional rather than what might be called practical lines. But that the interest in books of love and passion is not exclusive of numerous other interests is what I shall now demonstrate. In fact, placing book against book, there are a number of titles entirely free from any love appeal that are more popular than sex books. Taken as a class, and as might be expected, the popularity of books about love is greater than the popularity of any other single class. But this is not new; it is a fact that is self-evident among other books, in the daily press, on the stage, in the movies, and in everyday activities.

What is probably not as apparent, and what many of my readers may not know and will be surprised to learn, is that the quest for self-improvement along strictly educational and even academic lines is an outstanding aspect of Little Blue Book sales figures. The Little Blue Books prove that the desire for self-improvement on the part of American readers is not an idle dream. They prove that this desire is more than a wish to appear better than people perhaps really are; they demonstrate beyond any doubt that this desire is sincere, and that it is almost universal.

If a person goes to college and secures an academic degree there may be varying impulses behind this apparent wish for education. A degree is in some measure a fetish. A degree is sometimes thought of as an *Open Sesame*; it is wanted because merely by having it a man or woman may think that it will get him ahead in the world. College enrollments are no criterion of any desire for education for its own sake. Students in night schools are studying in the hope of making commercial progress, it is true, but these are not as numerous as is sometimes supposed. Again, the night schools themselves, and often those who employ the students, emphasize constantly the benefits to be derived from such education. These students do not show any spontaneous desire for education until they are urged into it.

Even the national correspondence schools, which widely advertise the increased salaries and greater social prestige that can be secured if one studies by mail, cannot claim that their enrollments prove a sincere American desire for self-education. It is a fact that only a small percentage of the people who enroll for such courses complete them. In some cases this may be because the expense is prohibitive; in others, it is because the students lose interest rapidly and possibly because the courses are not of a character to create and maintain interest in education as a fascinating adventure. There is still a schoolroom atmosphere – a tinge of compulsion – about taking lessons by mail.

But the Little Blue Books lack the usual drawbacks. They are not expensive; there is nothing of a formal *course* with required lessons about them; every purchaser may exercise his free choice. And it must be remembered that this choice is made in the face of the competition of other titles of all kinds – against the competition, indeed, of those very sex and love titles that I have already shown are so popular. As I have pointed out, the average purchaser of Little Blue Books has only a dollar or two to spend at a time. If in his selection of twenty or so Little Blue Books he has the discrimination to buy only ten or twelve Little Blue Books of sex or love, and buys eight or ten books of self-improvement or self-education, this is highly commendable. He may even buy only a half dozen books of love interest, and scatter the rest of his order among books of humor, biography, puzzles, games, and self-education. This is hardly cause for alarm, or any reason to suppose that the American reading public is sex-mad.

The Little Blue Books have from the beginning emphasized education in their policy. The series is known far and wide as the University in Print. The strongest part of the editorial policy has been, especially in recent years, the endeavor to add to the series a greater number of educational works. These are especially written for the series, conforming to the established length of a Little Blue Book, and prepared especially so that the reader can educate him-self without the aid of an instructor. I have said that I am a business man and not a philanthropist, and I explain in another chapter exactly what I mean by this. Therefore this educational phase of my editorial policy is not self-chosen. I do not print these educational books because I think the public ought to read them – but because there is a tremendous demand for them, and I find myself hard pushed to keep up with that demand.

Please bear in mind that the sales figures I am going to give represent the popularity of these books as people have picked them out from the entire list of 1,260 different titles. These figures have been based only upon orders from advertisements or the catalogue listing the entire series. These figures are a direct indication of popular preference; these books have been selected in these proportionate quantities – in orders of from twenty to thirty books each – in spite of the competition of all other titles in the series. These figures, in other words, are in competition with the figures I have given for Little Blue Books of sex and love. They are not an independent set of statistics, but should be regarded as just another part of the data from those orders for 25,000 books (explained in the preceding chapter).

First of all, what of the general titles that discuss self-improvement in a somewhat abstract fashion? I refer to these titles:

Book Title	Copies Sold
Success Easier Than Failure (E. W. Howe)	38,000
The Secret of Self-Improvement (John Cowper Powys)	36,000
Hints on Self-Improvement	24,000

The fact that a book setting forth the secret of self-improvement sells to the extent of 36,000 copies annually among American readers of today can mean only one thing – that there is a widespread desire for such improvement, that there is, indeed, a universal quest for self-education. Whether you call it self-improvement or success, it means the same thing. *Success* is open to varying interpretations, but the desire for betterment is certainly present.

Education through books must be by reading them. There are Little Blue Books that guide people toward a better reading method, or toward better books, or tell them how to read to get the greatest benefit from it. These books also sell well:

Book Title	Copies Sold
100 Best Books to Read (Powys)	32,000
Facts You Should Know About the Classics (Joseph McCabe)	25,000
How to Get Most Out of Reading (Georg Brandes)	17,500
How to Get a Liberal Education (Thomas Huxley)	15,000
How to Enjoy Reading (Isaac Goldberg)	12,000
Art of Reading Constructively (E. Haldeman-Julius)	10,500
How to Choose Books (Thomas Carlyle)	10,000

Another direct proof of my contention that the desire for self-improvement manifests itself more in the sales of self-teaching books than in the actual enrollment for formal university education is that a general guide on *How to Get a Liberal Education* sells 15,000 copies annually, while the Little Blue Book called *How to Work Your Way Through College* just about sells its required 10,000 copies per year. Few of these thousands of Little Blue Book readers could go to college even if they wanted to; of course, I do not mean that the colleges should be abandoned, or that it is a mistake to go to college. I mean that the desire for self-education is proven more soundly by the sales of these general books, and of the titles that I shall cite in the following paragraphs, than by any other statistics available.

All the Little Blue Books are educational, and by rights I should give the figures for all of the books if this chapter were to be really complete. A little book of biography or of history is just as educational as one of chemistry or physics. Works of fiction by the masters, anthologies of the world's greatest poetry, and even books of humor, are educational all in their own particular way. But for the sake of brevity, and in order to emphasize more particularly those books that are definitely educational in a limited sense along special lines, I shall consider here only books that are usually classed under self-educational headings in the Little Blue Book advertising.

Probably the most outstanding phase of this passion for self-education is the immense popularity of the books that enable one to improve one's English. *Better English* is the classification used in the advertising. This phase of self-education is fundamental; from this readers can go on to other subjects. And here are the figures:

Book Title	Copies Sold
How to Improve Your Conversation	77,000
How to Improve Your Vocabulary	76,000
How to Write Letters	53,500
Common Faults in English	47,000
How to Talk and Debate	38,500
How to Argue Logically	33,000

Book Title	Copies Sold
Most Essential English Words	33,000
Grammar Self Taught	31,000
A Dictionary of American Slang	29,000
Handbook of Useful Phrases	25,000
Spelling Self Taught	24,000
Punctuation Self Taught	23,000
Rhetoric Self Taught	14,000
English Composition Self Taught	12,000
The Romance of Words	10,500

The social influence can be plainly seen. The strongest desire is for improving conversation and the speaking or writing vocabulary. People want to appear well among their fellows, and they do not want a false superiority – they are after the facts. These books do not pretend to give anyone any magic key to conversational brilliance. But they do give the facts in an understandable way, and their popularity shows that there is genuine interest in maintaining our mother tongue in its best form. Even the popularity of the dictionary of slang does not lessen this, for slang is the laboratory in which new words are born and new uses for old words.

Pocket dictionaries that aid in bettering English are also very popular, as follows:

Book Title	Copies Sold
A Book of Synonyms	28,000
Words Often Mispronounced	26,500
Foreign Words and Phrases	24,500
How to Pronounce Proper Names	24,000

The Little Blue Book of synonyms, if viewed over the entire history of the series, has been inordinately popular. But this was due partly to the craze for crossword puzzling that swept the country. The figure given here is more exact, and shows more precisely the proper place of this book in the popular demand for books of this kind.

The logical next step in this discussion brings to mind the jest that everyone in America is trying to break into print with some screed or other. Harassed editors bemoan the fact that thousands of people are laboriously putting pen to paper in an endeavor to add to their income, or even, in a few instances, to win fame and fortune overnight by writing some best seller that will later be put into the movies. Probably no definite figures have ever been available on this question. Even popular contests, in which attractive cash prizes are offered for manuscripts, cannot feel the popular pulse to the extent that the Little Blue Books that offer aid to these people can tell how much interest there is in writing for profit. Of course, too, many people who enter prize contests are under the illusion that writing takes no training, people who believe that writers just dash off their stuff in mad moments of frenzied inspiration. Such people would not spend even five cents for a book to tell them something of the technique of the craft they hope to enter. But here are the figures that indicate how many people there are who would like to write for money, and who are anxious to find out how to do it:

Book Title	Copies Sold
Hints on Public Speaking	46,500
Short-Story Writing for Beginners	36,000
Hints on Writing Short Stories	23,000
How to Write Advertising	20,000
How to Prepare Manuscripts	17,000
Writing for the Market	14,500
Hints on Writing Poetry	11,000
Hints on News Reporting	10,500
How to Write Movie Scenarios	10,000
How to Write One-Act Plays	8,000
How to Write Book Reviews	8,000

In a general list like the Little Blue Books this is rather amazing – especially the popularity of the manual on *How to Prepare Manuscripts*. In fact, in view of the popularity of this book, I, as one of those same harassed editors, wonder why it is that so few people read the book and follow its plain instructions. These books, I wish to explain, contain nothing but facts. No claims are made that short-story writing is a grand road to fame and fortune. There is no assertion that the movies are clamoring for the work of amateur scenario writers and offering fabulous sums for it. There is nothing to induce the tyro to enter the writing *game* except the unvarnished essentials of the craft. In fact, these Little Blue Books include warnings against fraudulent organizations that claim to train amateurs to produce manuscripts that will sell for extraordinary amounts.

Proceeding to other titles of self-improvement intent, a wide field opens up under the general heading of Psychology. This recent science, which has made such rapid strides in the past few years, is not yet at a point where it can diagnose all the ills that human flesh and behavior are heir to, but it can help. Again, as always, the Little Blue Books in this field give the facts. It has somehow reached the ears of the general reader that psychology is a panacea of some kind or other, and that if he can study up on psychology and psycho-analysis he will be able to find the secret of success that he believes must be latent within him. Unfortunately, psychology cannot work magic. But these Little Blue Books stay within the limits of scientific knowledge, and make no false pretensions whatever.

There is much bunk about human personality that readers can get from some sources. I mean the *you-can-if-you-wish-to-hard-enough* personality drivel. There are Little Blue Books that deal psychologically with personality and I am sure they are helpful, but these books are not sold because they make any extravagant promises. No lures are held out that these books will make the rosiest dreams come true, not to mention the host of wayward fancies per-haps less rosy but none the less desired. These books are offered only as facts, and as such they are very popular. Here are the figures for some of the more general titles:

Book Title	Copies Sold
How to Psycho-Analyze Yourself	43,000
Psycho-Analysis Explained	38,500
Psychology for Beginners	35,000
Behaviorism: Newest Psychology	25,500
The Puzzle of Personality	21,000
Auto-Suggestion: How It Works	18,500
Psychology of Jung	13,000
Auto-Suggestion and Health	12,000

It is not quite true that any title containing the word *psychology* will sell well, but it is almost true. There are few exceptions, so widespread is the interest in this subject. That it is a quest for self-improvement or self-betterment and part of that eternal pursuit of happiness that makes psychology and psychoanalysis so popular, can hardly be disputed. The entire emphasis of these sciences is on improvement of the individual by better understanding of his weaknesses and his potentialities.

These are some of the titles with a more direct emphasis on self-understanding:

Book Title	Copies Sold
How to Fight Nervous Troubles	39,000
Facts About Will Power	38,500
Your Memory and How to Improve It	37,000
Your Talent and How to Develop It	35,500
Psychology of Leadership	32,000
How to Think Logically	30,500
Psychology of Character Building	29,000
The Conquest of Fear	27,500
Psychology of Laughter	14,000
How I Psycho-Analyzed Myself	13,500

The obvious conclusions are that people want to overcome their nervous disorders and acquire a steadied self-sufficiency, that they want to make the most of any talent they may have, that they would like to lead, if it is possible for them to do so, that they want to improve their characters, if there is such a thing as improving character, and that they really want to know what will power is, if there is any, and how it may help them solve their problems. There is no doubt that these readers are after the facts, whether they are in accord with their hopes or not. This is most encouraging.

The tally to the credit of American readers as desirous of self-improvement mounts up. Throughout the range of self-improvement books there is an excellent showing. The modern search is for knowledge, and the thirst for information will be satisfied. It will take time for this passion for knowledge to adjust itself to the needs and capacities of the individual, but there is great hope that it will not spend itself in vain.

What would you say if I claimed that I could get 10,000 American people every year to admit that they are stupid? Not only to admit that they themselves are stupid, but to state further that they are anxious to become less stupid if they can? You would not believe me. You would laugh me to scorn. You would remind me that everyone calls everyone else a moron, but never admits the possibility that he himself may be one.

Of course, I could not appear on a public platform and ask for a showing of hands on such a question. That would be ridiculous. The average American is a timid creature, and he hardly wants to parade his deficiencies, much as he may admit them in the privacy of his self-communion. Nor could I reasonably hope to secure any reliable statistics by asking for a ballot – unsigned votes – on the question. There would be insufficient inducement for honesty. But if I were to *sell* a possible aid toward reducing stupidity, I might reasonably assume that if 10,000 people bought the book they would be admitting at least some degree of stupidity in themselves.

There is such a book in the pocket series. It is called *How to Conquer Stupidity*. One reason why people do not hesitate to order Little Blue Books, and why they forget the inhibitions that personal vanity might set upon them, is that there is a soothing anonymity in the numbers of the Little Blue Books. People order by numbers instead of titles. They feel secure

40

– the timid ones – in the apparent meaninglessness of a list of numbers. So if people think themselves stupid, and want to remedy it, they will not hesitate to order *How to Conquer Stupidity* – for it goes by the three digits 759 and there is no self-reproach in these figures!

To come to the climax of this digression on stupidity, this book sells – not merely 10,000, but 17,500 copies annually! If 17,500 people every year in these United States are willing to admit that they have some measure of stupidity that needs overcoming, here is a nucleus around which to build something worth while.

These facts about a book dealing with stupidity bring to my mind again those vigilant censors that protect the delicate constitution of the *average American man*. This *average man* must not be led into temptation, and he must not, above all things, be the least bit offended. Indeed, one must not even risk offending him, if there seems the slightest possibility of such an affront. There are publishers who would not include in their list a book entitled *How to Conquer Stupidity*, objecting to it on the ground that their customers would be offended by such a suggestion – the suggestion that the publication of such a book would imply that book-buyers have among their number several stupid individuals who might buy such a book.

Perhaps you think this is fanciful, but I can quickly disillusion you. I have had a recent experience that excellently illustrates my point. Possibly you have seen some of my advertisements of a high school educational course, made up of fifty of the Little Blue Books that include high school subjects. This advertisement implies that there are many people who could benefit from study of these fifty books. A nationally known weekly periodical refused this advertisement, as worded in the original copy submitted, on the ground that they could not risk implying that any large number of their readers were lacking the essentials of a high school education! Yet this same advertisement, implying that a high school course of this kind will be very welcome to many people, is very successful nearly everywhere it appears. I am sorry, but I cannot sympathize with this constant exaggerated effort to avoid stepping on people's toes. People wear shoes, and besides, their toes are not nearly as tender as some of the guardians of our public safety seem to think. It is preposterous to suppose that an American

41

reader, however average, will give vent to hot and righteous indignation because someone suggests that a little more education may benefit him.

To get back to discussing improvement of personality and character, and such matters, I have another bit of interesting statistical news. Americans are being constantly condemned for their bad habits, and seldom praised, except in funeral panegyrics and political hypocrisy, for their good habits. I must admit that Americans as readers are not as interested in good habits as they are in bad habits. But do not leap to conclusions – the amazing fact is that American readers want to *overcome* bad habits to a greater extent by almost a half than they want to form good habits. Here are the actual figures:

Book Title	Copies Sold
How to Break Bad Habits	29,000
How to Form Good Habits	20,000

At that, there are 20,000 people annually interested in finding out how to form good habits. This is far from insignificant. And those 29,000 readers who are so earnest in their wish to break their bad habits – notice once again that they are ready to admit they have them and they eagerly demonstrate their wish to remedy such an appalling state of affairs. I am heartily in accord with these people; much as I decry small-mindedness and all kinds of the usual success and personality bunk, and the readiness with which people fall for such illusions, the people who are in quest of facts that will really help them win my sympathy – and, yes, my applause. They are a promising multitude, these readers of Little Blue Books.

So much for mental and emotional health—if psychology may be so regarded. Logically, the next phase to be considered is bodily health: physical well-being. Sex has already been discussed (in "Are Americans Afraid of Sex?"). The question now is, are Americans interested in keeping themselves physically fit? The answer of the Little Blue Books is Yes. According to the figures:

THE QUEST FOR SELF-IMPROVEMENT

Book Title	Copies Sold
Cure of Skin and Hair	52,000
Eating for Health (Vitamins)	36,000
Latest Food and Diet Facts	27,000
Everyday Health Rules	22,500
Home Nursing (First Aid)	17,000
Facts About Cancer	15,000
X-Ray, Violet Ray, etc	13,500
Tuberculosis: Causes and Cure	12,000
Diabetes: Cause and Treatment	12,000
Quacks of the Healing Culls	10,000
Truth About "Patent" Medicines	10,000
Childhood Diseases (Diphtheria, Scarlet Fever, Chicken Pox, and so forth)	10,000
How to Take Care of Your Mouth and Teeth	8,000

The record is not all one of glory, as you see. It is clear that American readers are far more interested in externals (*Care of Skin and Hair*) than in arbitrary rules for general health (*Everyday Health Rules*) – in fact, they are twice as interested in keeping an outside appearance of good looks than in mere health without emphasis on appearance, (As for teeth – the low figure for this manual may be because people read so much about teeth in toothpaste advertisements.) Vanity creeps into the figures, but it is rather a justifiable vanity. Yet I do not want it to seem that I am optimistic about this reading public we have in America today, though I fancy the facts I cite in my chapter called "The Morgue" will relieve me of appearing too confident of America's high intelligence in reading tastes. The point I want to make is simply that American readers as a class are not as hopelessly bogged in inconsequential choices of books as some critics would have us believe.

The fact that people are interested, to the extent of 36,000 copies per year, in eating for the sake of good health is true enough to human nature. Every wife knows how her husband likes to eat. That he should want to eat what is most healthful, however, she may not suspect – but the Little Blue Book record shows it. The book on food and diet is a close second. The idea seems to be that if one can eat and contribute to health at the same time, why not do it?

As I have said before, men are the chief purchasers of these Little Blue Books. It is masculine vanity, then, which jumps up that total for *Care of Skin and Hair*. Feminine vanity may be just as great, but women are not buyers of these books to the same extent that men are. It shows up clearly in the sales figures for a distinctly feminine title: *Simple Beauty Hints*, with an annual total of 22,000 copies.

As a side remark, I may say that I have reason to believe that American women as a class prefer to buy their cosmetics; though they may invest in a book on how to use cosmetics intelligently, they buy a book on how to make their own cosmetics only about half as often – *How to Make Your Own Cosmetics* sells only 14,000 copies per year. As for a defense of cosmetics, none is wanted! Max Beerbohm's *Defense of Cosmetics* is a failing title, averaging less than 5,000 copies annually in 1927. If something is not done about this book, it will go into The Morgue! Contributory factors in gaining health are sports and other forms of recreation. The sports classification of the Little Blue Books is weak at the time this book is written. This will be remedied in 1928, and meanwhile the figures available must suffice. They are very revealing:

Book Title	Copies Sold
How to Teach Yourself to Swim	27,000
How to Play Golf	17,000
Baseball: How to Play and How to Watch it	15,000
Camping, Woodcraft and Wildcraft	15,500
Handbook of Golf Rules	12,000
Helpful Hints for Hikers	10,500
How to Get the Most Out of Recreation	9,000

Golf wins by a slight margin over baseball. This may be because every small boy learns baseball as part of his adolescence. But golf is more an individual game, and must be learned later. Further, golf is still somewhat an expensive game to play, and there is perhaps a great deal of curiosity, independent of any strong determination to play, about the game and about the fun that may be had playing it.

Coming back to more academic educational subjects, suppose we examine the records of some of the courses found in high school and college curricula:

Book Title	Copies Sold
Facts to Know About Music	37,000
Psychology for Beginners	35,000
Astronomy Self Taught	30,500
Facts to Know About Painting	27,500
Outline of U. S. History	25,500
Chemistry Self Taught	25,500
Facts to Know About Architecture	16,000
Evolution Made Plain	16,000
Physics Self Taught	14,500
Outline of Economics	14,500
The Weather (Meteorology)	14,000
Botany Self Taught	13,000
Zoology Self Taught	12,000
Facts to Know About Sculpture	10,500
Sociology for Beginners	8,000

I am myself amazed at the popularity of the arts – music, painting, sculpture, and architecture. Who would have guessed that there are 27,500 people annually to be found in America interested in learning facts they ought to know about painting? Of the academic subjects, chemistry is more popular than physics, probably because it captivates the imagination to a greater extent. Chemists have been much in the press of late, what with their rayon and other wizardry with cellulose. But the stars win the most favor, with 30,500 people every year anxious to learn about astronomy. This is gratifying, especially when I glance at the record for *Facts You Should Know About Astrology* (really a debunking book), which sold 17,000 copies only. It pleases me to think that almost twice as many people are interested in the science as in the pseudo-science, though I know that those who read the Little Blue Book on astrology will get nothing but a scientific appraisal and exposure of the subject.

People will have the facts about astronomy and the sciences whether they can reconcile them with their religious beliefs or not, it seems. Even evolution, in spite of all the opposition set up against it, finds 16,000 people annually who want to have it clearly explained to them. If given the chance, people will accept the facts gladly.

Foreign languages, one might think, would have a fairly limited appeal in as general a series as the Little Blue Books. But even here the popular demand for books of self-education shows itself strongly. For these are the indisputable figures:

Book Title	Copies Sold
Spanish Self Taught	47,000
French Self Taught	46,500
German Self Taught	27,500
Italian Self Taught	21,500
Esperanto Self Taught	17,500
Latin Self Taught	10,500

French and Spanish are about tied for first place. It is easy to understand this. Perhaps most surprising is the popularity of Esperanto, the proposed scientific international language that exists nowhere in fact. It is dead like Latin, for it has never come to life – yet 17,000 People a year seem to want to learn it. It may be partly that interest in puzzles and *brainteasers* that so fascinates a large portion of the human race; it may be partly just curiosity. Even the interest in Latin, when it is remembered that this is a cross-section of the American reading public, is much larger than might have been supposed. Business plays so large a part in contemporary life that the popularity of commercial subjects could be logically presupposed. These are the figures:

Book Title	Copies Sold
How to Write Business Letters	37,500
Handbook of Useful Tables	33,000
Typewriting Self Taught	29,000
Handbook of Legal Forms	28,500
Handbook of Commercial Law	27,000
A Rapid Calculator	24,000
How to Own Your Home	17,500
First Aid for Investors	17,000
How to Save Money	16,500
How Wall Street Works	16,000
Arithmetic Self Taught: Part 2	14,500
Arithmetic Self Taught: Part 1	12,000
U. S. Commercial Geography	10,000
How to Budget Your Income	10,000

Americans, it appears, show a disposition not only to learn more about business itself, but also to find out how to improve their personal financial affairs. Few care to go to the trouble to budget their income, apparently, but many want to know how to save and how to invest their savings. The popularity of the second part of the arithmetic is probably due to its being regarded as more advanced than the first part. Finally, the exceeding popularity of the book of useful tables is due, not only to its commercial utility, but to its handiness in everyday activities.

As civilization grows more complex there is an increasing need for books of reference, handy manuals in which to look up a fact when it is wanted. Evidently people are not as afraid of such books of reference as the average professor thinks his students are. The pocket dictionaries to be found among the Little Blue Books are very popular:

Book Title	Copies Sold
Book of Familiar Quotations	34,500
A Dictionary of Scientific Terms	25,000
Pocket Rhyming Dictionary	23,000
A Dictionary of Musical Terms	21,500
Popular Shakespearian Quotations	17,000
A Dictionary of Biblical Allusions	16,000
International Dictionary of Authors	15,000
A Dictionary of Classical Mythology.	13,000
A Dictionary of Geographical Names	10,500
A Dictionary of Sea Terms	8,000

Anent the Shakespearian quotations, who thinks that Shakespeare is not popular in America?

Farming, in spite of the prevalence of agricultural colleges and the journalistic apotheosis of the American farmer, is not popular, comparatively, as a subject for study. I have had to withdraw one of my agricultural titles, and may have to withdraw one or two more. For this is the record:

Book Title	Copies Sold
Hints on Soils and Fertilizers	12,500
Poultry for Profit	11,000
Hints on Animal Husbandry	10,500
Home Vegetable Gardening	10,500
Hints on Farming	7,500
Beekeeping for Profit	7,000
How to Grow Fruits	6,000
How to Build Your Greenhouse	6,000

Home mechanics, or books that tell a person how to do things for himself, do fairly well. This classification is still in the experimental stage, so too much must not be assumed from the slight representation:

Book Title	Copies Sold
How to Tie All Kinds of Knots	27,500
Principles of Electricity	23,000
How to Paint and Finish Woodwork	19,000
Practical Masonry: Brickwork	17,000
How to Cane and Upholster Chairs	8,000
Elements of Woodworking	8,000
Bookbinding Self Taught	8,000

Apparently the Boy Scouts are not alone in a wish to know how to tie knots! Such books as those above are rather popular, I think, because of the average person's inclination to putter around the home, the back yard, and to tinker with the family car. Human hands itch to experiment with a brush and a can of paint, and I have heard that they also like to wield a monkey-wrench, so one of these days I'll have a Little Blue Book on how to repair your own car.

Interior decoration is a special phase of home-improvement. I think some mention of it belongs here, because these Little Blue Books prove that Americans are weary of unattractive homes. Thousands of people are trying their best to beautify their houses and yards, and they want to do this according to the best tradition and in accord with the best artistic taste. I cite these figures to support my assertion:

Book Title	Copies Sold
Interior Decoration for Small Homes	29,000
Practical Hints on Interior Decoration	27,000
How to Make Your Home More Homelike	14,000

Cooking, of course, is an indispensable art. The Little Blue Books have many collections of recipes, as follows:

Book Title	Copies Sold
How to Make All Kinds of Candy	45,000
Simple Recipes for Home Cooking	33,000
How to Make Pies and Pastries	29,000
How to Cook Fish and Meats	21,500
Better Meals for Less Money	17,500
How to Make Ice Cream and Gelatine	16,000
French Cooking for Amateurs	9,500

Thus, even the Little Blue Books contribute data to support the contention that America has a hungry sweet tooth – for the most popular book of recipes is that on how to make candy. Of specialized recipe books, that on making pies and pastries – more sweets – also surpasses the others.

Housekeepers, such of them as may be Little Blue Book readers, are anxious to be good hostesses. Among the men, all want to be socially correct quite as much as do the women. That is why *Hints on Etiquette* sells 72,000 copies per year. In fact, one reader wrote a letter saying that he had read this book and had assimilated all of it. He now felt ready for more particulars, and would like to obtain a much larger book of etiquette so that he might become really and truly cultured! Joking aside, however, American readers do want to conform to social strictures. They believe in social amenities because they serve in a large way the purposes of civilized intercourse. So *The Charming Hostess: How to Entertain* is also popular, selling at the rate of 32,000 copies annually. As part of the wish to entertain guests happily, I should add that *Party Games for Grown-Ups* is in demand to the extent of 46,500 copies per year. I shall have more to say about this demand for fun and entertainment in another place.

The figures I have given in support of America's quest for self-improvement will perhaps suffice to show that the desire for knowledge and the yearning for education are much more than a passing fancy. The demand increases if anything, with the years. I could go on to show that other books – books of poems, masterpieces of fiction, biographies of the great, philosophy, comparative religions, books of maxims and epigrams, and so on – bear out this widespread interest in self-betterment and advancement. In another chapter I explain how a classification called Cultural Helps has done much to sell certain *highbrow* titles in the series. The clamor everywhere is for education, culture, knowledge; surely these are signs of the times, and they point hopefully toward an ever brighter future.

The University in Print still has gaps. Some phases of self-education are still meagerly represented. For example, there is law. I have secured, so far, very little usable material to enlighten the general public in legal matters. But these gaps will be filled in as time goes on. The public wants the books, and I have no choice, in my capacity as editor of such a series, but to give them the books desired. I am optimistic about this demand for self-education, because it gratifies me to know that there is such a really general interest in acquiring knowledge. It must gratify anyone interested in the progress of modern civilization. For though it may take generations for this desire to take proper shape, and for this avid search for knowledge to work any real benefits for the race, it cannot ever work for harm or drag us back into those dark ages from which we so recently emerged.

It was fear of knowledge that held humanity back during the Middle Ages, and before. There was fostered in people's minds a fear of the printed word. Reading was an accomplishment few dared to undertake. The invention of printing did much to dispel this popular fear. Books were seen not to be very harmful, after all – except perhaps *some* books, which were kept carefully from the public lest the people be contaminated thereby. Censors still stalk among us, placing a taboo on this and another taboo on that. There are still books that moralists and reformers think *no one* should be permitted to read. But the individual's fear of the printed word has gone – probably that is why these self-appointed censors take their tasks so seriously. They know that people would read the books if they had the chance, and so they try to see to it that the public does not get the chance.

American readers are thorough in their quest for knowledge. I have demonstrated that. They place no taboos of their own on anything that may inform them, or help them to understand the world and themselves. One of these days *Mr. Average Man* may resent being deprived of a book he wants to read, just because some self-styled *Superior Man* says it won't be good for him. When that time comes, the desire for knowledge will at last have its way: its full, undenied, unhindered way.

A Note on Music

I cannot leave the subject of self-education and self-improvement without a word about music. So particular a phase of cultural development seemed to have no place in this chapter as I went along, so I put it here as a kind of postscript, and a worthy postscript it is. Music has been called the purest of the arts. Great music probably requires more education than any other single art to be appreciated to the fullest possible extent. But even the least educated may get something, however little, from great music. Music satisfies a hunger that none of the other arts can do so well or so universally. Perhaps it is because I am myself so very fond of music that the Little Blue Books have such a generous sprinkling of musical titles. It was with deep regret that I found myself obliged to withdraw some of the operatic titles – the stories of famous operas, with excerpts from the scores. Several remain in the list, I am glad to say, but I still think sadly sometimes of those that had to go into The Morgue.

The popularity of music in America cannot be questioned. The generous support given to such artists as Galli-Curci, Rosa Ponselle, John McCormack, Ignace Paderewski, and so forth, proves this. Paderewski, indeed, is a name that even a street urchin will recognize as a great musician.

It will surprise no one to learn that Little Blue Books of a musical appeal are popular, except perhaps when one remembers that there is a difference between the popularity of music itself and books *about* music. There is a vast gulf between, but it is not so wide that popularity cannot bridge it. For even liking music as they naturally do, American readers want to know more about it. They want to learn how to like it even more – they want to educate themselves into greater joy, and truer appreciation, of the greatest of all the arts.

Here are some of the titles, with their revealing sales figures:

Book Title	Copies Sold
Facts You Should Know About Music	37,000
Dictionary of Musical Terms	21,500
How to Learn to Sing	19,000
Story of Rigoletto	16,000
Old Favorite Negro Songs	15,000
Jazz: What It Is and How to Understand It	15,000
Harmony Self Taught	14,500
Story of Tannhauser	14,500
How to Teach Yourself to Play the Piano	14,000
How to Enjoy Good Music	13,500
Story of Das Rheingold	13,000
Introduction to Wagner's Music	11,000
How to Enjoy Orchestra Music	10,500
Old English Songs	10,500
Gilbert and Sullivan Guidebook	9,000
Great Christian Hymns	3,000

I assure you – for I will be accused of it – that I have not falsified the figures for *Great Christian Hymns*. Some of these hymns (if you leave the words out) are worthy of a place in the world's music, but the public in general has comparatively little interest in hymns. Indeed, they show three times as much interest in old English songs, and five times as much interest in Negro songs! If to some of us the 15,000 annual purchasers who wish to learn about jazz are a little depressing, we can surely brighten up when we know that more than 10,000 people every year want to know how to get greater enjoyment from orchestra music.

CHAPTER IV

AMERICANS WANT

FUN AND LAUGHTER

As Shown By Little Blue Book Sales Statistics

Everyone likes a good laugh. Laughter is sociable – like good wine. We are told to laugh, for all the world will laugh with us. Fun and laughter are catching. A theater full of laughter contains more enjoyment than one of the laughers could get if he saw the same things or heard the same words in the privacy of his apartment. Humor is funnier if two can laugh at it together, funnier still if three can laugh at it, and make a party. Yet for all this sociability, there is fun to be had even if one has to laugh alone.

Readers are solitary persons, while they are reading. A reader may be actually alone in a room, or he may be mentally isolated in a subway train, a public park, or the waiting room of the Grand Central station. Occasionally such a reader may be seen to smile, or he may so far forget himself as to give way to involuntary laughter. It may even be noisy laughter, for perhaps he is reading a Little Blue Book of jokes.

Humor has always been in the series of Little Blue Books – usually in the form of the work of Mark Twain, Artemus Ward, Josh Billings, Bill Nye, and so forth Stephen Leacock is a happy recent addition. But books of jokes came late, and their popularity was so immediately apparent that the group of collections grew promptly into a sizable classification. That there should be a demand for such books I did not for a long time suspect. I leaned toward the more lengthy humor, in the form of tales and essays, and let compilations of dialogue jokes wait until little more than a year ago.

Now there is hardly a form of wit or humor you cannot find represented in the series of Little Blue Books. The *fun-and-laughter* classification is well developed, and it is one of the strongest portions of the list. If there is fun to be found in the pages of a book, you are almost sure to be able to find it in the pages of some Little Blue Book or other. That is why the sales statistics for these *fun-and laughter* books have such comparative value – why they tell just what kind of a sense of humor American readers have most of, and how they analyze the well-known desire for fun and laughter of all kinds.

The jokebooks began with a simple enough title, wholly unpretentious: *Popular Jokebook*. To show you how late it came in the series, comparatively speaking, I may add that it is No. 972 in the list – and at the time the book was added that number was indicative somewhat of its youth. High numbers are not always younger than the low ones, for there have been many recent substitutions, but high numbers are often quite young. Those over 1000 are all less than three years old.

This *Popular Jokebook* was a good seller from the start. Its popularity made other jokebooks necessary, and yet, with a score or so of other books of jokes now competing with it for public favor, this first anthology of jokes still holds its own with an annual sales figure of 37,000 copies. Its title is what makes it so popular. The title insists that the book is popular, and so it is! American readers, you see, are in many ways a great deal like sheep – in buying books as well as in buying cigarettes or hosiery or theater tickets. If it is something they rather want anyway, and you point out that other people also want it – they clamor for it.

By way of contrast, this *Popular Jokebook* has a companion – a twin, born into the list at the same time, and given another title mostly for convenience and to avoid confusion. This twin's name is *A Book of Humorous Anecdotes*: its annual sales figure is – it rather appalls me, for I had not noticed its low ebb before – only 8,000 copies, or less than a fourth of that of the *Popular Jokebook*.

Suppose we examine more closely some of the annual sales figures for miscellaneous jokebooks:

Book Title	Copies Sold
Toasts for All Occasions	55,000
Best Jokes of 1926	50,500
Popular Jokebook	37,000
Broadway Wisecracks	29,000
Best College Humor	17,000
Masterpieces of American Humor	16,500
Best Jokes of 1925	15,500
Masterpieces of American Wit	9,000
Humorous Anecdotes	8,000

The best of them all is not jokes, but toasts! Is this, I wonder, because *toasts* suggest something said before drinking – and drinking suggests, well, wine and possibly whiskey? In the imagination, of course – certainly all in the reader's imagination. But why should not drinking be as popular on the printed page as love? Then, people may think also that toasts are funnier than just jokes. Such may have been their experience, due possibly to the mellowing effects of good liquor.

Second best is the *Best Jokes of 1926*; in 1928, of course, it will be the new collection, *Best Jokes of 1927*. Again there is that tendency to choose something someone points out as best. Indeed, here is the reason for all the superlatives you see on billboards and in magazine advertisements – say it is the best long enough, and you may have thousands agreeing with you, provided you have a good product in the first place. Even the *Best Jokes of 1925* is not considered too out of date for 15,500 people every year, though this may drop a little in 1928.

Of particular interest are the jokes about various nationalities:

Book Title	Copies Sold
Best Jewish Jokes	43,000
Best Negro Jokes	37,500
Best Irish Jokes	37,000
Best Scotch Jokes	34,500
Best American Jokes	16,000
Best Yankee Jokes	16,000

There are also books of the best Russian, Spanish, Italian and German humor, but these struggle hard to keep up their required 10,000 yearly. It is the Irish and the Scotch, and, seemingly, the Jewish people who are credited with the best laugh-giving characteristics. Negroes, though a race – like the Jews – instead of a nationality, speaking broadly, have their generous share of favor. It is a coincidence that American and Yankee jokes have equal popularity, but it is not a coincidence that they are less than half as popular as jokes about any other of the nationalities in the best-seller list. Americans, perhaps, are not quite ready yet to laugh at themselves so much as at others – the others being individuals with strongly marked racial or traditional idiosyncrasies.

What now of the professional jokes? These figures tell a story:

Book Title	Copies Sold
Best Jokes About Doctors	25,000
Best Jokes About Preachers	23,000
Best Jokes About Lawyers	21,000

I daresay that the much looked down upon man in the street shakes with glee at any chance to laugh at a doctor, a lawyer, or a preacher. He is so often victimized, or induced by his imagination to stand in awe or fear of these professions, that laughter is a welcome relief. He laughs long and heartily at jests implying a doctor's brutality or ignorance or carelessness – of all of which he is afraid. He guffaws boisterously at funny cracks suggesting that lawyers are liars, and that they have many weaknesses and faults common to all of their profession. He smiles broadly and haw-haws gaily at gibes aimed at the preacher's sanctimoniousness and overdone righteousness. But it is healthy laughter, and of course it has its foundations in fact. Humor could not exist without a basis of common humanity, and by laughing at our superiors – at these professional highbrows – we, as well as our inferiors, can recognize, whether consciously or not, a universal kinship. Other jokebooks have wide favor, as follows:

Book Title	Copies Sold
Best Jokes About Married Life	45,500
Best Jokes About Lovers	35,000
Best Jokes About Kissing	33,000
Best Hobo Jokes	23,000
Best Ford Jokes	22,500
Best Jokes About Drunks	18,500
Best Rube Jokes	11,000

Mr. Henry Ford's Model T died in 1927, but the jokes about it – see the figures immediately preceding – did not. If some 20,000 people or more continue to laugh at trials and tribulations incidental to owning a Ford Model T may pass but will hardly be forgotten. Though the car may die, the jokes go rattling on. It is not every man who can invent the butt of an everlasting joke!

I gave the figures for the jokes about love and marriage in the chapter dealing with the popularity of sex books in America. I repeat them here for the sake of comparison. These figures are immensely significant, and they strike deeper into the real nature of humor than any psychological analysis can probe. The most popular jokebooks of all, taken as a trio (with the exception only of the *Best Jokes of 1926* and the *Toasts for all Occasions*), are about what human beings have most revered, most idealized, and most consecrated – love and its relationships. Love is human, however, and it is universal. That is why it is such good material for humor, and why we can all easily and gladly laugh about it. We laugh, partly at lovers and partly with them. For if we have not been lovers yet, we have an inner voice that tells us we may soon be lovers, and it may be best for us to laugh while we may. For lovers themselves do not laugh – at love. Earlier or later they may; but not in the midst of the experience.

It is a good thing, too, this laughter, though it be laughter at love and loving, and all the affairs and circumstances that go with it. For it is not a world for long love, or continually and everlastingly blissful true love. Lovers may make fools of themselves in a harsh world like this. It is good that we know how to laugh at our own foibles, and our own humanity. And we laugh most at married life – at that attempt, as some wit (a Frenchman, wasn't he?) put it, to coordinate economics and emotion – in joke books as well as in the comic strips in the daily papers. We laugh loudest at what effects us most, provided we are given the graceful illusion of supposing the joke to be on the other fellow.

So much for jokes in general. What of humorists, those cynical observers of humanity who have turned to laughter for escape from thoughts that may perhaps have become too heavy to face seriously? I shall select a book or two by some of the outstanding names, so that the comparison of their popularity may be made readily. These will suffice:

Book Title	Copies Sold
Jerome K. Jerome: Funny Ghost Stories	33,000
Mark Twain: English As She Spoke	31,000
Humor of Abraham Lincoln	15,000
Stephen Leacock: Ridiculous Stories	14,500
Carles Dickens: Pickwick Papers	14,000
Jerome K. Jerome: Idle Thoughts of an Idle Fellow	13,000
Bill Nye; Humorous Essays	12,000
Josh Billings: Humorous Epigrams, etc	11,000
Petroleum V. Nasby: Let's Laugh	10,000
Artemus Ward: Laugh Book	9,000

Mark Twain is without doubt the most popular of the humorists; the rest have their followers, but none to equal his. The popularity of Jerome's *Funny Ghost Stories* is about half laughter and half shivers – the ghosts lure as many nickels as the chuckles in it. Of them all, Artemus Ward is the least popular; this is probably because Ward's was an older day, and he is not remembered because his humor is more superficial and not as well founded on those unchangeable qualities of human nature that make any creative effort enduring. The humor of Lincoln is, of course, traditional, like that of the Irish and the Scotch. It is none the less humor for all that, however.

Humorous verse, comic poems, and nonsense rhymes have their place in the great category of humor and laughter. Books of this kind are varyingly popular:

Book Title	Copies Sold
Casey at the Bat, Face on the Barroom Floor, etc	25,500
Book of Comic Poems	21,500
Comic Dialect Poems	11,000
Book of Humorous Verse	10,500
Book of Funny Limericks	10,500
Book of Nonsense Poems	10,000
Laughable Lyrics: Edwin Lear	8,000
Hunting of the Snark: Lewis Carroll	7,000

It has been up to mighty Casey to support this list and maintain a residuum of popularity for the versifiers. Mighty Casey, and that memorable face on the bygone barroom floor – this verse that is the most popular is, you should notice, verse in which tears mingle with the sounds of merriment. It is verse that, if you laugh at it at all, must impress you with a certain pathos. As humor, it is like the screen comedies of Charles Chaplin, so rightly called the pathetic comedian.

Edward Lear is all but forgotten; the limerick is passé; and even Lewis Carroll's reputation, sponsored by Alice, seems to be slipping. For *Alice in Wonderland*, too, sold only 8,000 copies per year. And the *Nonsense Stories and Pictures* of Edward Lear, though much better – at 16,000 copies annually – than any similar book, is not as popular as one would expect. His *Nonsense Alphabets*, also with his inimitable pictures, has not done as well as I had hoped. It is, I am sorry to say, really a failure, selling hardly more

61

than 5,000 copies annually as compared with the others mentioned here.

What, by the way, of the much despised pun, that lowest form of wit, as all good critics call it? There is a book called *Interesting and Amusing Puns*, and I know all punsters will be eager to learn how the public has received it. Punsters, of course, would not condescend to buy the book; its influence might cramp their style. That is the very reason, I suspect, why the book does not sell well – for who is not, or who has not been at sometime, a punster? We have all been victims, of course; most of us, I daresay, have committed the crime itself. For this book sold only – I almost suppressed this shameful figure! – 6,500 copies. That showing is its very best. I suspect it is because American readers are too busy making their own puns to buy any ready-made. Viewed in a dispassionate light, however, 6,500 purchasers for this book are appallingly many – one must meet one or more of them sooner or later in this small world of ours.

"Let's have fun," cry our boys and girls, our Babbitts and Rotarians, our Ku Kluxers and Masons, our Sewing Circles and our Ladies' Aiders. It is the desire of the average American to have all the fun he can get – as witness the playgrounds provided at Atlantic City, in Florida, in California, and nearly everywhere else. Chorus girls, vaudeville performers, radio announcers, *et al*, earn their livings providing fun – though it is often poor fun, unjust to the name and unworthy of fun-seekers. There are the movies, the basis of a gigantic industry. There are the grandstand and ringside seats at baseball games and prize fights. There are carnivals and fairs and circuses galore. And there are books –

Books of fun include games and other forms of recreation, but these I have already discussed, as a subdivision of health, in the chapter on self-improvement books. I shall not repeat those figures here. In this chapter I am more concerned with indoor sports – riddles, parlor games, puzzles, and so forth In the Little Blue Book lists these books come under the general classification of Entertainment.

First of all, there is that recent *fad*, intelligence, or rather, information quizzes – the question-and-answer game. In this there is mingled not only fun and entertainment, as in playing a game, but some desire for self-improvement as well. It may not be admirable to get a *kick* out of parading one's superior knowledge by getting a higher score than one's fellows – or desperately trying to get it! – but it is human nature. Three Little Blue Books of questions and answers sell as follows:

Book Title	Copies Sold
What Do You Know?	45,500
Who, When, Where, What?	30,500
General Information Quizzes	14,500

I strongly suspect that the *General Information Quizzes* does not appeal because of the matter-of-fact title. There is no suggestion of fun in such a title. The popularity of that first question-and-answer book that swept the country, and whose title became a slang phrase or was borrowed from a slang phrase – whichever was the hen and which the egg – owed much of its success, I am sure, to its title: *Ask Me Another!* Some such title is needed for this laggard Little Blue Book of mine.

Crossword puzzles were earlier in the popular favor for games with pencil and paper. There are two series in the Little Blue Books, and even now they sell like this:

Book Title	Copies Sold
Crossword Puzzles: Series 2	21,500
Crossword Puzzles: Series 1	21,000

At the height of the craze, the influence of a populace madly seeking new words to conquer was felt in the Little Blue Book series by the phenomenal sale of *A Book of Synonyms*. It was found necessary to keep two sets of plates of this book constantly on one press four or five months.

I had supposed that riddles belonged to the past, with square dances, the cat's cradle, and braiding rugs. But I learned that riddles were still popular, along with other puzzles:

Book Title	Copies Sold
Book of 500 Riddles	53,500
Mathematical Oddities	37,500
Curiosities of Mathematics	35,000
Puzzles and Brainteasers	33,500
Popular and Amusing Riddles	24,000
Riddle Rhymes	8,000

It is impossible to prophesy what the reading public may prefer. That book called *Curiosities of Mathematics*, for example, leaped into sudden and lasting popularity. It surprised me. I did not expect it to sell many more than the required quota to keep it in the list. Mathematics, I naturally thought, would hardly appeal to many people. But the suggestion of possible fun – even with figures – is apparently too attractive to resist.

Indoor games are always popular. These are the totals:

Book Title	Copies Sold
Party Games for Grown-Ups	38,500
How to Play Auction Bridge	37,500
How to Play Contract Bridge	30,500
How to Play Card Games	29,500
How to Play Checkers	21,000
Children's Games	18,500
How to Play Chess	17,500

There is, as you see, not a failure. Even chess, a game I thought was being forgotten, has some 17,000 devotees – and beginning players, at that – every year. And at last we have statistical evidence of the comparative popularity of chess and checkers; checkers leads by a margin of 3,500 annually.

Of amateur entertainment I have but a brief story to tell. My 1928 list will be expanded to include theatricals, ventriloquism, Hindu magic, sideshow tricks and all the rest. But there is one book on which I have figures, and these are the figures that determined me in an extensive enlargement of the list in this direction. I refer to *Amateur Magic Tricks*, which reached the total of 36,000 copies annually. Perhaps, speaking of amateur entertainment, this is the best place to insert a paragraph on fortune-telling and character-reading books. I believe, of course, that these are merely playthings — these attempts to read the future or divine *character* — and so these Little Blue Books are careful to explain that though it may be fun, it is quite without foundation in fact to *read* palms, the cards, the stars, or the bumps on the head. The books are popular, nevertheless, as these figures show:

Book Title	Copies Sold
Facts About Fortune-Telling	44,000
Facts About Palmistry	31,000
Facts About Astrology	17,000
Facts About Phrenology	12,000

Palmistry, it appears, is either the best known or the best liked method of *looking into the future*. It is a Halloween sport, and is but another bit of evidence of the fun-seeking tendency of American readers.

Hypnotism Made Plain, though as much a psychological treatise as a book of entertainment, owes its popularity, I feel certain, to a hope that there may be some fun in it. Its annual figure is 24,000 copies.

Photography is utilitarian and altogether practical, as a profession. But among amateurs it has all the lure of any other sport, and it becomes, like angling and the rest, just fun. It is not as popular as some of the other books of this class, but *Photography Self Taught* sells at the rate of 13,500 copies a year.

The popularity of radio goes without saying. For the sake of completeness, I tuck in here the statement that *The Simplicity of Radio* has an annual sales figure of 22,500 copies. Even *A Directory of Radio Stations* — which I abandoned because so difficult to keep up to date — sold 12,000 copies annually.

I feel on the verge of closing this chapter with a comedy note. For the last figure that meets my eye reminds me of the thousands of parlors along countless Main Streets where little Mary or tiny Bob is urged to stand up and "recite a piece for the gentleman," or "now say your little piece for the lady." This may be unkind, but I am sure the day of the recitation, whether from the center of the parlor carpet or from the front edge of the high school stage, is not past. There is still magic in talking about studying *elocution*, and it is taken as seriously as piano lessons for the growing boy or girl, whether there is any evidence of talent or not. It is, like Main Street itself, an American institution.

All of which has been inspired by the fact that *Popular Recitations* has an annual figure of 15,000 copies. I do not suppose that this means that very much uncomfortable reciting for the visiting lady or gentleman really goes on as a consequence of the sale of this book. I was merely reminded of it, and I wondered if it did. I sincerely hope that the book contributes to real entertainment, instead. At any rate, I think that the desire for entertainment and amusement on the part of American readers is strong enough to account for the book's popularity.

CHAPTER V
RELIGION VS FREETHOUGHT

Little Blue Book Sales Tell a Significant Story

Blinders are popular among some people, notably the incurable optimists, when by optimism they mean the triumph of their side of the question. That is, they like to think their side is on the way to victory, no matter what the facts may be. They fatuously blind themselves to the real situation, and refuse to admit any possibility of failure. Specifically, religious enthusiasts will not admit that there is any widespread tendency toward skepticism and freethought in America.

Yet recent developments in the world of books tell a different story. The trend is ever toward more progressive viewpoints, toward more free and unlimited thinking – toward what is popularly known as freethought. I could point to a dozen outstanding books of the past two years that tread ruthlessly upon religion's toes. Sinclair Lewis and his *Elmer Gantry*, for example – such a book would have been almost impossible a generation or two ago, where now it is a best seller.

Nine years ago books of skepticism, books against superstition and religion, were included in the pocket series. In those days they were almost alone, those forward-looking books of rationalism and agnosticism. Even now the Little Blue Books, in the half a hundred titles by Joseph McCabe, contain more outspoken arguments against religious dogma, ritual, and any form of blind faith than any other books available today. The Little

Blue Books are still in the vanguard, and it is because the readers want such books.

I have made no secret of my own heretical beliefs. For this reason I have been accused of saturating the Little Blue Book series with skeptical books because I wish to print propaganda that agreed with my own notions, and thus convert everyone to my own way of thinking. I have been called various uncomplimentary names on this account, and yet I may suggest mildly that even if this were true, it is only human that I should want others to see things my way.

However, aside from the fact that I am glad to publish books I agree with, the printing of free-thought Little Blue Books is not a phase of my vanity. I do not do it because I think it should be done, even if no one would buy the books. I do it because I think it ought to be done, and also because thousands of people buy the books eagerly and readily.

If these skeptical Little Blue Books did not sell well, I would drop them. I have dropped many titles that I like immensely, for I am not forcing upon the public anything it will not read. There was Sir Richard Burton's *Kasidah*. I like that poem, and I put off as long as possible the inevitable fate of that book. It was finally consigned to my Little Blue Book Morgue because American readers showed no interest in reading it. My great liking for it saved it for a time, but my business sense got the better of my personal preference and the book was withdrawn.

In fact, I am being more than fair in this question of religion. I am an avowed agnostic, or atheist, or rationalist, or whatever you wish to call me – for I subscribe to no religion (I use the word strictly in the dictionary sense, and have no sympathy with those backsliders who stretch out the definition to include anything whatever). I am against all religion – I think the Bible is a dull book. Yet I print the Bible, and in the face of an appallingly low annual sale I keep the book in the series. I do this out of stubbornness. I am determined, because I know I am prejudiced against the book, to give it more than a fair chance. Could supporters of the Bible ask any more of one who does not like it?

Take a specific case. Henry C. Vedder once prepared a two-volume work for the series called *The Words of Jesus*. He gathered all the words of Jesus

68

from the Bible and did modern readers the service of putting the sayings of Jesus into the English of today. I offered this two-volume work in the Little Blue Books for two or three years. But I could not sell it; American readers did not care about it. I withdrew it, finally, at a substantial loss. But I did not quit. I would not admit having failed to sell the words of Jesus, even. I thought it might be possible to make the book more popular by giving it a famous title. So I had a new one-volume work compiled, using the language of the King James version of the Bible, and called it *The Sermon on the Mount and Other Sayings of Jesus.*

This book of the sayings of Jesus is published without any adverse comment. There is no freethought propaganda in the book. It is offered for its own sake, on its own merits. Its title is a fair indication of what the book contains. It is what might be called a concentrated version of the New Testament. If Jesus uttered anything worth reading today, it is in this Little Blue Book. And by going to this trouble, which my religious enemies are hardly aware of, I saved Jesus for the Little Blue Book readers of America. This book, in its present form, sells about 12,500 copies every year.

Is it perhaps pertinent to ask if any Fundamentalist would have done as much for a book setting forth the tenets of an agnostic?

Other Little Blue Books from the Bible sold as follows:

Book Title	Copies Sold
The Essence of the Bible	8,000
The Gospel of Luke	5,000
The Gospel of Mark	4,000

I suppose I will be accused of doctoring these figures, but I can only sigh in the full knowledge that they are only too true. Those books represent an investment in editorial labor, type-setting, electrotyping, and so on. They take up warehouse space, and each one – Luke as well as Mark – requires its own separate pigeon-hole in the order-filling booths. The plates have to be stored in my crowded fireproof vaults, in compartments that, if released, might hold the plates for two much better sellers. As I said, I can only sigh and reflect that it is impossible to sell the Bible in five-cent doses, or in blue covers. The Bible must be black and complete, and expensive. It cannot be sold for a nickel, and it cannot be given away, even to the heathen.

Yet the figures I have just given would be meaningless if I could not make comparisons. What of the other great religious books? Here are their sales figures:

Book Title	Copies Sold
The Essence of the Koran	15,000
The Essence of the Talmud	13,500

These figures may alarm some people. It looks as though American readers were more devoted to Mohammedanism and Judaism than to Christianity. But the real reason for the popularity of these titles is curiosity. Readers want to find out what other religious books contain. They have been brought up on the Bible, perhaps, and they are curious to see whether the Koran and Talmud are anything like it. They are broadening their outlook, these curious readers, and learning lessons of tolerance. They are escaping from the cramped limits of bigotry into wider and freer opinions.

Suppose we go back and consider some other Little Blue Books that espouse Christianity or Christian principles, and see how popular they are as compared with books of other religions or beliefs:

Book Title	Copies Sold
The Wisdom of Confucius	21,000
The Essence of Buddhism	16,000
The Essence of Catholicism	14,500
The Essence of Judaism	12,000
Life of Martin Luther	12,000
Life of Jesus (Renan)	11,000
Life of Mahomet	9,000
Life of St. Francis of Assisi	8,000
History of the Modern Church	8,000
Bryan's Prince of Peace	7,000

Book Title	Copies Sold
History of the Ancient Christian Church	6,500
Poems About Jesus	5,500
History of the Medieval Christian Church	5,000
Great Christian Hymns	3,000

The evidence, again, seems to indicate a great curiosity on the part of American readers to learn what other faiths have been like. It comes to a climax in the interest shown in the sayings of Confucius (who was an agnostic), which is almost twice as great as that shown in the sayings of Jesus. Too, the life of the infidel Ingersoll is more than twice as popular as the life of Jesus.

Let us see whether this curiosity continues as we examine more skeptical titles, especially books that deal with the facts underlying Christian faith. These figures tell us a great deal:

Book Title	Copies Sold
Did Jesus Ever Live?	42,500
Self-Contradictions of the Bible	33,000
Reasons for Doubting the Bible	31,000
Forgery of the Old Testament	30,000
The Myth of the Resurrection	30,500
Thomas Paine's Age of Reason	29,000
Life of Robert G. Ingersoll	25,000
Paine's Revolt Against the Bible	21,000
How the Old Testament Was Made	16,000
Sources of Bible Myths and Legends	10,500

For every copy of the life of Jesus sold in the Little Blue Books, nearly four copies are sold of a book that suggests that perhaps he did not live at all. For every copy of Essence of the Bible sold every year, four copies of Self-Contradictions of the Bible are sold. And Thomas Paine's Age of Reason, it appears, continues its work of exposing superstition even in this twentieth century, when most of the religionists of Paine's day are

71

all but forgotten and whose books are cherished only by collectors of rare examples of colonial publishing. I should not think, for example, of ever putting any of the work of Cotton Mather into the Little Blue Books!

We are living in an age of skepticism. It is an age when people are seeking the truth. Facts are being weighed against tradition, to the cost of the latter. Faith is no longer quite sufficient to substantiate belief in this or that dogma. But of course these manifestations of a healthy skepticism are true only of readers. People who do not read books are still slaves to the faiths of their fathers. That is why the leaders of religion have always regarded most books askance, and feared the literacy of their followers. One may be led astray by reading, they say.

The demand for Little Blue Books of freethought and skepticism is real. I was venturing into unknown harbors when I first published such books. But the venture was worth the gamble, as you are beginning to see by the sales figures for these books. Free-thought is more profitable, from a publisher's point of view, than the most devout creed. The emancipation of American readers has begun. There can be no doubt of that. The day of any possible Index Expurgatorius is, I am sure, far in the past. You cannot say to the reader of today, "Here is a book you must not read because it is dangerous to accepted opinions," and expect him to leave the book alone. On the contrary, he will probably read it all the sooner.

Take skeptical titles at random. Pick them out as you will. The figures all tell the same story:

Book Title	Copies Sold
Luther Burbank's Why I Am an Infidel	64,000
Voltaire's Skeptical Essays	25,000
What Can a Free Man Worship? (Bertrand Russell)	24,000
Controversy on Christianity (Debate: Ingersoll and Gladstone)	22,500
Rome or Reason? (Debate: Ingersoll and Cardinal Manning)	19,000
Rupert Hughes' Ghastly Purpose of the Parables	19,000
What Atheism Means to Me	17,500
Clarence Darrow's Voltaire Lecture	17,500

Book Title	Copies Sold
Ingersoll's The Gods	17,000
Wit and Wisdom of Voltaire	16,500
Why I did not Enter the Ministry	14,500
The Necessity of Atheism (Shelley)	13,500
Nature of Religion (Schopenhauer)	12,000
Anatole France on Life and Destiny	10,500

The sensational sale of Luther Burbank's *Why I Am an Infidel* indicates a popular curiosity about the man, but this curiosity, it is only fair to explain, was aroused by the wide publicity given the horticulturist's declaration of agnosticism shortly before his death. Preachers, of course, made much of the death of an avowed agnostic. Being thus reminded of it, I cannot help pointing out the vicious parallel of the death of William Jennings Bryan – not as divine punishment, of course, but because "his work on earth was done."

But even the curiosity about Burbank's reasons for being an infidel is more than a hopeful sign of American reader emancipation. The fear of reading heretical books is gone, now that the shadow of the rack has faded into nothing. People dare to doubt today; they dare to read to find out whether there are justifiable reasons for doubting. Perhaps some are strengthened in their faith, but I like to believe that for every such person there are a dozen others who are inclined toward the free and healthy atmosphere of modern skepticism and free-thought.

It was the success of these scattered Little Blue Books of skeptical trend that set a great scholar to work turning out a complete history of religious controversy, written for the first time from the agnostic angle. The scholar was Joseph McCabe, and he did fifty-odd Little Blue Books in somewhat over a year, comprising *The Story of Religious Controversy*. These fifty books represent a substantial investment. Is it fair to my business judgment to suspect me of putting Joseph McCabe at this task just because I wanted to flood America with anti-religious propaganda? And remember, please, that these Little Blue Books are not distributed gratis as are many religious tracts. They cost five cents apiece, you know, and just exactly as much as hundreds of other books offered in competition with them. American readers do not have to buy these books unless they really want them.

The reception of these Joseph McCabe Little Blue Books by the American reading public gratifies me. I do not deny that. It will gratify anyone interested in enlightenment and progress. It is only when there is a clash of ideas that there can be any intellectual advance. Readers must be ready to peruse other men's views if they are to get out of the rut in which tradition has left them.

What is the verdict, in actual figures, of American readers when offered heretical works by Joseph McCabe? The verdict is as follows:

Book Title	Copies Sold
My Twelve Years in a Monastery	46,000
Seven Infidel U. S. Presidents	43,000
Horrors of the Inquisition	41,000
Absurdities of Christian Science	36,000
The Degradation of Woman	35,000
The Jesuits: Religious Rogues	34,500
Lies of Religious Literature	28,000
Galileo and Medieval Science	27,000
The Future of Religion	25,000
Pagan Christs Before Jesus	25,000
The Conflict Between Science and Religion	23,000
The Beliefs of Scientists	23,000
The Myth of Immortality	21,500
Religion's Failure to Combat Crime	21,000
The Futility of Belief in God	20,000
The Churches and Modern Progress	20,000
The Triumph of Materialism	17,500
Failure of Christian Missions	17,000
Myths of Religious Statistics	16,000
The Fraud of Spiritualism	13,000

I have, of course, not given the figures for the entire fifty-one or fifty-two books. But I have endeavored to select those titles that indicate most forcibly the interest in rationalistic books. I have listed all of the out-and-out agnostic titles. That these titles have not scared away thousands of readers is clearly evident. Bear in mind, too, that these are annual sales figures and not the total sales for the entire time these books have been in print. Some people wonder if Little Blue Books of this kind do not make more enemies than friends. Probably they do make some enemies. I receive letters from religious devotees who get a package of Little Blue Books and then happening to notice that the series contains such titles as those discussed in this chapter, they put the whole shipment into the stove. The passion for burning *dangerous* books still survives, even if this is the twentieth century. But these fanatics are the exception rather than the rule. American book readers as a group seem to be tolerant and ready to let everyone have a hearing.

In the chapter I have called "Business Man or Philanthropist?" I point out that, though I am strictly a business man when it comes to publishing these Little Blue Books, I am sincerely endeavoring to guide my editorial decisions by the dictates of my convictions. Obviously, had I been entirely mercenary, I might never have dared to offer Joseph McCabe the contract for writing fifty books or so of this nature. I would not have printed any skeptical or freethought books in the first place, thinking that they might hinder a few sales here and there. But I did print the skeptical books, and they were successful, and I did employ McCabe, and his books have been successful too. If that is philanthropy, I am glad of it – though my part ended when the demands of the public began.

But what if the books based on the Bible and Christian traditions had been more popular than Ingersoll and Paine and Voltaire and McCabe? Would that, you ask me, have made the story different? Perhaps. It is a supposition that can never be brought into the realm of workaday facts. If American readers had been so shackled still that they would not read Thomas Paine and his sympathizers, I might never have begun the Little Blue Books in the first place. I might have turned to the manufacture of chewing gum, or something equally free from intellectual dynamite.

It is clear that the genesis of the Little Blue Books is bound up closely with a belief in American readers of today. The whole aim of the series is false unless I believe, and you agree, that American readers will support a series of good books at a low cost price by the tens and hundreds of thousands of copies of each title annually. I had a suspicion, or a hope, that American readers would grab at five-cent books printing good material, free from the usual trash. It was a hunch, but it was the kind of a hunch that made the venturing into freethought and rationalism not only possible but inevitable.

If the Bible had sold by the hundred thousands, would I have quit? Again I cannot answer the question, because it is not in point. The Bible was already selling by the hundred thousand, as a piece of merchandise, thought desirable as a fetish if nothing more. I would hardly have hoped to sell the Bible, at a nickel a selection, as a fetish. I published it as literature – or as *entertainment* – just as I published all the other Little Blue Books. It failed, as compared with other more popular books. Had it been otherwise, there would have been something wrong with American readers, or with my estimate of them. As I said, the readers would have been different. The whole publishing field would have been different. I would not have had the idea of the Little Blue Books in the first place. This success of skeptical and heretical books is but one phase of the realization of a dream based upon a sound foundation in reality.

I did not start the Little Blue Books at some wild tangent. It was not a crazy notion unrelated to the world, without any connection with life as it is today. I thought I saw a demand – I did my best to fill it. Skepticism, rationalism, free thought – these were part of the bill of goods necessary to fill the demand. I interpreted the demand aright. If I myself had not been agnostic, of course I would not have seen it. That is all.

CHAPTER VI
SIDELIGHTS ON
READING TASTES

Some Miscellaneous Facts About American Book Buyers

There is one book that I suppose will always be in the best seller class. It is justly popular, and yet it has become the bugbear of many a book lover, exactly as it has also been the constant inspiration of publishers of gift books, special editions, and such. I refer, of course, to *The Rubaiyat of Omar Khayyam*, as translated by Edward Fitzgerald. Yes, it is in the Little Blue Books—and it is No. 1! It is the oldest title in the series. It has never been crowded from its numerical first place, and I don't suppose it ever will be. For the Rubaiyat, in this edition, sells 50,000 copies annually – and in competition with 1,259 other titles!

If anyone had wanted to lay a wager, before I published this book, I might have been tempted to vote against it, on the grounds that nearly everyone must own a copy already. I have three in my own library: two are gifts. Someone is always giving a copy of the Rubaiyat to someone else. Gift editions are too plentiful, and too superficially attractive, to be resisted.

Not that the Rubaiyat is not a great poem. It is. I like it; I even have admiration, mingled with some affection, for Omar Khayyam. He was a man after my own inclination or perhaps I should say, after some of my inclinations. But the Rubaiyat has been done to death by so many unappreciative mouthers that many readers of books feel urged to hide when it is mentioned. Clarence Darrow quotes it often and effectively, and quite without affectation. But he is the only man of such high attainments who dares to do it.

My liking for the Rubaiyat is clear, because it was the first Little Blue Book I sent to the linotype. That my liking was shared by thousands of others accounts for the fact that it is still No. 1. The sale of the book during its nine years approached the half million mark.

A Word About Poetry

Poetry in general is hard to sell, even for five cents. I am sorry for this for a very practical reason – something like ninety different volumes of poetry were in the Little Blue Books at one time. Many have been withdrawn, and I explain all this in another chapter ("The Morgue").

Of popular poetry, Rudyard Kipling leads:

Book Title	Copies Sold
Gunga Din, and Other Poems	25,500
Mandalay, and Other Poems	19,000
The Vampire, and Other Poems	14,500

The leadership of the first of the trio is accounted for, I expect, by the familiar phrase: "You're a better man than I am, Gunga Din!" The second is a favourite song, and the third – ah, yes, the "rag, a bone, and a hank of hair." Phrases like these capture popular fancy, sometimes worthily and sometimes not, and they cling tenaciously. For I am, of course, under no illusions. These three little Blue Books of Kipling's poetry are sold because of three leading titles identifying each of them. If they had been called *The Rubaiyat of Omar Khayyam*, Vol. 1, Vol. 2 and Vol 3, respectively, they would not have sold nearly as well. For every man who knows the name Kipling, there are a dozen who will respond to *Mandalay*.

The only immediate rival of Gunga Din is the mighty Casey – *Casey at the Bat, and Other Poems* also has an annual sales figure of 25,500 copies.

Humorous verse is popular, but not as popular as comic poems. I am not contradicting myself. This is the explanation:

Book Title	Copies Sold
A Book of Comic Poems	21,500
A Book of Humorous Verse	10,500

The psychology of this may be that *comic poems* is shorter and more to the point than *humorous verse*. The word *comic* perhaps suggests something funnier than does the word *humorous*. The contents of both books are quite similar. The only explanation of the fact that one is twice as popular as the other is that the title of one is twice as appealing as the title of the other.

Other books of comic poems are:

Book Title	Copies Sold
A Book of Comic Dialect Poems	11,000
A Book of Nonsense Verse	10,000

American poets can now be measured properly as regards their popularity, for here are the indisputable figures:

Book Title	Copies Sold
Poems of John Greenleaf Whittier	17,500
Poems of Edgar Allan Poe	14,500
Poems of William Cullen Bryant	14,500
Poems of Walt Whitman	11,000
Poems of Ralph Waldo Emerson	10,500
American Poetry of Today (Anthology)	9,000
Courtship of Miles Standish (Longfellow)	8,000
Poems of Oliver Wendell Holmes	7,000
Vision of Sir Launfal (Lowell)	6,000
Poetry of the Southern States	5,500

I have tried the manner of the Kipling titles – using some popular poem as the lead – with Poe (*The Raven*), Bryant (*Thanatopsis*), Holmes (*One Hoss Shay*), and so forth, with mild success. General anthologies do not go very well, as can be seen by the low figures for the last two books listed above. Whittier is first, and Poe and Bryant are tied for second place in the reading hearts of their countrymen, with Whitman and Emerson close thirds. Yet, if you had been asked, you might have guessed Longfellow as first. Now you have actual sales statistics to guide you.

British poets are in demand as follows:

Book Title	Copies Sold
Harlot's House, and Other Poems (Wilde)	40,000
Poems of Robert Burns	21,000
Poems of John Keats	13,500
Tennyson's Enoch Arden	13,500
Scott's Lady of the Lake	13,000
Poems of Percy Bysshe Shelley	12,500
Alexander Pope's Essay on Man	12,500
Macaulay's Lays of Ancient Rome	12,000
Coleridge's Ancient Mariner	10,500
Great English Poems	10,000
Goldsmith's Deserted Village	9,000
Ballad of Reading Gaol (Wilde)	9,000
Elizabeth Barrett Browning's Sonnets from the Portuguese	7,000
Sonnets of William Shakespeare	7,000
Poems of William Wordsworth	5,000
Poems of Alfred Tennyson	5,000
Poems of William Morris	4,000
Robert Browning's Pippa Passes	4,000
Robert Browning's Lyric Love	4,000
Ballads of Sir Walter Scott	4,000

Robert Burns wins first place without any argument. I leave out Oscar Wilde's book because of the title – it is *The Harlot's House* that jumps up the demand for that selection (see the chapter entitled "Are Americans Afraid of Sex?"). Keats and Shelley sell on the merits of their names alone. *The Ancient Mariner*, *Lays of Ancient Rome*, *Enoch Arden*, *The Deserted Village*, and *The Lady of the Lake* are famous titles. Pope's *Essay on Man* does not suggest verse, and sells so well largely because it implies a discussion of mankind – or so I interpret its popularity. Speaking of famous titles, Browning's *Pied Piper* and Whittier's *Snowbound*, in the same volume, together sell 11,000 copies every year.

Of foreign poets, Dante is by far the best with his *Inferno*. The Little Blue Book edition is in two volumes, and the sale runs to 20,000 sets annually. Francois Villon is next best, though he sells only 9,000 copies per year. *Famous German Poems* sells about 8,000 a year. *The Life and Poems of Catullus* is a book scheduled, one of these days, to go into The Morgue – at this writing its annual sales total is only 3,000 copies.

The Bard of Avon

What of the popularity of William Shakespeare in this twentieth century? On the stage, if sympathetically presented, I can vouch for him – Otis Skinner as Falstaff in *The Merry Wives of Windsor* can get as hearty laughs from a present-day audience as ever an actor did in Shakespeare's own time. Humor was the same to the sixteenth century Londoner in the pit as it is to the twentieth century American in the orchestra. But do Americans read Shakespeare?

The Little Blue Books devoted to Shakespeare's immortal plays are a portion of the series of which I have always been proud. The editions are complete and verbatim – though they often run to 96 and 128 pages each, which are almost prohibitively expensive in these days of a five-cent price uniformly postpaid to any address in the world. The plays sell as follows:

Book Title	Copies Sold
Romeo and Juliet	14,500
Julius Cesar	9,500
The Merchant of Venice	9,500
Hamlet	9,000
Macbeth	9,000
As You Like It	9,000
The Taming of the Shrew	9,000
A Midsummer Night's Dream	8,000
The Comedy of Errors	6,500
The Merry Wives of Windsor	6,500
The Tempest	6,500
Othello	6,000
Twelfth Night	5,000
Much Ado About Nothing	5,000
King Lear	4,000
Measure for Measure	2,500

Romeo and Juliet is the only play that does the necessary minimum or better per year. I shall probably keep all his plays in print that sell 5,000 copies or more a year. All of the historical plays – the Richards, Henrys, and King John plays – will go into The Morgue, for they all do scarcely 1,000 copies a year. *Venus and Adonis*, the poem, sells about 7,000 copies annually.

Other Dramatists

Henrik Ibsen is probably the best-known name among more modern playwrights. I am also proud of offering his leading plays in Little Blue Book form. They are in demand, too, as can be seen from these figures:

Book Title	Copies Sold
Ghosts	22,500
A Doll's House	15,000
Hedda Gabler	12,000
Pillars of Society	10,500
The Master Builder	9,000
The Wild Duck	7,000
Rosmersholm	5,000

The first three plays are the most famous, which undoubtedly accounts for their popularity. It is but another sign of the reader-curiosity in America about the most famous classics, when such titles are put readily within people's reach. The dramatist with the next best representation in the series is Moliére. His plays sell like this:

Book Title	Copies Sold
Ridiculous Women	11,500
The Show-Off (The Nobody Who Apes Nobility)	10,000
The Misanthrope	8,000

Other miscellaneous plays reach these sales totals:

Book Title	Copies Sold
Love's Redemption (Leo Tolstoy)	29,500
The God of Vengeance (Sholom Asch)	11,000
Lady Windermere's Fan (Oscar Wilde)	11,000
The Land of Heart's Desire (William Butler Yeats)	9,000
Woman of No Importance (Wilde)	8,000
One Act Plays (August Strindberg)	7,000
Importance of Being Earnest (Oscar Wilde)	6,000

Plays are about on a par with poetry – they are rather hard to sell unless the titles are particularly appealing. They can scarcely be sold at all, as plays. The public likes to see drama on the stage, but apparently cares little about reading plays.

I had a terrible time with the ancient classical dramas of Greece and Rome. I tell the story elsewhere, when I recount my failures and shed tears over the books that had to be withdrawn. Of the plays remaining in the list, it may be apropos here to list some of the sales figures for them:

Book Title	Copies Sold
The Bacchantes (Euripides)	12,000
Prometheus Bound (Aeschylus)	10,500
King Oedipus (Sophocles)	9,000
Electra (Sophocles)	9,000
Antigone (Sophocles)	8,000
Electra (Euripides)	7,000
The Frogs (Aristophanes)	7,000
Medea (Euripides)	6,000
Hippolytus (Euripides)	5,000

Prometheus Bound was the earliest classical drama to be added to the series, and, from the indications of these figures, it looks very much as though it will be one of the last to be withdrawn – if it ever is. *The Bacchantes* of Euripides, undoubtedly because its title implies joyous dancers or some similar idea, is the most popular classical drama of all. It was the second to be added to the list. Basing hopes on the success of these two, many others were added; too many, as I tell in another place.

Other Ancient Classics

People are curious to know how Plato and his Socratic dialogues, and some of the other classical selections from antiquity, sell as compared with other books in the series. The figures, though often low when placed against the sales figures for more popular books, are still large enough to amaze many readers. For example, here are the sales totals (annual, remember) for some books frequently regarded as *dry*, and thought destined to be read only by professors and other pedants:

Book Title	Copies Sold
Meditations (Golden Sayings) of Marcus Aurelius	22,500
Trial and Death of Socrates	15,000
Plato's Republic	13,500
Decadent Rome As Seen by Tacitus and Juvenal	8,000
Dialogues of Plato	8,000
Xenophon's Memorabilia of Socrates	6,000
Moral Discourses of Epictetus	6,000
Morals of Seneca	5,000
Cicero As Revealed in His Letters	4,000

It certainly speaks well for American readers to buy 22,500 copies of a book of the thoughts of an ancient Roman emperor, Marcus Aurelius, whose works, though remembered by the embellishment of a glittering title – *Golden Sayings* – one would think likely to be little read in modern circles. It is even hopeful that 4,000 people every year can be found who want to read about Marcus Tullius Cicero. I wonder, too, if the poor showing of this isn't partly due to bad memories of the orator, hanging over from high school regimens. I'm afraid I shall have to withdraw Cicero, if his name is not in any more demand than this – but I'm letting him stay through 1928, as a special extension of life.

Some Famous Books

Do books survive because people want to read them, or because of some arbitrary decision on the part of college professors? The question, though it may sound foolish, is frequently in the minds of readers. Many famous books are compulsory reading in the schools. Some are read by conscientious readers for *background*, or because of some petty notion of self-duty. But if such famous books sell for a nickel apiece, it is fair to assume that they are bought to be read only for two reasons: either to satisfy a natural curiosity, since it isn't costing much or, finding other classical titles unforbidding, additional ones are bought because they may prove to be good reading.

Selecting more or less at random, here are some interesting figures:

Book Title	Copies Sold
Dr. Jekyll and Mr. Hyde (Stevenson)	29,500
The Man Without a Country (Edward Everett Hale)	27,500
Voyage to the Moon (Jules Verne)	19,000
Autobiography of Cellini	18,500
Confessions of an Opium-Eater (De Quincey)	17,500
The Pilgrim's Progress (Bunyan)	17,000
Aesop's Famous Fables	16,000
Poor Richard's Almanac	14,500
Andersen's Famous Fairy Tales	13,500
Travels of Marco Polo	13,000
Tales from Arabian Nights	12,000
Rip Van Winkle (Washington Irving)	11,000
She Stoops to Conquer (Goldsmith)	11,000
Adventures of Baron Munchausen	10,500
A Child's Garden of Verse (Stevenson)	10,000
Thoughts on the Meaning of Life (Joseph Joubert)	9,500
Burton's Anatomy of Melancholy	8,000
Meditations on Man (Pascal)	7,000
The Mikado (W. S. Gilbert)	7,000
A Christmas Carol (Dickens)	6,500
Robinson Crusoe (Defoe)	5,000
Boswell's Life of Dr. Johnson	5,000
An Apology for Idlers (Stevenson)	4,000
The Beggar's Opera (John Gay)	4,000

A number of conclusions can be drawn from these miscellaneous totals. Here are valuable secrets – here, in short, are revelations of the right classics to issue in handsome editions. *Robinson Crusoe*, it can be seen clearly, has been done to death; everyone has read this story, in childhood or later. There is little reader-curiosity about such a book, so constantly accessible to nearly everyone.

But Jules Verne still appeals to the adventurous imagination, even with his extraordinary *Voyage to the Moon*. Likewise the famous travels of Marco Polo, the Venetian who made his way to the great Kubla Khan in distant and marvelous Asia. The adventures of that greatest of liars, Baron Munchausen, still hold fair sway over modern readers. And the Arabian Nights – Sinbad, Aladdin, Ali Baba, and the rest – even today, in a twentieth century full of wonders, 12,000 people want to know more about the magical land of Bagdad and the mysterious East.

I have put in some of the failing titles deliberately. This chronicle is not entirely one of success. I tell in the chapter called "Rejuvenating the Classics" how it has been possible to resuscitate, as it were, many of these weaker titles by changing the listing in some way. I am disappointed, I assure you, with the poor showing of Boswell's biography of beloved old Sam Johnson. But something may yet be done with this book – I am thinking about it, and it may be saved from The Morgue, where it surely does not deserve to go.

At Stevenson's *Apology for Idlers* I am not as astonished. After all, America is certainly not a land of idlers, as the Rotary and Kiwanis Clubs will hastily assure you. America has no hankering to read about excuses for *laziness* – yet more's the pity, for what Stevenson is really talking about is leisure for cultural betterment. Ah, that is perhaps it – the elusive title, the hope of a bad seller! I have happened upon it by chance, while the keys of my typewriter clatter busily away – something about leisure in which to cultivate the mind and pursue that elusive culture that modern Americans are so anxious to capture.

John Gay's *Beggar's Opera*, though plainly listed as comic, does not do well either. Perhaps the word *beggar* is objectionable to busy Americans, who are ever at their work making progress in the world. Perhaps it is the word *opera*, which suggests formality, highbrowism, white gloves, and the agony that so many husbands are dragged to endure. In an earlier section of this chapter, I have pointed out that plays – which include operas – do not sell well. Oliver Goldsmith's *She Stoops to Conquer* is one of the exceptions. Its title is excellent, and even if it is a play, people are curious to find out what it is about.

Benjamin Franklin's *Poor Richard's Almanac* still has its adherents, new ones every year, 14,500 of them. No one knows how many editions this book has gone through, in the hands of hundreds of publishers. No one can tell into how many languages it has been translated. Yet still it goes on, among the most popular of the famous books, a perennial, even an everlasting, favorite. Its maxims are American, strictly – "early to bed and early to rise will make a man healthy, wealthy, and wise" – what Babbitt could ask for anything nearer the glorious One Hundred Percent? Franklin knew what he was talking about, and he had also a sense of humor – no wonder he is still popular. The two best among the famous titles listed above are *Dr. Jekyll and Mr. Hyde* and *The Man Without a Country*. In the first we have a story of dual personality – horror mingled with a liking for the occult and mysterious. The story is world famous. In Hale's story there is more than the appeal of a good yarn well told. There is that propagandistic note that Stephen Decatur strikes in his lines about his country, may she always be in the right, but his country right or wrong. Patriotism is the lure – and something deeper, too, for mere chauvinism could not make the story as enduring – something that is revealed in the lines that cause poor Nolan to fling a copy of Scott's *Lay of the Last Minstrel* into the sea: "Breathes there the man with soul so dead who never to himself hath said. This is my own, my native land!" It is provincial, even primitive; it is the Home, Sweet Home chord. It is, in short, so much hokum – but it always has its appeal, and is therefore consistently popular.

In the eagerness to read Cellini's memoirs I detect something else. It is that lure that I discuss at some length in the chapter called "Are Americans Afraid of Sex?" For Cellini – and he is so described in the Little Blue Book catalogue and advertisements – was a notorious murderer, lover, and miscellaneous sinner. He took a great deal of joy in life, and he pursued his notions of happiness with much fervor and zest. He killed willingly, but he risked his own life with as little compunction as he took that of someone else. He tells us he was a hero, and he is not slow to make himself out a good one. Hence he is good reading.

SIDELIGHTS ON READING TASTES

Who Is Your Favorite Philosopher?

In the Little Blue Book poll of philosophers a genuine insight is given into reading preferences. There is no guesswork here, nor is there any need for analytical supposition based on the supposed character of American readers. These are facts, and from them I am in a position to state positively that America readers select (by preference) the following philosophers in the ratio of these figures:

Book Title	Copies Sold
Story of Friedrich Nietzsche's Philosophy	45,000
Story of Plato's Philosophy	39,000
Story of Anatole France and His Philosophy	32,000
Story of Aristotle's Philosophy	27,000
Story of Arthur Schopenhauer's Philosophy	26,500
Story of Baruch Spinoza's Philosophy	25,500
Story of Francis Bacon's Philosophy	25,500
Story of Immanuel Kant's Philosophy	24,000
Story of Voltaire's Philosophy	24,000
Story of Herbert Spencer's Philosophy	19,000
Story of Mark Twain's Laughing Philosophy	10,500
Story of Ralph Waldo Emerson's Philosophy	8,000
Story of Henri Bergson's Philosophy	8,000

There is no question about Nietzsche's taking first place. The book in the above list is the one by Will Durant. Emily Hamblen's *How to Understand the Philosophy of Nietzsche* does nearly half as well with an annual total of 20,000 copies. Even Nietzsche's epigrams, in a book by themselves, sell 13,000 copies per year.

Plato is second choice among American readers. His books of philosophy, apart from Will Durant's account of him, are also popular (see the figures in a preceding section of this chapter). Third is the Frenchman, Anatole France. France's *Reflections on Life and Destiny* sells 10,500 copies annually. The total for his *Wisdom of the Ages and Other Stories* is 10,000 copies, and his *Epigrams of Love, Life and Laughter* does not do as well, ag-

89

gregating hardly 6,000 copies yearly at this writing. (Books of epigrams are another group that is hard to sell in large quantities.) France's *The Human Tragedy*, however, vindicates him with a total of 16,000 copies.

Emerson and Mark Twain, two American philosophers, are low in the scale. Emerson is strongly represented in the series, however, and his books, if taken all together, mount up to a substantial total. Mark Twain is more usually thought of as a humorist than as a philosopher. Of the Europeans, Henri Bergson is least popular. Will Durant's *Contemporary European Philosophers* sells 19,000 copies annually, while his *Contemporary American Philosophers* reaches a yearly total of 28,000 copies. This is in direct contradiction to the figures for Emerson and Mark Twain, but the reason I have noted may help to explain it. Will Durant's name, also, is an inducement.

Books that have subject matter allied to philosophy are fair sellers as a whole. In general, those books that deal with life and mankind are in regular demand. For example, here are some comparative figures:

Book Title	Copies Sold
Is Life Worth Living? (Darrow Debate)	33,000
The Art of Happiness (John Cowper Powys)	31,000
Is the Human Race Getting Anywhere? (Darrow Debate)	30,000
Facing the Plain Facts of Life (Maxims of La Rochefoucauld)	13,500
Has Life Any Meaning? (Debate)	13,000
What Life Means to Me (Jack London)	10,000

The debates in which Clarence Darrow took part are, of course, so popular because of his name. But their popularity is also due to their subject matter. For example, his debate on prohibition sells only 15,000 copies, or only half as well as either of the two titles listed above. His debate on capital punishment jumps up to 28,000 copies. Again, his dry law debate with Wheeler sells only 14,500 copies. Subject matter has its influence – and incidentally, prohibition is not so vital an issue to American readers as capital punishment.

Americans are clearly interested in how to secure happiness. The sale of Mr. Powy's book is exceeded only by his *Secret of Self-Development* and *One Hundred Best Books*, both discussed in the chapter entitled "The Quest for Self-Improvement."

E.W. Howe, the *Sage of Potato Hill*, has contributed several booklets of worldly wisdom that could come under the life-philosophy grouping, though I generally list them, for better effect, and quite as appropriately, under Humor. It is interesting here to compare the effect of the titles. For book against book, when the author is the same, is a competition of titles alone:

Book Title	Copies Sold
Success Easier Than Failure	77,000
Sinner Sermons	20,000
Preaching from the Audience	13,000
Dying Like a Gentleman and Other Stories	11,000
Notes for My Biographer	5,000

Obviously, *Notes for My Biographer* is, as a title, responsible for the book's low sale. It is being changed to *Stepping Stones Up from Failure*, which really describes the book better. Mr. Howe wanted to call *Success Easier Than Failure* – which has a sensational sales figure, due to the American's everlasting quest for success – *Preaching of a Brother-in-Law of the Church*, which is much too literary and recondite. I am sure that, with these figures against him, Mr. Howe will be glad the change in title was made.

Comparisons of sales totals on philosophers, by the way, are also given in the chapter entitled "A Comparison of Advertising Mediums." I add here by way of an aside that the figures may differ, and pause only to call the attention of the reader to the fact that the figures in these chapters discussing what America wants to read are based on sales from the list as a whole and not from particular advertisements. The results necessarily vary, depending to some extent on the medium and whether the book is in competition with 1,259 or only 299 other titles.

Story Collections

Little Blue Book statistics are available, too, on various types or classifications of stories – adventure, mystery, and so on. These data are alike a commentary on and a revelation of American reading preference. You can get an inkling of it from the newsstand magazines that cater to such specialized – and stereotyped – fiction as these groupings often imply. But here the result comes from offering good literature, some of it in classified groups for the sake of discrimination. Let the figures tell their own story:

Book Title	Copies Sold
Funny Ghost Stories (Jerome)	33,000
Tales of Far North (Jack London)	25,500
Great Ghost Stories	21,000
Adventure Stories (Jack London)	17,500
Great Sea Stories	17,000
Tales of Big Snows (Jack London)	16,000
Mystery Tales of the Sea	16,000
Tales of Mystery (Poe)	14,500
Ridiculous Stories (Stephen Leacock)	14,500
Civil War Stones (Ambrose Bierce)	13,000
Great Detective Stories	13,000
Masterpieces of Mystery Stories	12,000
Masterpieces of Adventure Stories	11,000

The ghosts have it. The funny ghost stories, of course, have the additional attraction of humor. Adventure – including the sea and the far north – comes next, helped out to a good extent by the name of Jack London. War stories, at least not Bierce's iconoclastic glimpses of the Civil War, are not as popular as current whitewashed episodes appearing in certain periodicals. But the copies of the Bierce books will do more good than harm. They deserve to be read, for they tell of war as it is – or more nearly do that than much similar fiction.

The detective stories of Arthur Conan Doyle – featuring the ever popular Sherlock Holmes – do about as well as the general detective title given above. The average is about 14,000 copies annually, which is not so bad, considering that there are seven different books of Sherlock Holmes tales in the list.

Foreign fiction, grouped by nationality, does not sell as well as might be expected. The well-known names – such as Guy de Maupassant, Emile Zola, Honor é de Balzac, Remy de Gourmont, and so forth, for France; Anton Chekhov, Leo Tolstoy, Maxim Gorki, Leonid Andreyev, and so forth, for Russia – always do rather well. But I am referring more particularly to such collections as the following:

Book Title	Copies Sold
Famous Russian Stories	16,000
Yiddish Short Stories	13,500
African Negro Folk Tales	12,000
Spanish Stories	11,000
African Jungle Tales	9,000
Irish Fairy Tales	8,000
Brazilian Stories	5,000
Costa Rican Tales	5,000

Costa Rica and Brazil do not attract United States readers, it seems. French and Russian fiction are always the most popular of the European possibilities. I am rather amazed at the showing of the Yiddish stories; the success of this book pleases while it surprises me. Ireland is poorly represented here with fairy tales, which, as a class, are not as popular as more realistic fiction.

The Proverbs

A unique feature of the Little Blue Books has been the collections of national proverbs. I began, rather practically, with the English proverbs, and ranged far over the world, finally including even Persian proverbs, African black proverbs, and so on. The venture, as a whole, has been, I regret to say, a failure. I mention it again in "The Morgue," but here it may be well to give the actual sales figures of those books of proverbs still in the list January 1, 1928:

Book Title	Copies Sold
Irish Proverbs	11,000
English Proverbs	8,000
Chinese Proverbs	6,500
Spanish Proverbs	5,500
Turkish Proverbs	5,500
Hindu Proverbs	5,000
Scotch Proverbs	5,000
Modern Greek Proverbs	5,000
Japanese Proverbs	4,000
French Proverbs	3,000
Italian Proverbs	3,000
Arabian Proverbs	2,500
Persian Proverbs	2,500
Russian Proverbs	2,000

I should add here that I tried to save these books – which contain the epitome of national or racial wisdom – by calling each, instead of *Proverbs*, the *Wit and Wisdom* of the English people, French people, and so on. These sales figures must be viewed in the light of the change in title, which increased them all somewhat. Many of them were near ciphers before the change. But keeping the change in mind, it appears that American book-buyers feel that Russians, Arabians, and Persians have the least propensity for wit or wisdom in their national proverbs. The Irish, apparently, are credited with the most wit, and possibly also the most wisdom.

Maxims and Epigrams

Once upon a time I had a classification in the Little Blue Book catalogue named Maxims and Epigrams. It was not a success. Readers do not care for short, pithy sayings in too large doses. So now they are scattered about, and they sell better. However, as a venture in itself, epigrammatic collections are not exciting. Here are some of the figures:

Book Title	Copies Sold
Epigrams of Oscar Wilde	13,500
Epigrams of Bernard Shaw	9,000
Wit and Wisdom of Disraeli	8,000
Wit and Wisdom of Thackeray	8,000
Epigrams of Henry David Thoreau	7,000
Wit and Wisdom of Dickens	7,000
Epigrams of Remy de Gourmont	6,500
Wit and Wisdom of Charles Lamb	5,000
Epigrams of Henrik Ibsen	4,000
Maxims of Napoleon	3,000
Epigrams of George Moore	2,500

Oscar Wilde has a reputation as a wit, from the looks of the above figures, even in America.

Personalities

Whom most do Americans want to read about? Whose lives most appeal to American readers? What biographies should be the most successful in America?

I have some interesting statistics toward answering such questions. The Little Blue Books have a large list of *short* biographies especially written for the series. The sales figures tell what personalities are of strongest appeal to American readers of today:ye

Book Title	Copies Sold
Thomas Paine	21,000
Oscar Wilde	19,000
Napoleon Bonaparte	17,500
Abraham Lincoln	13,500
Leo Tolstoy	12,000
Jesus Christ	11,000
Machiavelli	7,000

Book Title	Copies Sold
Benjamin Disraeli	6,500
Thomas Paine (a second biography)	6,000
Michelangelo	5,000
Frederick the Great	4,000
Thomas Jefferson	4,000

The list given here is small. I have selected it principally to show that biography as such does not sell widely enough to justify much of it in a series that must go into the tens of thousands annually. Some of the better titles are discussed elsewhere. A few of the better ones listed above are influenced as much by the title as anything – Oscar Wilde, for instance, whose life is characterized in the advertising as tragic. The notoriety of Wilde's later years is probably recalled, which makes the story of his life take on a sensational aspect. Napoleon, Jesus, and Abraham Lincoln are the best so far as their names alone are concerned – three sharply divergent ideals of human character. In each of these three men, too, it is more the traditional or legendary character that appeals, than the real flesh-and-blood man.

In other chapters the differences made in sales by changes in title, variations in placing titles first among one group and then another in the catalogue, and so on, are thoroughly discussed. Selling books by the ten thousand is not a simple matter of listing the books and announcing that you can take your pick for five cents. An American reader will not spend even five cents until he is quite sure what he is getting in exchange for his nickel.

CHAPTER VII

REJUVENATING THE CLASSICS

The Cause and Justification of Changing Titles of Books

Firirst of all I want to ask and answer the old question. What is a classic? In schools and colleges a classic is a book that students may be allowed to read with safety – without damage to their moral integrity or to their patriotic zeal – because it has become a part of literary tradition and has ceased to be startling or new or interesting even. A classic, according to the students' idea of it, is a boresome and tiresome book that *must* be read just because it is a classic. A classic, in the usual acceptance of the term, is a work written some time in the past, probably by an author now dead, and that is still being read by those who are supposed to have literary discrimination. This is very arbitrary, but it gives the popular idea.

Now I have not the space to go deeply into the accusation against academic English departments that they spoil the classics for our younger readers. I will say, however, that there is no doubt that many a good book has been spoiled forever by this very academic poison for people who would otherwise read it with enjoyment. This poison is so insidious that it is seldom recognized for what it is. It is poisonous because it suggests or implies that classics ought to be read simply because custom has accepted them and given them their very proper niches in the world's literature.

I have never argued for or against classics as such. To me, as to Oscar Wilde before me, a book is either well written and worth reading or badly written and not worth the trouble. Most classics, I am glad to agree, are well written and worth reading. The judgment of time is for the most part sound and trustworthy. But is it possible to offer such books – such classics – to the reading public with the bare assertion that they have stood the test of time and therefore should be read avidly? I contend that it is not possible to do any such thing.

You can sell the classics as classics, all dressed up in handsome bindings, with gold tops and all that sort of thing, as merchandise. But merchandise is not read. It is put on the library or parlor table for show, along with a china elephant, an amber-colored ash tray, Lincoln book-ends, and a family photograph or two in gilded frames. These classics are bought not for what is inside but for how they look on the outside. The sales patter that puts such books into American homes is particular to stress the appearance of the books – their luxurious binding, their artistic distinction from a mechanical point of view, and so on. It is an old jest that such a set of books, such merchandise, never has the pages cut if they come uncut. I repeat, merchandise is all right as merchandise, but it is seldom if ever read.

It is another thing altogether if a book is sold strictly on the merit of its contents, to while away a spare quarter of an hour, or to educate oneself, or to satisfy a wholly legitimate literary curiosity. It is a practical certainty that a book bound in paper or card covers is not bought to fill a bookcase or to adorn a piece of furniture. I can reasonably make the statement that no purchaser of the Little Blue Books has ever bought his assortment out of any superficial vanity. He has always bought Little Blue Books because, for some reason or other, he wants to read them.

Nor do I mean to say that Little Blue Books are cheap or disreputable or need to be kept out of sight. It has been my experience, in so far as I have been able to find out about Little Blue Book owners, that readers of the Little Blue Books are rather proud of them. They prove the very point I have been making – they buy Little Blue Books for one reason only: to read them. Readers of books are always, and with sufficient excuse, proud of their reading. The Little Blue Books are neat, though inexpensive. There is nothing cheaply flamboyant or sensational about their appearance. The blue covers are quiet instead of some flaming color. The covers have only conventional type printed in black, for there are no startling jackets or flaunted pictures of blood or nudity or pageantry.

Little Blue Books are bought to be read, *and* now the question is, "Do people buy classics in Little Blue Book form in order to read them?" This is the nucleus of the whole discussion. This is the critical point. This is what I have been driving at all through the preceding paragraphs. And the answer is that some people buy some of the classics in Little Blue Book form in order to read them.

When I began the series of pocket classics to become internationally famous as the Little Blue Books, I began it with the idea that I would print the classics in a form everyone could afford. From the first, in my advertising, I made the most of the word *classics*. I subscribed to the notion that to call a book a classic was a sufficient endorsement of its worth – or at least that such an appellation would be a strong selling argument in offering the book to the reading public. I still think that the argument is in many ways a strong one, but, as I have already pointed out, it is also a kind of boomerang. Sometimes classics is a selling point. At other times it is a handicap, for people would rather read something they know will interest them, instead of gambling with something merely on a reputation fostered largely, they think, by old fogy college professors and bespectacled students of literature.

One of the first things I learned in my publishing experience is that the reading public is a critical audience. I mean this in more than one sense. I mean that readers are often skeptical of what is offered to them. They will by no means swallow a thing hook, line and sinker. They want to be told exactly what they are going to buy, and they prefer to decide for themselves whether they really want to read a particular book or not – classic or no classic.

If anyone will take the trouble to investigate the first two or three hundred Little Blue Books that were offered at ten cents apiece, he will learn that I carried my belief about low-priced classics for every man into complete reality. I put out almost nothing but classics at first. That was the idea with which I started, and it was not a halfway plan that I had in mind. I selected classics that I had read and liked, and I also put in a number of classics that I had read and did not like. I had a conviction that any classic

99

offered at ten cents a copy would sell by the tens of thousands.

The early experience in Little Blue Book publishing seemed to bear out my belief about low-priced classics. I ventured only so far, and then, finding that the idea was working out, I went farther. The whole expansion of the Little Blue Book series has proceeded by this simple principle – find out what the public wants and give it to them. I would do myself an injustice if I did not point out, at discreet intervals, that the field of dime or nickel books in America was an entirely unexplored one. Much of the progress was made in the dark, with only glimmers of light here and there.

But always, as with a constant hammering, one dominant precept was written down in the Little Blue Book editorial archives. Each rebuff repeated it; each success emphasized it anew. *Buyers of the Little Blue Books can be induced to purchase only what they earnestly desire to read.* This is not because they are afraid of wasting their money. The low price rules that objection out immediately. But it is because there is no other conceivable reason for buying a Little Blue Book. There is never any pictorial or luxury appeal whatever. There is no such thing as a Little Blue Book famous for being a best seller, and therefore bought because it is the thing everyone else is buying and reading. In fact, it is not even because Little Blue Books are books, but just because they contain printed reading matter.

This last point needs a brief aside. One of the handicaps that the Little Blue Books have always had is that they are not substantially books in the mechanical sense of the word. Occasionally some aloof and hypercritical person will contemptuously call them *pamphlets*. Of course, a booklet containing 15,000 words of text is not exactly a pamphlet, but the objection is there, nevertheless. For a surprisingly large number of book-buyers, upon whom American publishers depend for revenue, buy books because they are books. They would not think of reading the Rubaiyat of Omar Khayyam in a *pamphlet*, but they would – having money to spare – spend five dollars to have it in a handsome library edition. Little Blue Books are not sold, as a usual thing, to a buyer of this class.

There are, naturally, some classics that large numbers of people want to read. These classics have been consistent good sellers in the Little Blue Book series. Edward Everett Hale's famous story, *The Man With-*

out a Country, is an excellent example. So is Washington Irving's *Rip Van Winkle*, and also Mark Twain's *English As She Is Spoke*. These titles are so well known that they arouse in the mind of a prospective reader what may be called a literary curiosity. He has heard about these books – heard about them rather favorably, probably – and so he wants to read them, and therefore buys them.

But when a survey is made and the results are tabulated, it is found that the number of well-known classics that tens of thousands of people will buy just in order to read them is disappointingly limited. This number is an arbitrary one, of course. I could not venture to give an absolute figure, but I might say that it is certainly less than one hundred separate titles. This, obviously, could not long be a sound commercial basis on which to publish a series of classics the only appeal of which would be a desire to read on the part of the purchaser.

One way to help the sale of the less familiar classics is to educate the readers about them, and endeavor to create a compelling curiosity about them also. This can be done, to a small extent, with educational volumes, reading outlines, and such. It was not long before the Little Blue Books had such volumes, together with biographies and critical studies of leading literary personalities. But this phase of promoting the classics is also limited. There are strict boundaries beyond which it cannot go.

Keeping always in mind that a well-written book is much to be preferred to a poorly-written book, and remembering that if only a reader could be induced to start many a famous or at least established classic he would probably enjoy reading it, I saw only one course open to me. I refused to be discouraged in my project of publishing classics so that everyone not only could afford them, but would read them. If the title of the classic, as it had come down through the ages, did not itself arouse sufficient curiosity in the reader, then it must be changed in such a way that it would arouse such curiosity.

Another important point, a thoroughly practical consideration from my point of view, must also be kept in mind. The larger the list of Little Blue Books grew, the more of a problem it became to advertise them. A product costing a tenth part of a dollar, or less, certainly could not be given individual and expensive advertising display. It is impossible, in other words, to give each Little Blue Book a persuasive blurb. The title, and perhaps the author, must sell the book or it is lost. When the total number of titles reached the thousand-mark, the space allotted to each book in national advertising became approximately one agate line. Even at that, it took a thousand agate lines to advertise the complete list. It is easily seen, then, why it became necessary for the title of every Little Blue Book to combine identification, blurb, and all the sales persuasion there could ever be.

This is the explanation of how the practice of altering titles came about. The changing of titles became an important part of Little Blue Book publishing. It was a fascinating gamble. It took on the glamour of laboratory experiment. Juggling words about was an editorial and commercial necessity, as well as a sort of amusing pastime. Sometimes it did not work; many times it did work.

A New Way to Treat Old Books

Tampering with the classics, in some aspects, is dangerously like playing with fire; but again, this notion of it is largely a myth. Conventional book-lovers pose at throwing their hands up in horror and crying out in anguish when any beloved classic is altered in any way whatever. To apply editorial shears to a master, to blue-pencil a literary tradition, to issue an editorial edict about some immortal book – all these, say the defenders of classics, are to court swift and sure disaster.

I remember that when I first scheduled for publication an abridged version of Sir Walter Scott's *Lady of the Lake*, I had an agitated feeling about it. I likened the venture to carrying dynamite through a burning building. Readers might rebel against it. The precedent of publishing an abridgment of a narrative poem of such established fame might hurt the whole idea back of the Little Blue Books. It was a dare. It was a risk.

But nothing happened, except that the book was sold. Yes, it was sold and it continues to sell. Even schools buy it now and then and use it for a text. There has been no literary uprising; there have been no indignation meetings about it; the integrity of the Little Blue Book publishing idea was not jeopardized. As a matter of fact, people seemed rather to like the abridgment – the duller portions were taken out and, for him who runs as he reads, the Little Blue Book version is ample. It is not a summary, for the best of the poem is there. It does Sir Walter Scott justice, and little if any harm.

Well, I breathed easier after that. I watched the first edition go with a little fluttering of the editorial pulse. But there was no shock. My causes for alarm vanished like dreams, bad dreams. I found that the public was receptive to intelligent presentation of the classics along modern lines entirely removed from the academic and the traditional. To be sure, no change was made in the title in this instance – as it happens, Sir Walter Scott's own title is a very good one. It is much better, I may say, than the title of either The *Lay of the Last Minstrel* or *Marmion*. If I ever put either of these into the Little Blue Books I am sure the titles must be changed.

The title-changing had not come yet. I was still publishing classics under their accepted banners or, at least, under the banners they had always carried. It began to be apparent that such banners were not always accepted by a large majority of today's readers.

But before the title-changing became an editorial privilege and duty thoroughly sanctioned by success, there was another experiment I should describe briefly here. I had always cherished the notion that the classics of antiquity, Greek and Roman classics, needed to be given a modern angle, or at least to be put into up-to-date language, and offered to modern readers. It has always seemed to me that a literal or even an approximately literal translation is of little merit for the needs of most readers. For scholars or prospective scholars such hairsplitting is all right. But ordinary readers, who are really avid for knowledge and an approach to wisdom, need something less precise and more interpretative.

If you have ever read a fairly literal translation of almost any one of the Socratic dialogues of Plato you will know exactly what I mean. In literal English such a dialogue is full of repetition and constant circumlocutions. Such distressing superfluities depress the ordinary reader and drive him away from classical literature in perhaps justified disgust. He refuses to wade through literary barbed-wire entanglements for the sake of empty words like Classics, Tradition, Antiquity, and all that. He wants healthful pabulum for a man in his senses or no food of that kind at all.

It is not the matter or text of the classics to which I object. The substance is exactly what it is desirable to preserve and perpetuate for readers of all time. But it is hard to make the modern reader, whether he has had what is called a classical education or not, perceive that there is anything in the literature of antiquity to interest or benefit him. It is precisely this difficulty that the professors of classical Greek and Latin run up against in handling their groups of high school and college students – or rather I should say pupils, since few are students in the real sense of the word.

Perhaps it is a mistake to have Latin high school curricula at all, when this difficulty looms up in its really prodigious proportions. It takes a mature individual with some knowledge of the world and the various phases and experiences of life to see clearly that classical literature can be really an esthetic pleasure if read in the original – and that there is even a large chance of carrying some of that esthetic essence, or whatever you want to call it, over into English if the translator has some really creative imagination in him. Certainly it is better to read some intelligent English version and get something out of it than to memorize Latin and Greek vocabularies, conjugate verbs, and all that sort of thing, with never an inkling of what it is all about.

The whole objection is epitomized, too, in the old-fashioned idea that a classical education was safe because far removed from the hedonism and other satanic temptations of contemporary life. A classic that is like some empty husk – some transparent shell or chrysalis from which the living butterfly has flown – cannot be expected to interest anyone, least of all an adolescent. Translators have emphasized too much the togas and other paraphernalia of an older and departed day, forgetting that clothes are a costume quite empty when, without a human body in them, they are hung on a hook to droop lifelessly. We do not wear togas, and even though the Romans did, what is there in that except an indication of time? For the Romans certainly loved and hated, connived and condoned, and bled as red blood as any of us. Unfortunately, it is the loving and hating and the rest of life and human nature that most versions of the classics neglect to emphasize or surreptitiously suppress.

Too much effort cannot be expended in making it clear to modern readers that when Aristophanes and Sophocles and Euripides, for example, wrote their powerful dramas they appealed to their people not because they were writing *great plays*, but because they depicted life in a manner that the Greeks of their day could recognize and understand. A man went to a good play – a convincing, realistic play that intensified life – then, as now, to be loved and hated and conspired against and redeemed and so on vicariously. He went, let us say, because in the ordinary run of his daily activity, life more or less passed him by. At the play he could, without endangering his profits or his domestic peace, get by proxy many a thrill and realize to some small extent some of the major experiences of human life. But we today are capable of the same feeling – and if we read the classics as they should be read we will find in them much that the Greeks of old found in them. Putting *Hamlet* on the New York stage in modern dress was not as asinine a thing as some people contend – and the classics as far back as ancient Greece certainly deserve to be put to some extent in modern language and dress.

If there is some way of telling modern readers, and making them believe it, that there is real life in any great piece of literature, no matter when it was written, I am all for it. A happy twist to the title may do it sometimes by suggestion. Or the substance of the book itself may be given new life by modern presentation – by the treatment that will make it clear that the characters in the piece are not puppets long dead, but living human beings just as we are, though playing their parts on a stage with rather different scenery and props from ours.

I think this latter treatment is particularly suitable for the classical literature of antiquity, because it is so far removed in time from our own day. I would not lay this precept down as an absolute to be applied to all classics – one must pick and choose, carefully deciding, so far as possible, whether the audience is really widened by such treatment.

The way to put the dialogues of Plato, to take but one instance, into such a popular form did not immediately present itself. Every idea must for a time lie in the back of the mind, awaiting the manner of its realization in fact. I had experimented enough with some of the ancient classics to learn that there was a market for them. With proper treatment and presentation they could well be a permanent part of the Little Blue Book series. I was glad of this. It proved my original contention that the classics could be sold at a low price if they were published and advertised in the right way.

When I saw my way clearly outlined for presenting these classics of Greek and Roman antiquity in a popular form, the carrying out of this plan took three distinct directions through three differently equipped writers. These three contributors to the Little Blue Book series undertook their work at approximately the same time. It was at the opening of a new period in Little Blue Book publishing – just about at the beginning of the policy of having original manuscript provided especially for the series and its purposes.

One of these writers is by now known throughout the United States because of a best seller. His name and his book are household objects. It will amaze many people to learn that the contents of this book first appeared in the form of Little Blue Books. The writer to whom I refer is Dr. Will Durant, author of *The Story of Philosophy*, which for so many months has been one of the best selling non-fiction books in America – at five dollars a copy. I do not mean to imply that the price of this clothbound book is anything against it. I merely wish to indicate that virtually the same material, though in altogether different dress, first came out in Little Blue Book form, and still is in Little Blue Book form. Dr. Durant helped along my popularization of Greek classics with his *Guide to Aristotle*, and *Guide to Plato*. Later, when the value of story in the title of a book of knowledge was demonstrated, these books were called *The Story of Aristotle's Philosophy* and *The Story of Plato's Philosophy*, respectively.

Another phase of popularization among ancient classics was new and vigorous translations of the dramas of Greece and Rome. I found in Alexander Harvey exactly the man to do this part of the work. He seemed to catch the spirit of the original and somehow carry it over into English. The zest was still there, though in a new tongue and in a new manner. This was the idea exactly. Alexander Harvey enabled me to offer *The Bacchantes* of Euripides, the *Antigone* of Sophocles, the *Electra* of Sophocles and of Euripides, and so on.

106

Then there were the dialogues of Plato, the written record of the famous philosopher, Socrates, who walked the streets of Athens expounding his particular wisdom. All the translations I had ever seen of these had the same faults I have already mentioned. It did not seem that it was exactly a new translation that I needed. Rather I wanted a new version, an interpretative version. When Lloyd E. Smith wanted to try the job I had my doubts. I was skeptical. I wanted to be shown. But in two books Mr. Smith did a good job. He gave the dialogues something they lacked before. He put them into language everyone could follow with interest and complete understanding. He performed a service for the Little Blue Book idea of rejuvenating the classics that was completely in accord with my plans. The two books, still in print, are *The Trial and Death of Socrates*, and *Dialogues of Plato*.

All of this experimenting and its successful exploitation steadily led the way to the title-changing policy – a policy that is probably the most drastic ever adopted by any publisher of established reprints and in many ways, I feel confident in stating, one of the most daring departures from accepted custom. Only one thing could justify this tampering with the classics – and that is their wide distribution. If by altering a title here and there a good book would be more widely read, then the end certainly would justify the means. There could, if the policy succeeded, be no argument whatever about it.

Please understand me. I emphasize that in a large measure the changing of Little Blue Book titles has concerned what are loosely called *classics*, and it is in this respect that a policy of title-alteration is unique. Usually, and in an altogether regular and accepted publishing etiquette, publishers of *popular classics, the best classics, famous books, gems of the world's literature*, and so on, keep the titles intact. For example, the novel *Beulah* by Augusta J. Evans keeps that title without change – the blurb, very likely, gives the book a description that is made as persuasive as possible. But my immediate question, after my Little Blue Book experience, is: "What does the title *Beulah* tell? Is there any suggestion in the title itself of what the book is about – particularly if a person has never heard of either book or author before?" Certainly the title is as ambiguous as any title could be. It tells nothing whatever. But I have yet to see this book offered under any other name.

Changing the title of a book is a common occurrence in an editorial office. Authors are proverbially poor guessers when it comes to titles. They lack practical knowledge of how a book is presented to the public and how the public is likely to receive it. That is why a contemporary book is called one thing in America and another in England, as frequently happens. Editors also help authors – especially when the royalties are figured – by providing apt and striking titles for books. There is nothing new in this – but where is there an editor of *reprints* of fairly well-established classics, classics that have titles that were supplied, conceivably, to appeal to the audiences of an older and bygone day, where is there an editor, I say, who has had the courage to alter in the twentieth century the title of some book whose fame and worth were won in the eighteenth or nineteenth century? Frankly, I know of none.

You clamor for an example. I select the story that Guy de Maupassant chose to call *The Tallow Ball* (*Boule de Suif*). This story is famous, and deservedly well known and genuinely appreciated. That is why I put it in the Little Blue Books. Certainly, *The Tallow Ball* is a thoroughly reserved, dignified, and assuredly proper title for any story. But what does it *say*? I answer my own question with a word – it says *nothing*. Even if the story is about a ball of tallow, who on earth cares to read a story about a ball of tallow? Indeed, in these modern times, even tallow as a substance has ceased to be of compelling importance. Tallow candles have gone the way of hoop-skirts and kerosene lamps. *The Tallow Ball*, as a title, serves only to identify the story to someone who has heard of it, or whets the appetite of a devoted admirer of Guy de Maupassant. It has no appeal whatever to anyone else.

But this story ought to be read. I wanted to keep it in the Little Blue Book series, and so I cast about for some way to remedy a bad situation. The record in 1925 of orders for *The Tallow Ball*, listed in my catalogue under that title, was 15,000 copies. This was good, but Guy de Maupassant's Love and Other Stories sold 37,000, and likewise his Mademoiselle Fifi. These last two have titles that suggest more of life – the first names love, and the second is obviously about a woman. As an experiment in titling, therefore, I gave *The Tallow Ball* a new and rather startling listing – I called the story *A French Prostitute's Sacrifice*. That, after all, is what the story is about. Behold, that when a similar sales record of orders was made in 1926, *A French Prostitute's Sacrifice* showed a total of 54,700, or more than three times the selling power of *The Tallow Ball*! Now it surpasses the other two mentioned Guy de Maupassant books.

As an example of the modern method of helping the author – which editors are doing all the time – I cite the example of the Little Blue Book of poems by Arthur Davison Ficke. This was called at first *The Sonnets of a Portrait-Painter*. Under that title it was practically at a standstill as far as sales went. It was another indication that the public does not rise to the bait of painting unless some suggestion of the red blood of life is made also. I tried, as a substitute title, *The Love Sonnets of an Artist*. This helped a little – not nearly as much as the de Maupassant book just described, but from zero the book went up to about 6,000 copies annually. I remember that Mr. Ficke saw it advertised under the new title and objected strongly on the ground that the title vulgarized his poetry. When I told him the situation, however, he was appeased. Even a poet prefers to have his poems read to not being read at all, though it mean the hint of life and love in his title!

Other figures are given in another place, but these will serve to show, at this early stage of the discussion, just what I mean by a drastic policy of title-changing, especially as applied to books that are known as classics. I mean more than editorial suggestion and improvement relating to contemporary work. I mean more than the difference in appeal between an American and an English audience. I mean more than a blurb that tells what a book is about. In short, I mean that it is possible to inject some of the modern zest for living into a book otherwise dead from a commercial point of view – provided only that the book is still readable if some new quirk or twist to the title, or even a new title altogether, will induce in buyers of books a desire to read it. As I once metaphorically expressed it, if a book is sent into my editorial Hospital, I seek to revive its sales record by pumping some of the life-juice of romance or adventure into it.

Naturally, an important consideration would be how the reading public would receive the innovation. But I had gone through my days of trepidation with Scott's *Lady of the Lake* in abridged form. That had told me that the public is receptive to new methods – that, in short, the public is not afraid of new things even when applied to what is already in a measure old and established, but on the contrary advances rather eagerly to meet them halfway. The first half of the battle therefore was won.

I decided, too, at the start, that there would be no tampering with such classics as had shown themselves to be successful sellers without alteration. I have already named some examples. But Shakespeare's works are probably the best examples of any. I would not think of tampering with Shakespeare – to change Shakespeare would not be sacrilege, for I don't regard things in that way, but it would make something else out of Shakespeare, and, as I have already pointed out, Shakespeare is still sufficiently in touch with life of today to make it worth while to read him unaltered. Shakespeare is more than a name – Shakespeare is Shakespeare, indeed.

Shakespeare has become such a noble part of our literature, in a sense so permanently his own, in a perfection unapproachable, that it would be folly to attempt any sort of metamorphosis. I intended to offer Shakespeare for his own sake, unadorned, even without a suggestion of blurb – it is the only way Shakespeare should ever be offered to anyone, from the youngest up. *Romeo and Juliet, Hamlet, The Taming of the Shrew, Julius Caesar*, all of these are titles fully adequate in themselves. They have the advantage of fame that nothing added can ever increase.

Saving, then, something less than a hundred titles, so well known as to need no change, I was launched on a definite policy of altering titles of classics to fulfill the requirements of identification and persuasive description. The title of any book should tell something about it. I am in favor of only those titles that tell something definite about the contents of a book. If an otherwise ambiguous title, such as Rudyard Kipling's *Gunga Din*, is in its way a tag for the thing it names, because known for so long as such, I consider that a descriptive title. But if the title is both ambiguous and comparatively unknown – then it has to be changed, or the book must be withdrawn.

Always, for obvious reasons, it has been necessary to keep the reader in mind. Any change in title must be validated by the actual contents of the book. The change must serve enlightenment, not deception; the change must advance some particular information as to exactly the book's contents. It would never do to retitle Chaucer's *Canterbury Tales*, for example, unless the titles were also to indicate that the tales were still in archaic verse.

CHAPTER VIII

THE HOSPITAL

How Little Blue Books Are Given New Zest By New Titles

W hen the Little Blue Books were approaching the thousand mark in number of different titles in print and on sale at the price of five cents per book, there was a great deal of investigating and tabulating going on in Girard. Any number of influences was constantly being brought to bear on the selling totals of various books. A book that was a good seller in a list of 300 titles became a very poor one in a list of 800 titles. There must be reasons for such discrepancies. Figures were obtained. Inventories were scrutinized. And there grew up what I rather like to call The Hospital, an editorial sanctum sanctorum into which were sent those books that were not selling their quota.

In any scheme of mass production and a low-priced product a certain average distribution must be maintained. In the Little Blue Books, it developed that any single book must be sold in a minimum quantity of at least 10,000 copies every year. This was not exactly a fixed figure, but was flexible to the extent that a book might sell 8,000 or 7,000 copies annually and still be kept in the list. But it meant chiefly that any book running consistently below 10,000 copies annually was sent to The Hospital for consideration of the selling points shown in its title-and-author listing in the catalogue and advertisements.

When The Hospital began it was overcrowded with book-patients. The list of Little Blue Books had grown with such leaps and bounds in the five years it had then been in existence that a number of titles had been passed along the way and left dying in a ditch behind us. That is, it was not noticed until very suddenly that some of the earlier books were losing their place – they were not selling, or, when they came to be investigated, it was found that they had never sold quite as many copies as they ought. The first thorough tabulation of figures sent a hundred or so books to The Hospital for a complete examination and going over.

A good title is a work of genius. I have no hesitancy in saying that, for it is genius whether it is the inspiration of a lucky moment or the painful elaboration of a faint idea through an hour of deep thought. I have always made the final decision as to the title of any Little Blue Book, but I have never confined the search for a new title entirely to my own efforts. An editor must have recourse to more than one method for achieving any desired result. Often a Little Blue Book sent to The Hospital would be read by two or three editorial assistants, and they would all comment on it, making suggestions. Out of that a new title would be born and given a trial.

Alice, my ten-year-old daughter, has even played her small though significant part in the birth of new titles. Children are voracious readers, and they usually read with such directness of viewpoint that they have something definite to say about what they read. They approach books with freshness, and a book must be vital and alive to hold their interest. As any writer for children knows, children make the most critical audience in the world. For example, I gave Alice a copy of Captain Marryat's *Privateersman*, which had not been going well. Perhaps people did not know what a privateersman might be. Alice did not know. Yet it was a good story, and it is still in the list because Alice said, after reading it: "It's about a seaman and battles." It was rechristened *The Battles of a Seaman*, with a marked improvement. In 1925 it sold 7,500; in 1926, 8,000—and in 1927, with the change of title, it sold 10,000 copies.

One of the first books to go into The Hospital was Theophile Gautier's *Fleece of Gold*. This amazed me; in fact, it nearly floored me. There were two good reasons why this book should be a top-notch seller. First, the author was a Frenchman – American readers have a *weakness* for tales by French authors. Second, it is an excellent story, full of love interest and everything that should place it high among the stories of love and sex. But a moment's consideration of the book shows at once what is wrong. What could *fleece of gold* mean to anyone who had never heard of Gautier or his story before? Little, if anything. It suggests Greek mythology instead of modern France. Gautier's title is picturesque, even poetic, but it lacks informative value. It tells nothing whatever. A happy thought brought this title to mind: *The Quest for a Blonde Mistress*, exactly the sort of story it is. The record is, in 1925, under the old title, only 6,000 – in 1926, under its new banner, this jumped almost unbelievably to 50,000!

Some skeptics will raise the objection – I know, for I have already considered it – that such retitling cheapens a book. In refutation I offer an example or two from classical literature where authors showed more precision in titling their own works. Is there any great difference between the tone of *The Quest for a Blonde Mistress* and *The Taming of the Shrew*? The latter is by William Shakespeare, unaltered. And how about *The Merry Wives of Windsor*, an accepted Shakespearean title? Such an objection vanishes into thin air when parallel examples are cited. The reason that a new title such as I gave Gautier's story *seems* to cheapen the book is that it is, at first, rather startling. Again, consider Balzac's *A Study of a Woman*, or his *Splendors and Miseries of a Courtesan*. These titles could not be more apt. Even Gautier himself was particular and to the point in his titling of *One of Cleopatra's Nights*, a title that cannot be improved upon.

Then there was Moliere's play, *Les Precieuses Ridicules*. For a long time this was in the Little Blue Books under the French title, with the name of Moliere to recommend the book. The French title was bad for another reason – it intimated to some readers that the whole play was in French. By a happy chance the best possible English title was hit upon for this book: *Ridiculous Women*. This conveys the idea exactly; comedy and irony are both suggested. I do not think this play has ever been given a better English title. Something like *The Highbrow Ladies* is usually used but I don't like that. It is rather too pompous; it sounds *genteel*. But *Ridiculous Women* connotes the whole spirit of the play – and it sells the book. Under the French title, as the list grew in variety, this book dropped to almost zero. The new title raised it to better than 10,000 annually. Another Moliere play, *Le Bourgeois Gentilhomme*, was also a problem. A lame attempt was made to make use of *The Nobody Who Apes Nobility*, but this was awkward and wholly inadequate. There is no real idea in this title that can be grasped at a glance. You can figure it out, to but sure, but what reader is going to regard titles as riddles? The right title for this book, in modern American slang, is *The Show-Off*; and that is what it is now being called. In yearly sales it has jumped from slightly above zero to almost 10,000.

At one time in the history of the Little Blue Books, as I have said, little attention was paid to titles. The enterprise was growing so fast that the most important thing was to get new books into print – the public demanded books and, before its choice was spread over so wide a range of subjects – before it had a real choice to make, in other words – the title did not matter as much as long as the book was a good one. But as soon as choice became paramount in making out an order for Little Blue Books, the title leaped into first-place significance. Now the title is considered from every possible angle before a Little Blue Book is put on sale. In those early days two volumes of the collected essays of *Llewelyn Powys* were put into the series. I was glad to do this – the essays are eminently readable and I was sure Little Blue Book readers would enjoy them. And I let Mr. Powys give his own titles to the books. So the books appeared as *Honey and Gall*, and *Cupbearers of Wine and Hellebore*. This was very pretty, and appealed to a few readers – but only a few, in fact, almost none. Something had to be done to save these essays from an untimely death. They are now called, with fair success, *Studies in Mystic Materialism* and *A Book of Intellectual Rowdies*. The first sold 15,000 in 1926, the second 11,000. For those who may like them, the older and less informative titles are still on the covers of the books.

A similar poetic mistake was made when several volumes of Jack London's stories were put into the series. One book, because I fancied the phrase from one of the stories, was called *Tales of the White Silence*. This seemed to me particularly expressive. I really thought the book would go. Of course, the name of Jack London carried the book satisfactorily, but still it seemed to me that it should do better. At last I was forced to give up my fanciful preference for the *white silence*, and now I think that the newer title is really the better. It is: *Tales of the Big Snows*. The difference in expressiveness is instantly apparent.

It is really amazing what the change of a word may do. The mere insertion of a word often works wonders with a book. Take the account of that European mystery of intrigue and political romance, which Theodore M. R. von Keler did for me under the title of *The Mystery of the Iron Mask*. This title was fair. It certainly tells what the book is about. But there is something aloof about it. It may, says the reader to himself, be another one of those poetic titles. It may fool me, he thinks, and so he bewares. But I changed it to *The Mystery of the Man in the Iron Mask*, and now there can be no question for the record is 30,000 against 11,000 copies per year. Two other *slight* additions come to mind. Victor Hugo's drama, *The King Enjoys Himself* (*Rigoletto*; translated by Maurice Samuel), and Zorilla's, the Spanish Shakespeare's, *None Beneath the King* (translated by Isaac Goldberg) were both rather sick – 8,000 for the first and only 6,000 for the second. In 1927, lo and behold, the miraculous cure of title-changing brought 34,000 sales for *None Beneath the King Shall Enjoy This Woman*, and 38,000 for *The Lustful King Enjoys Himself*! Snatched from the grave! Then there was Whistler's lecture, fairly well known under the title *Ten o'Clock*. But readers of Little Blue Books are numbered by at least ten thousand for each title yearly. Due to the concentrated interest shown in self-education and self-improvement, this helpful lecture on art should be read widely – following this reasoning, the proper explanatory title evolved into *What Art Should Mean to You*. Readers are more interested in finding out what art should mean to them than in discovering what secret meaning may lie behind such a phrase as *ten o'clock*. In 1925 the old title sold less than 2,000; in 1927, the sales, stimulated by The Hospital's service, mounted to 9,000.

Francis Bacon's *Apothegms*, under that name in the Little Blue Books, was one of my cripples. Here is a great book by a great philosopher. And yet, so listed, it was practically at a standstill – less than 2,000 copies yearly when I came to investigate it. What is wrong with it? The fault lies on its face – the average person, even many a person above the average, does not understand what the word *apothegm* means. I know I had to look it up in the dictionary the first time I came upon it. Many people do not like to go to the dictionary. They prefer to pick up their new words in conversation, where the relation of one word to another will indicate something of its meaning. This is not commendable, perhaps, but it happens to be true. Not one person in a thousand knows what *apothegm* means.

People are not afraid of meaty reading, of a substantial reading diet. I can prove that. But they fight shy of the utterly strange. A book by the same Francis Bacon entitled *The New Atlantis* was doing a little better than 7,000 yearly – not satisfactory, but on the brink of success, so to speak. There is hope when a book gets some distribution, even if it is less than one has hoped. But when it practically stands still, the burden is unnecessarily heavy.

This collection of apothegms is a splendid book, in which a great philosopher gives several hundred brief sentences, many of them sparkling epigrams, about this thing we call life. The sentences are interesting, because they tell us about what interests us most – life. What is an apothegm, then? Simply a terse truth. Look it up for yourself. So, taking the problem in hand, I remedied the situation by retitling the book: *Terse Truths About the Riddle of Life*. The following year (1926) this book climbed to a sales total of a few copies over 9,000 – which is worth selling, I am happy to say.

Robert Louis Stevenson belongs, to a large extent, with those accepted literary giants – in the sense of world fame, for I do not propose to be critical here – who should not be altered. Certainly I have proved by the success of the pocket edition of *Dr. Jekyll and Mr. Hyde* that this is a title that cannot be altered with impunity or benefit. Even the movies kept this title, which is a good sign of its widespread effectiveness. But with *Will o' the Mill* and *Markkeim* (both in one volume) a question arises. Are these two stories sufficiently familiar to make them desirable books to read? The sales record of this book indicated that they were not. The latter story is a psychological study of a murderer and his crime – yet the man's name alone does not convey this at all. It might be any sort of story from the title as Stevenson had it. I called it *Markkeim's Murder*, which gives it a definite classification, and from practically a cipher the book leaped to 7,000 copies annually. It is still shaky, as you see! Perhaps something more drastic should be done to it.

Rudyard Kipling has several good titles of his own that I would not venture to touch. What could be better, for example, than *Without Benefit of Clergy*? Certain of his poems, too, are so famous that they are clamored for as they are – *The Vampire, Mandalay*, and *Gunga Din*. Some of the stories, as *The Man Who Would Be King*, go very well also. But there is a lure in these stories that is not expressed in the title, and that I have no way of suggesting except by the title. By this I mean the fascinating adventures of the British soldiers in India – those unforgettable episodes of happy-go-lucky army life. So I am experimenting with some titles like *Tales of British Soldiers in India* and *Stories of Army Life*.

It seemed to me that there could be no reason why Oscar Wilde's *Pen, Pencil and Poison* should not sell. That title appeals to me. But it apparently does not appeal to the public at large, as the records of this book showed. And anyone can see, now that the change has been made, that *The Story of a Notorious Criminal* is much more likely to aid the wide distribution of the book. It is another good example of the change from the poetic to the practical, for from 5,000 annually, the book rose in 1926 to 15,800 copies!

A number of definite tendencies in titling have come up in this experimenting with what banner a book shall go forth under. All of this is, of course, a revealing commentary on the reading tastes of the American public. There is, for example, the yearning for the truth about things. Americans want to know the truth, even if it hurts – and if you tell them that you are giving them the truth they will at least believe you long enough to read what you offer them under that name. Take, for example, Dr. Arthur J. Cramp's *"Patent Medicine" and the Public Health*. This is a purely academic, professional-thesis sort of title. It indicates what the book is about, but it suggests nothing of controversy, nothing that anyone ought to know. Yet *The Truth About "Patent Medicine"* tells the reader that there is some sort of exposure here, something that he may owe it to himself to find out about. This book sold scarcely 3,000 copies in 1925; in 1926, being the *Truth*, it did a trifle better than 10,000 copies. That is why *The Truth About New*

York's Chinatown is a better title than simply *New York's Chinatown*. That is why, too, such a book as *The Truth About Los Angeles* is read throughout the United Slates.

There is another magical word in titles. It is Life. The American reading public of today is intensely interested in real life. Witness the success of the confession type of magazine, which tells in loud language that it is offering the truth about real lives. Witness the dominance of love and sex books over all others in the sales record of Little Blue Books as a whole. Sex is undoubtedly the most intimately connected with everyday living of any subject you could name. The interest in life is clearly evidenced by the repeated selections of books that have that word in the title. There was Charles J. Finger's book entitled *Addison and His Times*. This title is too scholastic: it sounds too much like a thesis written before graduation from a university. But *London Life in Addison's Time* indicates that the book may be at least interesting. As a matter of fact, before the change I moved this book only in complete sets; now it squeezes by with 7,000 per year.

Dan Hennessy's *On the Bum* never was a bad seller. As a matter of fact, it is one of the steadiest selling books in the entire list. But the addition of *Sketches of Tramp Life* to the more figurative title helped it even more. There is even one of my books, *The Color of Life*. My own books in the Little Blue Book series are on the whole poor sellers, as I have more than once candidly admitted. But this book, since it has so good a title – and its contents, I venture to hope, live up to it – is a very fair seller as compared with the others. And such combinations, of course, as *Love Tales of Italian Life*, *French Tales of Passion and Cruelty*, and Boccaccio's *Tales of Love and Life* cannot be beaten.

The ever present tendency of the public toward self-improvement has naturally influenced many a title in the series. I have already mentioned one or two examples. People want to improve their conversation, their vocabulary, or they simply want general principles of self-improvement, as in John Cowper Powys' lecture, *The Secret of Self-Development*. Arthur Schopenhauer is a forbidding name to the uninitiated. His *Art of Controversy* never did go very well. But now it is called *How to Argue Logically* and has earned its permanent place in the list. This is another one of those *naughts* that leaped suddenly, through the magic of words, to 30,000 copies per year. The *how to* beginning for a title is still another magical catch phrase. Piano playing is all right, but notice how much more dynamic and compelling *How to Play the Piano* is, or even, if there is space to print it, *How to Teach Yourself to Play the Piano.*

The book on conversation has an interesting anecdote to be told about it – at first it was simply Thomas De Quincey's *Essay on Conversation.* When this book came into The Hospital past experience showed immediately that it ought to be called *How to Improve Your Conversation.* But De Quincey's essay is a bit too studied and scholarly to be offered to an unsuspecting public under that title, at least by itself. It is still in the book, but half of the book is now taken up with Lloyd E. Smith's portion, written especially to fit the title *How to Improve Your Conversation.* That is one of the inside stories of how one popular Little Blue Book was born! Arthur Schopenhauer's *Art of Controversy*, mentioned in the preceding paragraph, is more practical and did not need such a preamble.

An entirely separate field of title experimentation was opened in the general classification of biography. Biography seeming to be less colorful, I have been trying out Personalities as a catalogue division. My experience has been that names alone, even if world-famous, are not sufficient to sell Little Blue Books. It appears that the book-buyer is one of the laziest persons on earth when he examines a catalogue of books. He may know perfectly well that Leo Tolstoy is a Russian story-writer, but he refuses to identify that name for himself. I know that this is so because I used to offer Garnett's *Life of Tolstoy*, and I am able to compare it with the records of the book under its present title: *Tolstoy, Russian Novelist.* It is 2,500 against the present average of 6,500 copies per year. The book is not yet secure – but the change in sales is nevertheless significant.

The general rule in titling biographies has been to name the person and identify him. Fanciful titles will not do at all for five-cent accounts of the life and works of various prominent people. The prospective reader must be reminded, in so many words, of precisely whom the book is about and, if possible, the title must also tell the book's particular bias or motivating thesis. Thus, Joseph McCabe's biography of Ingersoll is called *Robert G.*

121

Ingersoll, Benevolent Agnostic. You can see at a glance that this is ever so much more effective than simply *Life of Ingersoll.*

There are cases where the simpler and more obvious title will sell a biography. This is usually true of only what may be called *standard* biographies, however. I refer to *Life of Jesus*, by Ernest Renan, *Life of Lincoln, Life of Napoleon*, and so forth.

Often the biographical titles require a great deal of experimenting. When the Little Blue Books were young, I put in as Number Ten in the series that delightful essay by Francis Thompson on Percy Bysshe Shelley. That jewel of literature always seemed worthy of perpetuation to me, and I wanted to have it read by thousands of people. I cannot say that my hope for it has been fulfilled, although the book is still in print and available. But I am trying it under the title of *Shelley, Idealistic Dreamer*. If I called him a poet I hardly think that would help; few people are compellingly interested in the life of a poet. But Shelley was more than a poet, and if I can only get people to buy Thompson's essay, I'm confident each one will feel that it is five cents well spent. At any rate, the new title does four times as well as the old – 8,000 against 2,000 copies annually.

A classic example of failure to comprehend the man a book is about is the *Life of Barnum*. When Charles J. Finger wrote this book for me he offered the forceful title: *Barnum, the Man Who Lured the Herd*. Unfortunately, viewing the matter in the light of my later experience, I am afraid the public thought that Barnum was either an eccentric cow-puncher or a rustler of cattle! Consequently, this book was sent to The Hospital, and it came forth with the brand-new appellation of *P. T. Barnum and His Circus*. This is not only much better, but it tells exactly what the book is about. It jumped the book from 4,000 copies in 1925, to 8,000 in 1926.

Martin Luther is another case in point. A life of Luther without any other recommendation did not appeal to readers anywhere near to the same extent as does *Martin Luther and Protestantism*. On the other hand, it might seem that a life of Benjamin Franklin could succeed very well with such a name alone. But of late years it has become desirable to accentuate the human qualities of our great men, and that is probably the reason that I have found *Benjamin-Franklin, Printer and Statesman* slightly less popular than *Franklin, Lover of Life.*

I would have gambled a great deal on Clement Wood's biography of Casanova, especially since it was deliberately entitled *Casanova and His Loves.* The universal popularity of the *sex books,* so called, would seem to indicate that this book on Casanova automatically should be a best seller. It did not work out that way. The diagnosis of the failure was that people did not know the name Casanova, and so they did not care a nickel's worth about whom he loved or did not love. There was a mild revolution in the sales record of this book when it was advertised as *Casanova, History's Greatest Lover!* Witness the figures – 8,000 before the change: a yearly sale of 22,000 after it! A similar example is Ralph Oppenheim's life of George Sand. It is now called, with a gain of 6,000 copies a year, *The Love-Life of a Frenchwoman.* This proves, if anything, that the public would rather buy a book about an unknown Frenchwoman, when reminded that she is French, than one about someone whose name suggests neither nationality nor familiarity.

Scientific titles have also needed elucidation and popularization from time to time. Science has the reputation, with the general public, of being very dry reading. A few magazines, featuring the strange and bizarre, particularly in mechanical inventions, have managed to make science commercially popular as reading matter. But among books there is still great progress to be made. The *outlines* did a great deal to remove the stigma, and now the *stories* of this and that phase of knowledge are helping us all to progress in the humanizing of scientific knowledge. (I might say, in passing, that the titles of the individual numbers of my *Key to Culture* series have been carefully chosen with this point in mind.)

There has always been a market for books that make things plain, such as *Evolution Made Plain.* Then I tried introductions to this and that, and scientific subjects for beginners, but neither of these variations of title has been quite as successful as the facts you should know caption. An important secret of successful titling is to be imperative, to insist in the very name of the book that the reader should have it! Now *Life Among the Ants* was much improved in its distribution by extending it thus: *Facts You Should Know About Life Among the Ants,* or sometimes, when less space is available, *Fascinating Facts About Ant Life.* I took a tip from the *Fact Compendiums* of some years ago, and from the *Handy Books of Facts* which are still commercially profitable reference books. The public of today wants facts, and it likes to be told that it is getting facts.

But there is no general rule applicable to all cases. There is always room for experimentation, and I have changed a title of one book as many as half a dozen times. What works in one place is just as likely to be a failure in connection with some other book. For example, *Facts About the Moon* does not have nearly the selling value of *Is the Moon a Dead World?* The latter has romance in it, adventurous suggestion in it, and all the force of the continual controversy about whether or not there is life on other globes besides the earth. The same characteristics may be discerned in this title: *Solving the Mystery of the Comets.* Maynard Shipley, the author of the last-named two books, deserves a great deal of credit for his work as a popular-izer of such subjects.

Poetry I have left until the last because it has been something of a bug-bear in my editorial life. I may as well confess that I read almost no poetry from inclination, although I recognize its place in the literature of the world and would not for anything bar it from any Utopia I could conceive. For this reason, knowing that other people have a wholly justifiable liking for poetry, and due to a sense of my own *blind spot,* I have been led into the weakness of including too many books of poetry in the pocket series. At one time I had nearly a hundred different volumes of poetry in print. I even had – but some of this part of the story belongs in the chapter headed "The Morgue"! No publisher needs to be told that poetry is not a com-mercial literary commodity except in a very few exceptional cases. The old masters do very well in gift editions, text-books, and the like. So I find that there is every reason to keep in print Little Blue Book anthologies of *Best Poems of John Keats, Best Poems of Robert Burns, Best Poems of Walt Whit-man,* and so forth. But it is not true that contemporary poetry is salable in mass quantities just because it is poetry. *Today's Poetry* is fair as a general compilation. But it was necessary to call John Davidson's volume *Ballad of a Passionate Nun, and Other Poems* to make it earn its place in the list. I have found it wise, too, to pick out a well-known title, like *Thanatopsis* or

The One Hoss Shay, to feature on the cover of the book and in the advertising. But the general conclusion from my experience with poetry is that the
audience for poetry in America is still greatly in need of broad and hearty
development.

While discussing titles, I should give some answer to the question
sometimes put to me whether the length of a title makes any difference.
I am not able to give figures to bear out any of my opinions on this point,
and I can only present my own ideas – though these ideas are born, even if
unconsciously, from constant experience with the publishing and selling of
Little Blue Books. There are, too, some definite strictures determined by
the nature of the Little Blue Books themselves, and by mechanical limitations as well as advertising costs.

First of all, I state flatly that there is a great deal of nonsense in the
notion that brevity is the soul of wit or anything else. In naming certain
commodities, such as cigarettes, an attempt has been made to use a short
name that will easily roll off the tongue. Thus, Camel was decided upon,
no doubt, with the idea that the man who wants a package of Camels
will step into the shop and say one word: "Camels." That is highly theo-
retical, and anyone knows it is not proved by what actually happens. The
man goes in and delivers a lengthy speech something like this: "I want a
package of Camels," or, "Give me a pack of Camels," or, "Fork over some
Camels." The human animal is incapable of being as brief and wordless as
to say merely: "Camels."

As applied to books, it is necessary to consider other things. If the book
is going to be given plenty of advertising space the title does not make as
much difference. Descriptive phrases, catchwords, slogans, sales talk, and
so on, can be plastered all over the advertising and even on the jacket of
the book. The title sinks into obscurity, except when ordering the book or
asking for it in a bookshop. Even then the purchaser is likely to use some
advertising phrase in lieu of the title, and the clerk who handles the order
is expected to be up on his stuff sufficiently to interpret the customer's
jargon and get the right book for him with the least possible delay.

I recall a case in point from my own experience. By stuffing circulars
in outgoing packages of Little Blue Books listing some carefully selected

clothbound books, usually picked to appeal to readers of Little Blue Books, I sell a surprising number of more expensive books in the run of a year. *Havelock Ellis*, the recent biography by Isaac Goldberg, was one of these – especially since Goldberg is known to Little Blue Book readers. On the circular advertising this book, however, the headline was used: "The man who debunked sex!" Beneath this catchline the title of the book and the author were given in large type – but the name Havelock Ellis, without explanation, meant little to many people. Several orders came in for the book entitled *The Man Who Debunked Sex*! Now to me that is a better title for the book than the man's name.

But it can never be decided once and for all that a short title or a long title is the best. It is seldom a question of length. The real difference is one of appeal – of what the title tells, of whether it gives a clear idea of the nature and contents of the book. As I have said, if there is space to add a description of the book, the title matters much less than if the book must be sold by its title and author alone. I think of Will Durant's *Story of Philosophy*. Here is a title in three words, or with the definite article, four. This book could have a shorter title, for it could be called *Philosophy*. Yet the difference between the short and the long title is not one of words; the longer one clearly is better because it suggests a continuous, interesting narrative (story). To go to the other extreme, this book could have a longer title, for it could be called *A Comprehensive Survey of Various Systems of Philosophy from Antiquity to the Present*. Here, the difference is again not one of words; the shorter title is better because it avoids any suggestion of pedantry, and emphasizes that philosophy as a whole has a story behind it that can be told in a fascinating and informative way. The effectiveness of titles cannot be measured with a yardstick!

As for the Little Blue Books, the cost of advertising per agate line (the space occupied by a line of agate or $5^1/2$ point type [14 lines to an inch] set a column wide, the unit of measure in advertising space) has always been an important consideration. Now there are 1,260 Little Blue Book titles. If all these are listed in one advertisement and each book is allotted one agate line, for that listing alone 1,260 agate lines are required! In this case, the titles of the books in this advertisement are automatically limited to the number of words that can be set in agate type a column wide. The wording must be chosen to fit the space and at the same time to describe the book persuasively so that it will be bought.

Brevity is valuable as a characteristic only when it is more effective than something longer. There is Fannie Hurst's story called T. B. This is all right if the book is listed under Fiction, but what does it tell in a numerical list if someone does not know the name Fannie Hurst? It may suggest that the book is a medical treatise. But this, I may point out, is the shortest title in the present list of Little Blue Books, and I cannot say that its brevity is of any merit. I am of the opinion that a much better title could be found for this story.

There is room for housecleaning in the matter of titles. The whole atmosphere of titling is shrouded with cobwebs of myth and convention and what might be called superstition. On the one hand it is told that Shakespeare had a great contempt for titles – calling one of his plays *As You Like It*, and another, *Twelfth Night, or What You Will*. On the other hand, some of Shakespeare's titles are very apt, as *A Comedy of Errors*. *The Taming of the Shrew* and *The Moor of Venice* are strongly descriptive and distinctive.

Authors seem to take pride in writing things without titles and then casting about with loud wailing and painful moaning for a title that will fit. Other writers hit upon some pretty group of words that catches their fancy, or some title with a symbolic or metaphorical implication – to cite a blatant example, Harold Bell Wright's *The Mine with the Iron Door*. Such titles are handles, well enough. They serve for identification and do very nicely for listing in the huge card indexes of public libraries. But if they had to sell the books they caption they would, most of them, fail pitifully.

I have indicated many of my conclusions – the lessons I have learned – from my experimentation with titles. I pointed out that there are magical words like Truth, Life, Love, How to, Facts You Should Know, and so forth. I think I have made it clear that titles with hazy poetic haloes will not work, and that titles that state the plain facts about a book are in almost all cases the best.

In general, my own rules for titling a book are few, but they are much to the point. Particular books often demand particular treatment, but there are one or two lessons of general application that I have learned at some cost, and that I am glad to pass on to others for whatever they may be worth. For even though a book will have a large and lurid blurb, and plenty of bolstering with advertising space, I see no harm in giving it a title that will carry it alone if necessary. If the title does describe the book it will help to eliminate confusion in the minds of prospective readers, and clarify for them just the book they may decide to buy.

In that last sentence is my first rule: make the title describe the book. The title should contain some dominant word that clearly indicates the subject of the book. If it is a biography or criticism, I think the title should also indicate what the man stood for or what the matter criticized chiefly represents. If human nature can be put into the title, well and good. Every effort should be made to tie up the book with real life, or with the average person's desire for romance, adventure, and fun.

My second rule is: make the title as distinctive as possible, so as to compel attention and awaken interest. I subordinate this to the descriptive requirement. But I have a notion that many publishers put my second rule first – they seem to prefer the bizarre and startling to the suggestive and revealing. But by putting this first it is necessary to add the description on the flap of the jacket or in the body of the advertisement. I cannot do this, so I am obliged to consider the description of first importance, and distinction second.

In a series such as the Little Blue Books, description can be given first importance for another reason. Any publisher is aware that there is a constant demand for certain books of information, education, and such. That is to say, there is a fairly constant interest in a manual of Parliamentary Law. Several of these are always on the market, differing chiefly in price. There is a Little Blue Book on Parliamentary Law, and here the title is descriptive only. It is not necessary for it to be distinctive, since any attempt to distinguish this Little Blue Book manual from other manuals is obviously superfluous – the distinction lies in the fact that this is a Little Blue Book for five cents, whereas the others are bigger books costing much more money. The first rule only is necessary in titling such books.

As a final word, I might hint in a loud whisper: take a leaf out of the page of the movie-titler's ritual. Titles of books and stories are nearly always changed for the motion picture version – due undoubtedly to the necessity to make a much wider appeal. Allow me to ignore the merits of the photoplays themselves, and cite two of the titles as examples. John Barrymore began work on Francois Villon, but this was released under the much more popular title of *The Beloved Rogue*. Or consider that other Barrymore film, from Antoine Francois Prevost's *Manon Lescaut* (which would have been a total failure as a movie title), which was called *When a Man Loves*. Considered merely as titles, these are both more descriptive and distinctive than the originals.

CHAPTER IX
WHAT A CHANGE OF
SCENERY WILL DO

Sick Books May Be Helped By Changing Location

Though changing titles is a publishers' practice with a well-established reputation, there is an aspect of this Hospital to which sick Little Blue Books go that I am sure is unique. Keeping the figure, this phase of the treatment of books that need new life put into their sales may be called giving the book a change of scenery. A doctor may say to his patient: "You're really all right, old man. There's not a thing I can do, but I think a change of scenery might pep you up. I suggest that you run down to Florida for a month or so." If the patient improves in the Florida climate he may move there permanently. That is the way it happens with a Little Blue Book.

By scenery I mean the classifications used in listing Little Blue Books, either in the regular catalogue, in a sales catalogue, or in the advertisements. These classifications are being changed, more or less, all the time – new classifications are being tried and old ones discarded. In general, however, these classifications were at first specific and rather dry, such as the thoroughly established divisions of reading like Biography, History, Fiction, Debates, Epigrams, Drama, Essays, Science, Religion, Philosophy, and so forth. Later on it was thought advisable to liven up these classifications, and Biography became Personalities, Fiction was broken up into many smaller groups, Science became Wonders of Science, and so on.

131

As my latest advertising shows, I have found that these classifications are important. They are a vital part of the selling of the Little Blue Books; in their way, they are also titles. In certain advertising I have found that it pays to use such words as Fun, Jokes, Entertainment, Murder, Mystery, Horror, and so on, in listing the books. More and more of this form of classifying is likely to characterize Little Blue Book advertising of the future.

The change of scenery, in treating a failing Little Blue Book, is to move it from one classification to another. Astonishing as it may seem, this has actually worked wonders in the sales records. Take, for example, a book by my wife, Marcet, which was first called *What the Editor's Wife Is Thinking About*, and was reprinted from the *Haldeman-Julius Weekly* in response to numerous requests. This book sold well only at first, among the more steadfast of Little Blue Book readers. It then dwindled to almost zero. The title was changed to *Intimate Notes on E. H. J.*, without noticeable result.

The first classification under which this book appeared was Biography, and later, under Personalities. I kept the book in the list because there were numerous personal requests for information about me that it was easiest to answer by sending a copy of this Little Blue Book. Its annual average was, nevertheless, appallingly low – something around 1,000 copies, which would be partly accounted for in complete sets of Little Blue Books. Then I experimented with a classification called Confessional Autobiography, and this book of Marcet's was moved there. Still it did not show any signs of life, doing scarcely 2,000 copies in 1927.

As a last resort, during 1927, this book was listed under the classification Famous Women, as follows: *Marcet Haldeman-Julius' Intimate Notes on Her Husband.* This, amazing as it really is – I was quite flabbergasted when I learned it – sold 16,000 copies of this book in 1927!

There was another book that gave me a great deal of concern. This was an anthology called *Poems of Evolution*, really an unusual collection and deserving a better fate than The Morgue. The title seemed to be what was the matter with it – it did not tell that these poems are interesting, artistic (in spots), useful and amusing, intelligently done. The first poem in the book, indeed, is Langdon Smith's famous *Evolution*, with its fairly well known line: "When you were a tadpole and I was a fish" – which is a lively and excellent piece of poetical journalese.

Then a trip to The Hospital brought forth a major operation, with gratifying success – the patient lived! *Poems of Evolution* was changed to *When You Were a Tadpole and I Was a Fish*. The jump in sales from a mere 2,000 in 1925 to nearly 7,000 in 1926 amused the doctor, for he has always been especially stubborn about any threatened child. He did not want to euthanize any youngster with the word *evolution* in its title (The Dayton, TN, farce was at its height at the time). Sheer stubbornness and the inspiration of a happy title saved the creature.

This book came back to The Hospital, though, for it did not quite total 10,000 annually. There was another consultation. I, as the doctor in this apt metaphor, took the patient's pulse and noticed its healthy beat, with no little satisfaction. The triumph of 7,000 copies in 1926 proved that the child was well on the road to health. There was only one thing to do – to prescribe a change of scenery! It means that the book, which had once been listed under Poetry, and was now under Evolution, was moved to a new listing under the broad banner of Humor. The end of 1927 shows that about 21,000 copies were sold!

In general, I have found the classification of Juvenile Books unsatisfactory. Children do not buy from my advertising, though young people do. But it seems that young people do not identify themselves with the word juvenile – though they might like to read *Robinson Crusoe* or *Gulliver's Travels* or tales from the *Arabian Nights*, they are turned away by a Juvenile listing. They do not even care to be referred to as Young People, I have found. So these books are now distributed through the various classifications, and no separation is made for age. Each group or generation can find the books it wants for itself, and it is working out much better so. The change of scenery for books that were formerly listed only under Juvenile has certainly done them good. It has widened their scope, and thereby increased their sales.

There has always been a group of books – essays, belles-lettres, odds and ends of literature – which it has been difficult to classify. In the days of sharp division, a classification headed Miscellaneous or simply Literature was used for these. They never sold very well, largely, I am sure, on that account. Later, with the newer and livelier classifications, it became necessary to place these books more definitely and more alluringly. Some of them went readily under Mystery, or some such general head, but others – particularly things like *Great English Poems*, or Joubert's *Thoughts on the Meaning of Life* – needed other treatment.

The classification, now being used extensively, called Cultural Helps has been most successful. Books that before were close to the zero mark – books that have earned their right to be in the world's literature – have picked up wonderfully with this change of scenery. The desire for culture on the part of reading Americans is thus clearly shown. If there is anything in these books – and surely there is cultural help in any piece of literature – that will help them to find a sound basis for culture, American readers want it.

That Cultural Helps classification was an inspiration and a good one. It emphasizes the idea of culture behind the University in Print – that culture for which the American reading public is ever clamoring. The books are cultural, whether attention is called to the fact or not, but it is a sound assumption that the prospective purchaser will not use his imagination. It is better to name the thing for what it is – if the books are cultural, say so.

A number of Little Blue Books readily fall into this classification. The beauty of it is that they do not readily fit into any other classification. In early days (in 1922 and earlier), I was often *lazy* and made use of a Miscellaneous classification – which, of course, is quite meaningless and weak. I also used a Literature classification, which was simply another way of saying Miscellaneous. Books that could not reasonably be put under any other heading were placed under either one of those. Then the list was so small that people willingly went through the entire 200 or 300 titles; but now, with 1,260 titles, anything under Miscellaneous or as general a heading as Literature would be completely overlooked. The first attempt to find a compelling classification for those *miscellaneous* cultural books was too poetic. It was Door to New Worlds, which was apt enough, but hardly in sufficiently plain English to be forceful. I also tried Explanations of Life, which was better, but not as well suited to several of the books. I made shift with Doors to New Worlds, but the books listed there under – including *Spirit of Brazilian Literature, Spirit of Yiddish Literature, How to Enjoy the Humor of Rabelais,* and so forth – continued to hover exasperatingly and disappointingly around the zero mark.

The Rabelais book, by the way, was first titled *A Guide to Rabelais,* which suggested little if the name of the author of *Gargantua and Pantagruel* was unfamiliar. Then I tried *How to Understand Rabelais,* but even this did little better than 2,000 copies annually. The success of *How to Enjoy the Humor of Rabelais* (which is to say, or intimate, *Rabelaisian* humor) is partly due to the word *enjoy* in the title, for we all want to enjoy things, and to the word *humor,* for we all like to laugh as part of our enjoyment – but it is due also to the emphasis on self-improvement in the classification Cultural Helps, where it sold 13,000 copies in 1927.

Even Percy Bysshe Shelley's *Defense of Poetry,* with the emphasis on culture, sold 6,000 copies in 1927 – not very good, but far better than the 1,500 it sold in 1926. I. B. Stoughton Holborn's *Need for Art in Life,* now listed more personally as *Why You Need Art in Your Life,* under the Cultural Helps classification sold almost 14,000 copies in 1927, when it was facing withdrawal the year before. *The Spirit of Brazilian Literature* showed improvement only – it is still far from a successful book, for it scarcely sold 4,000 copies during the last year, and *The Spirit of Yiddish Literature* did less than 3,000 – but you must take into account the fact that both of these books moved less than 1,000 copies each in 1926. I am afraid that these two books will sooner or later find themselves in the great abyss of my Morgue. But my point is clear – Cultural Helps is a definitely successful classification. The change of scenery has done all of the books some good – it has prolonged their lives, if it has not always made them immortal.

My list of books under Poetry and the books under Biography grew rapidly, and they became unwieldy and forbidding in appearance to the prospective purchaser. Shorter and more alluring classifications have proved their worth. The development of the catalogue-classification of Little Blue Books has proceeded until I can positively assert that it serves more than convenience in listing a book – it is a constructive form of salesmanship.

Usually it would be thought that classifying books must always conform to set rules. If there is a heading Biography, it would be assumed that all the biographies in the series would necessarily group themselves under that heading. That is what I did, for a time, until I experimented and found a better method. Now the classifications of Little Blue Books are loose rather than strict – the Biography group, Personalities group as it is now, is representative only; some of the better biographies in the Little Blue Books are classified as such. Other ostensible biographies are given other places, and for very good reasons.

Take the Little Blue Book life of Jean Paul Marat, for example. This was always put under Biography until lately. But biography, to be significant and appealing, must build itself around famous figures, outstanding personalities. Who, at a venture, knows the name of Marat? Even identifying him and keeping the book under Biography or Famous Personalities is not as good as putting this life of him along with other radical books – for this biography is really a *study in radicalism*. The book was a failure for two years; in 1927, with the radical emphasis, it sold 9,000 copies!

The same is true, substantially, of Constantine Volney's famous *Ruins of Empires*, of which the Little Blue Books contain an excellent summary. This also is a radical book, in many ways a devastating book. By putting it under Skepticism, Iconoclasm, or some similar classification – for the place of no Little Blue Book is quite permanent, but in different catalogues and advertising moves about, though keeping the same general emphasis – this book also reached a sales total of 9,000 in the past year.

Other biographies have been scattered in a similar fashion. The life of Pasteur is now put under Health or Hygiene, because his name really is better known in the word *pasteurization*. Lives of Franklin and Jefferson and Paine find themselves linked successfully with United States history – but if they are placed with general biographies they are lost. Paine and Voltaire, too, are put with the skeptical books, the books of free-thought and iconoclasms for which I have learned hundreds of thousands of Americans are hungering. You see the idea – instead of allowing Biography to become too solid a mass of type, I have found it better to put many of the biographies under subject classifications.

I have done the same with poetry. Longfellow's *Courtship of Miles*

136

Standish does better under Love than anywhere else, and the same is true of Elizabeth Barrett Browning's *Sonnets from the Portuguese* – a bad title if there ever was one! Oliver Wendell Holmes' *One Hoss Shay and Other Poems* does much better under Humorous Verse – almost 7,000 against the previous 3,000 as an annual figure – than under Poetry with the weaker title, *Poems of Holmes*. And *Poems About Jesus*, a failure so far, is being put, for 1928, under the general heading of Religion, and under the sub-heading of Christianity – where I have real hopes that it may do well enough to stay in the list.

To go back to my experiment with Doors to New Worlds – in 1926 Francis Bacon's *The New Atlantis* was in this classification and came to my Hospital for resuscitation. I had begun to think this was one of those *literary* masterpieces that could not be sold widely, but I quickly found that I was killing the book by keeping an unhealthy aroma of *classic* about it. The rare atmosphere of highbrow literature was smothering this book. When I got it out and away from the dust of dry tomes, into fresh air and sunlight with books of adventure – along with the *Arabian Nights* and *Robinson Crusoe* and Gulliver's voyage to Lilliput – and called the book simply *The New Atlantis: Lost Island*, it leaped up to 16,000 copies in 1927.

Everyone knows that Swift's scathing satire, *Gulliver's Travels*, can be read as pure fanciful adventure. If one does not wish to think about the satire, one does not have to think about it. The same is true of *The New Atlantis* – as my Little Blue Book experience has proved beyond any possible doubt. The story can be read simply as a story; you can even do that, to some extent, with John Bunyan's *Pilgrim's Progress*, overburdened as it is with allegorical dogma and ritual – a book that, by the way, sold 11,000 copies in 1927 in the Little Blue Book edition, listed under Famous Tales.

This change of scenery is after all just a device to compel attention and center the spotlight on certain books. The fundamental purpose of Little Blue Book classifying is nothing else but putting the books on good display, as in a store window – putting those on Fifth Avenue that seem to do best there, and those on Seventh Avenue that do best there, and those in the Bronx or down by the Battery or along the Bowery that do best there, always remembering that the high and the low will to some extent gaze in the windows of all these localities!

Some books are lost in some classifications and stand out brilliantly and enticingly when placed elsewhere. When George Moore's *Euphorian in Texas* – an abominable title from my point of view for such a fascinating story – is placed in a list of general fiction it is lost, but when it is given an explanatory subtitle, as *An Unconventional Amour*, and put with other stories of love or amorous dalliance, it stands out and, in 1927, it sold 22,000 copies. The record for 1926, I am sorry to report, was less than half of this; and for 1925 the sales of the book had sunk almost out of sight. The vanishing point was reached under George Moore's own recondite title – the old image of hiding a light under a bushel basket.

Few people nowadays will run through the entire list of 1,260 different Little Blue Books when making up an order for a dollar or two. They scan the list in a cursory fashion, and if twenty or thirty books catch their eye at once, they perhaps order them without looking further. It behooves me, in selling these books, to see to it that in so far as possible all of the books are given adequate display and emphasis – for two reasons. First, so that the same books will not be sold in excessive quantity, squeezing out others just as worthy, and unbalancing the list; second, so that those who have bought twenty or thirty books – those that readily caught their eye—will not toss aside a new catalogue after glancing at it, in the false notion that it contains nothing to interest them.

This is the real reason why a change of scenery so surprisingly affects the sales record of a book. In the new classification, in a later catalogue, going to old buyers of the Little Blue Books – who are circularized at least twice every year – a book catches the eye of those who probably overlooked it in its less effective classification in the previous catalogue or circular. Americans have the reputation for being miserly of their time, and are great lovers of time-saving devices – no less in a Little Blue Book catalogue than elsewhere.

And there is another important point in this connection. My list of biographical titles, as I have said, was always too long in comparison with other classifications in the catalogue. The fact that such listings as Biography and Fiction ran far too long to be useful was one reason for changing the classifications from conventional divisions according to the literary form to the nature of the material in the books as the basis for division.

Biography had reached a low level when these changes in classification were tried. Some of Biography, for example, was satisfactorily split up into smaller groups like Famous Lovers, Beacon Lights of History, Benefactors of Mankind, Famous Women. Confessional Autobiography, and so forth. The lives of humorists were put directly after Humor, with the heading Great Humorists. The biography of Torquemada, the famous torturer, was put under Horror. The religious biographies, or the lives of rationalists, went under Comparative Religions or Skepticism, as the case might be. In another place I mention the improvements made with biographical titles by identifying the person in the title. But the sales of these books have increased wonderfully by these changes, in nearly every instance.

I have found, however, that the Thing is more interesting than the Person, in treating biographical books. By that I mean that people are more curious about a set of ideas or notions than about the person who may have discovered, invented, or sponsored them. For example, *Sarah Bernhardt's Philosophy of Love* sold 14,000 copies in 1926, which is very good. But on the principle that Sarah Bernhardt might not be as interesting as her profession, the listing was changed to *The Code of a Parisian Actress* – with the startling result that the book sold 29,500 copies in 1927.

Or take the 1927 figures alone, and compare three books of a similar nature. *The Truth About Christian Science* sold 26,000 copies, in round numbers. Joseph McCabe's *Absurdities of Christian Science* sold 36,000 copies. But *The Real Mary Baker Eddy* sold only 22,000 copies. This indicates that fewer people identify Mary Baker Eddy with Christian Science than might be supposed, or else, which I believe, it shows that people are indeed more interested in the subject than in the personality behind it. Thomas Carlyle did a brave thing to romanticize history by writing it around heroic figures, but my own experience seems to show that the people would rather have the history than the historical characters. For example, I have a book giving brief lives of all the U. S. presidents. This sold about 14,000 copies in 1927 – but *An Outline of United States History* sold twice as many. Even *A Short History of the Civil War* did close to 15,000 copies, and that

139

is only a portion of U. S. history. Of course, the lives of the presidents also represent only a portion of the country's history – but the fact remains that interest in persons does not dominate interest in the thing or things with which the persons are concerned.

Take Einstein and his theory of relativity. This book was put into the list under the title of *An Introduction to Einstein*. It readily sold 15,000 copies, but it seemed possible to improve it. The change in title was not as drastic as you might think – the new listing was *Einstein's Theory of Relativity Explained*, which sold 42,000 copies in 1927. The thing, Relativity, is of more interest than the man, Einstein.

The same thing happened with Friedrich Nietzsche and his philosophy – Nietzsche is, by the way, the most popular of all the philosophers the world has yet produced. I have a book that was called at first, *An Introduction to Nietzsche*. I did well, for the name Nietzsche is known. But I was amazed to find that by linking the name with the thing, and calling the hook *How to Understand Nietzsche's Philosophy*, the sales leaped up – to 19,000 copies in 1927. Even Will Durant's book on Nietzsche, which was at first called *Nietzsche: Who He Was and What He Stood For*, doing barely the necessary 10,000 copies annually, sold in 1927 no less than 45,000 copies under the title *The Story of Nietzsche's Philosophy*.

Another significant comparison is that of Fascism against its founder, Mussolini, The figures tell the story, and bear out the general conclusion that the man is of less interest than the thing. In 1927, *The Truth About Mussolini* sold only 14,000 copies, as compared with 24,000 copies of *The Facts About Fascism*.

Or take the book that was called *E. Haldeman-Julius: The Man and His Work*. This was marked for The Morgue, when, acting on this principle of the thing being better than the man, the book was listed as *The History of the Little Blue Books* – of which the sales were 13,000 copies in 1927.

Compare again the sales total of *The Jesuits: Religious Rogues*, 34,000 copies in 1927, with the record of *Loyola: Founder of the Jesuits*, which sold only 8,000 copies. It is not hard to understand that if Joseph McCabe had written *The Story of My Life*, the sales record would have been far less than his *My Twelve Years in a Monastery*, which, in 1927, reached the wonderful sales total of 46,500 copies. The thing – life in a monastery – is beyond a doubt more interesting than merely the life of Joseph McCabe would have been.

I might summarize all this by saying that the men die and are forgotten but the things that they discovered, invented, or established go on forever. The fickleness of human memory may be food for cynicism or not, just as you happen to look at it, but it is none the less a fact. We remember gravitation, but forget Newton. We have steam engines, and Watt is already slated for oblivion except in school texts and question-and-answer games. It will not do to write a book about radium and name it after Madame Curie, any more than it would suffice to list the Little Blue Book on Behaviorism under the name of John B. Watson. Modern health boards approve of pasteurization without ever thinking of Louis Pasteur, and there is more interest in the psychology of sexual dreams than ever could be aroused in Sigmund Freud.

CHAPTER X
THE MORGUE

What Happens to the Failures Among Little Blue Books

This is the most painful part of my story. Those books that go into The Hospital and do not come out are consigned, with regrets, to The Morgue. The Morgue is filled with books that have not found a large audience among the readers of today. It is also filled with many a bitter lesson, and some experience, though negative, the value of which cannot be measured in dollars and cents.

I have never had a complete failure, if by that you mean a book that did not sell at all – a copy at least now and then. It appears that there is always someone to buy a few copies of any book you could possibly print and offer for sale, provided it is a good book of its kind. But I had as near a failure as I ever care to come with the *Short Poems of Friedrich Holderlin*. It was a good book, but it was poetry, plus the fact that no one knew – or cared! – who Mr. Holderlin might be. I printed 10,000 copies of this book. My confession is complete when I add that I finally baled, after a year and a half, 8,000 of these. This book went into The Morgue and stayed there, for it was certainly dead. One book that went into The Morgue is still a profound regret in my memory. I hated to delete such a title from the list. I argued with myself, and for a time I let the book ride along merely for the prestige and the satisfaction it gave my *amour propre*. For Sir Richard Burton's version of *The Kasidah* has been a favorite of mine ever since I first read it as a young man. I always wanted to make an edition of that book available to the public at far less than the several dollars it usually costs.

But *The Kasidah* kept coming into The Hospital. There seemed nothing that could be done with it. At last it was consigned to The Morgue. But one of these days I'll find a way to sell *The Kasidah*, at a fraction of a dollar, and it will be brought back to the light.

Just when does a book go into The Morgue and any remainder into the bales of waste paper? Well, as I have said, in order to sell Little Blue Books at a nickel apiece it is necessary for each title to sell to the extent of at least 10,000 copies annually, speaking in round numbers. If every book sells at least its quota, then, with 1,260 titles the total distribution must be 12,600,000 – in one or two bad years, and at first, the sales for a year fell below this figure, and in 1927 exceeded 20,000,000. Some books sell far better than 10,000 copies a year, and help to support those that fall behind and that it is, for one reason or another, desirable to keep in print.

In general, the rules that slate a book for The Morgue are not too drastic. But if a book sells less than 5,000 copies annually and nothing can be done to increase that total, it goes into The Morgue and any remainder is sent to the baler. If a book sells 6,000 copies in a year I may keep it on sale, especially if it is a thoroughly good book, and lends prestige to the series. I may try to jump up that sales total – but the book may not immediately go to The Morgue even if it does not do better than 6,000 a year.

In a sales test made in 1925, in 400 orders selected for the test, ranging from twenty books each and over – up, in some cases, to as many as 100 books in a single order, – not one order was received for the following books. These were, in other words, at the zero mark – most of the stock of them was standing still in the warehouse and accumulating dust. This is the list of dead-heads discovered in October, 1925:

Herbert Spencer: His Life and Works
Defense of Poetry. Percy Bysshe Shelley
Rudolph Eucken: His Life and Philosophy
+Witticisms of Madame de Sevigne
Aphorisms. Thomas Huxley
Literature and Art. Goethe
Poems. Robert Southey
*Addison and His Time. Charles J. Finger

144

+Guide to Stoicism. St. George Stock

+Yugoslav Proverbs

+Literary Stars in Scandinavian Firmament. Julius Moritzen

+Essays on Rousseau, Balzac and Hugo. John Cowper Powys

+Essays on Emily Bronte and Henry James. John Cowper Powys

The Unworthy Coopers. E. and M. Haldeman-Julius

+Essays on Euripides. Alexander Harvey

+Essays on Aeschylus. Alexander Harvey

+Essays on Sophocles. Alexander Harvey

+Poems of Carew, Sucking, Lovelace and Herbert

+Matthew Arnold's Literature and Dogma

+Proverbs of West Africa

A Guide to Aeschylus. Henry T. Schnittkind

Camoens: Central Figure of Portuguese Literature. Dr. Isaac Goldberg

+Georg Brandos' Main Currents of Nineteenth Century Literature

Essays on the Friends of Jesus. Alexander Harvey

Gotterdammerung. Theodore M.R. von Keler

The Gospel of Luke

The Gospel of Mark

+Prince Hagen. Upton Sinclair.

*A Collection of Apothegms. Francis Bacon +Poems and Prose of William Blake

*Cup-Bearers of Wine and Hellebore. Llewelyn Powys

+Short Poems of Frederich Holderlin

+Poe as a Literary Critic. Dr. Isaac Goldberg

+Hauptmann and Sudermann: Two German Dramatists. George Seibel

+Talks with Lamb, Coleridge and Goethe

+Revolt in German Drama. Pierre Loving

+Perkin Warbeck and Other Poems. Lord Alfred Douglas King Henry VI. William Shakespeare

*A Ballad of a Nun, and Other Poems. John Davidson

*What the Editor's Wife Is Thinking About. Marcet Haldeman-Julius

+Mexican Poetry: An Anthology. Dr. Isaac Goldberg (editor)
  +The Acharnians. Aristophanes
  +Proverbs of Turkey
  *Sonnets of a Portrait-Painter. Arthur Davison Ficke

Those starred (*) were saved by title changes as discussed in the chapter entitled The Hospital. Those with a dagger (+) against them are in The Morgue, or soon will be. The others are still awaiting remedy or removal.

A glance at this list shows that it is crammed with titles of limited or rather scholastic appeal. Many of these sooner or later went into The Morgue. But I should explain that although not one person out of the 400 selected at random for this test ordered a copy of any one of these books, they did not actually stand still without a single copy ever being sold. Some of them, taking it by and large over a year with thousands of orders pouring in, would do around 5,000. Some of them were saved by the efforts of The Hospital, already described.

Then, too, it is never possible to make replacements wholesale. There is always a waiting list for The Morgue – unfortunately this will always be true in a list as large as that of the Little Blue Books – and as a rule those go into the discard first that somehow or other show on the inventory at 5,000 copies or less on hand. That is why some books are still waiting for The Morgue. Others, which it is necessary to drop, reach the deadline sooner. Some day, if a few of these books do not move at all, they will be dropped forthwith. I have baled, in one or two instances, as many as 28,000 or 30,000 copies of a book. This is expensive, but I needed the warehouse space and it is better to list a book that moves a little than to waste space on one that does not move at all.

In the preceding list you will notice, if you look carefully, two books taken from the Bible. It is customary to cite the Bible as the best selling book in all publishing history – but I must be intrepid enough to point out that this does not mean it is the most widely read book in print. On the contrary, for, as I have already proved, a Little Blue Book is purchased, if any book is, in order to be read – and no one, generally speaking, will buy the Bible in Little Blue Book form. I have both *The Sermon on the Mount and Other Sayings of Jesus* and *Essence of the Bible*, besides the two listed above, and all are poor sellers.

I once had a compilation of the *Words of Jesus*, made by Henry C. Vedder, in two volumes, nicely couched in the best of modern English. I think that modernizing the language of an ancient book is desirable – but people do not care for the Bible in modern English. They do not want to *read* it anyway, you see – or at least they don't want to make any sense out of reading it, and want it just because it is the Bible and one really ought to have one somewhere on the premises.

To sell the Bible you must publish it between *black* covers. The standardized stiff blue card covers used for the Little Blue Books mean, in the eyes of purchasers, that it is not the Bible. For the Bible is not a book – it is an object, a fetish, a piece of furniture. A large mail-order house once tried to sell a clothbound Bible – in blue or red covers. They were forced to abandon the project – people did not want the Bible just as a book.

But criticisms of the Bible – ah, that is something else entirely. People eagerly purchase all sorts of adverse comments on the Bible, the truth about its origin, the sources of its myths and legends, a collection of its self-contradictions, facts about forgeries of some of its books, discussions of whether Jesus ever lived or not – as the Little Blue Books of this kind have shown. The facts about this will be found in Chapter V.

Among the recent consignments to The Morgue there is Oscar Wilde's *Critic as Artist*, which I kept in the list for a long time as two volumes in the Little Blue Books. At an earlier date it was found necessary to eliminate Poe's *Marginalia*, and *Critical Excerpts from Poe*, and *Poe as a Literary Critic*. It is disappointing to have to remove these books, but there was no alternative. They are not books that it is feasible to sell on a basis of mass production.

I did not so much regret the passing of the *Poems of Philip Freneau*. I readily saw that Freneau was in the same depths of obscurity as Holderlin. It was a bad mistake to put such a book in the list in the first place. The same is true of Sainte-Beuve's essays on Chesterfield and Rabelais. Good as they are, they were out of place in the general scope of the growing series and they could not be effectively grouped for the best selling emphasis. Likewise, the *Essay on Swinburne*, by Sir Arthur Quiller-Couch.

In a somewhat different class was the *History of Printing*, by D'Israeli. This simply seemed to be an example of limited interest. An original work, published in the Little Blue Books for the first time, called *A Newspaperman's Estimate of the Fourth Gospel*, by Olin Wellington Archer, met the same fate for the same reason. I should also list here Charles J. Finger's decidedly interesting brochure entitled *England in Shakespeare's Time*. It went the way of the others, for no other reason than that it had limited appeal.

Certain expansion-centers in the growth of the Little Blue Books would now and then stray beyond the precise boundary set by commercial success. I mean by this that the public would express a desire for a certain class of books, and, to meet this desire, new books being printed of the same class would exceed – when things had quieted down and the first flutter of popularity was over – the capacity that mass production would justify. A clear example is the Greek and Roman drama classification, translated chiefly by Alexander Harvey. It became necessary to withdraw some of these books, including *Iphigenia at Aulis*, by Euripides, *Oedipus at Colonus*, by Sophocles, *The Clouds*, *The Birds*, *The Knights*, *The Achamians*, *The Wasps*, and *The Peace*, by Aristophanes, *The Captives* and *The Pot of Gold*, by Plautus, *The Self-Tormentor*, by Terence, and so on. A few of these classics, in accord with the popularization of the works of antiquity, as discussed earlier in this chapter, are being retained. There is a real demand for a very limited list of this kind of reading.

At the end of 1927 I find that the series of proverb collections in the Little Blue Books, as a series, is a failure. At first there were only nine of these books – Chinese Proverbs, Irish Proverbs, Russian Proverbs, and so forth. People were much interested in the early days – these collections have always been a unique feature of the University in Print, embodying, as they do, the crystallized wisdom of various races and nations. But as a wider range of popular books was offered, interest in this form of reading dwindled, until now only three or four of these books are successful – notably the Proverbs of China and those of Ireland. The others – there are nineteen books of proverbs in all as I write, and I may retain half a dozen – are slated for The Morgue. They have to go. Even pointing out, by the

148

catalogue listing, that these proverbs are the best wit and wisdom of large groups of humanity has done no good. In general, it has been shown that readers are not interested in such collections.

Occasionally I have found it necessary to send a biography to The Morgue. As a general principle, however, a biography can usually be saved with proper attention to the title, provided it is a good piece of work. The *Life of Keats* was one of the first to go, and also *Whistler: the Man and His Art.* For some reason not altogether clear to me, the lives of painters and poets, as individuals, do not interest the greater portion of the reading public. I also killed a lengthy critical study of Shakespeare and his plays. Among others, there were *Diderot and the French Encyclopedists*, probably too pedantic in tone and, withdrawn for much the same reason, *Hauptmann and Sudermann*, by George Seibel. Among the first to go, incidentally, was an old-timer, *The Trial of William Penn.* Another old-timer, a *Life of Columbus*, was sent to The Morgue, only to be replaced, with fair success, by an edition of *The Diary of Columbus in 1492.*

As I have shown from the beginning, the general development of the Little Blue Books has been along broad lines. Few books of a particular nature, isolated from others similar to it, get into the series. Now and then this has happened, sometimes successfully and sometimes not. Among the failures were such titles as *When the Puritans Were in Power* (although there is now Rupert Hughes' *Facts About Puritan Morals*), *Voices from the Past, Satan and the Saints, State and Heart Affairs of Henry VIII*, James Anthony Fronde's *Science of History*, and so forth. Others of this class, successful and still in the list, are *Twenty Years Among African Negroes*, Max Beerbohm's *Defense of Cosmetics*, Burton's *Anatomy of Melancholy*, and so forth. I cannot, of course, predict how long some of these titles will stay in the list. Some of them I am determined to keep, but others will have judgment passed upon them by the actual verdict of the buyers of the books.

There is one general rule The Morgue taught me. At one time I thought that longer works, like Upton Sinclair's *The Jungle*, could be issued in a half dozen or so volumes of the Little Blue Books, making the whole work cost much less than a dollar. I tried this idea out with two-volume, three-volume, and four-volume works particularly. Every one of them has been a failure and principally for the reason that when books are offered in this way, your choice at five cents, readers will buy the first volume only, to see what it is like, and then never get around to ordering the rest. A contributory objection, no doubt, is that there is something forbidding about a work in several small pocket-sized volumes. If a book is to be carried in the pocket, and that is one of the points in its favor, then it must be in some sense of the word a brief book.

Among the many-volume works sooner or later to be found in The Morgue are *The Jungle*, aforementioned, and Frank Harris' *Man Shakespeare* (4 vols.), *Psychical Research* (2 vols.), *Words of Jesus* (2 vols.), *Dante and Other Waning Classics* (2 vols.), Upton Sinclair's *Millennium* (3 vols.), and so forth. Although the objection may be advanced that some of these books are, by their nature, as compared with other single-volume works in The Morgue, destined to such a fate, I can also cite the example of the *Memoirs of Madame de Pompadour*, which was formerly in two volumes and not a satisfactory success. It is now in one volume under the title: *Memoirs of a French Royal Mistress*. The only best seller in more than one volume is Dante's *Inferno*.

A solution of the difficulty has been to give the separate volumes their own titles. This was done with the *Arabian Nights*, and it is at present being tried with the four volumes of Emerson's *Representative Men* and the four volumes of Frank Harris' *Contemporary Portraits*. These latter two, being biographical in nature, are being identified by the men treated in the separate volumes, in the manner of single biographies. This treatment has not always been possible, I am sorry to say.

The story of The Morgue has been a long one. It has, indeed, been much longer in existence than The Hospital. Buried in it is more than one corpse, long since a skeleton to haunt the editorial closet. Such ghastly relics as these I hesitate to exhume. But I have vowed that I would tell a straight story, and tell it honestly. In some ways it is ghoulish, but I owe it to the demands of this chronicle to state the facts.

In my younger days I was a Socialist journalist. I mean this in a political and something of a fanatical sense. All young men who dream dreams are fanatics. When I was in my twenties Socialism was a more important issue, under that name, in America than it is now. People were interested in Socialism. It was being talked about. People wanted to read about it. But the interest passed and Socialism waned, until now it is really a dead issue from any bird's eye point of view you may choose. It lives only here and there. I cannot go into the causes of this decline here. That would make an essay by itself, if not a whole book.

But in The Morgue you will find the remains of an early Socialistic debauch of mine in the Little Blue Books. I can call it nothing else, for the list of such titles is, as I look back at them now, appalling. They went into The Morgue because they ceased to sell. I have space to mention a few of them, and I think the titles are of enough interest to justify it. There was, for example, Kate O'Hare's *Prison Letters*. That brings back many an almost forgotten memory. Then there were the following: *The Socialist Appeal, From Terror to Triumph* (Soviet Labor Laws), Jack London's *Dream of Debs, Shall Church Property Be Taxed?* (A Debate), *Socialism vs. Catholicism, Socialist Pepper-Box, Keir Hardie Calendar, Fight for Your Life, Solution of the Trust Problem*, and so forth, and so forth. In the Little Blue Books as they are today you will find issues of the hour treated in a practical, truth-telling way, visionary aspects aside. For example, Anna Louise Strong, in a series on Russia, gives the facts about the Soviet Union, as in *How the Communists Rule Russia*. Arthur Garfield Hays tells his side of the story in *What I Saw in Russia*, and so on. Two debates on Socialism are also still in the list, so that the subject has fair representation.

So much for one large area in The Morgue. Another generous group brings back another phase of the Little Blue Book idea in the process of growth and transformation. Many of the titles consigned to The Morgue have been dropped to make room for better books. I mean this in a strictly critical sense, entirely aside from whether the books will sell or not. For there are some books in The Morgue, about which I now propose to tell, which were very good sellers – and yet they were withdrawn.

I refer to a series of a dozen or so books dealing with the improvement of the mind, the personality, and that sort of thing. *How to Strengthen Mind and Memory* was the title of one of these books; *How to Be a Leader of Others* was another. I withdrew these books because they were false. They

151

did not give the facts, but drew rosy pictures, fostering erroneous views of life – in short, these books were nothing but bunk. They were killed, all of them.

Then, later, it became possible to approach similar subjects from a more scientific point of view. I found a way to offer the facts, instead of falsities, and you will find most of those earlier books replaced in the series as it is today by books that are sound and authoritative and tell the truth about life. For example, William J. Fielding discusses personality in *The Puzzle of Personality*; Leo Markun has written *The Psychology of Leadership* and *Facts You Should Know About Will Power*, and so on. The Morgue has taught me that the public does not want large doses of highly-colored propaganda. Some people regard any presentation of facts as propaganda, but I use the word here to signify books that abandon reason and logic and facts and set about creating fanciful notions based entirely on the imagination. The Morgue has also taught me that the public does not want bunk if it can get the truth. I feel entirely justified in killing those earlier *self-help* books, for the new Self-Improvement books thoroughly live up to their aim and do honor to the series as a whole.

The Little Blue Books have taken shape as a series of wide appeal. The policy expanded to be nearly all-inclusive; those were dangerous days, full of publishing risks. In those days I talked of going on and on, to two thousand titles, even to ten thousand titles. But I soon saw that the only outcome in that direction would be a gigantic warehouse, full of an assortment so large that no one could make a real choice, and so expensive that no one could get any real benefit from it. From a rather indefinite intention to publish almost anything to sell for a nickel, the conflicting forces brought to bear upon the Little Blue Books, as they were offered in the market, chiseled out for them a policy of their own.

The Morgue has removed from the list, and is still removing from the list, those titles that do not coincide with this policy of good books with a wide appeal. That is why Ernest Dowson's *Pierrot of the Minute* is in The Morgue. That is why the literary criticism of John Cowper Powys, his essays on Emily Bronte and Henry James and the rest, are destined for The Morgue. That is why Theodore M. R. von Keler's concise summaries of many of the lesser-known operas will all find themselves one of these days in The Morgue – some of them are already there. These are good books, but they are not of wide appeal.

There has at times been a current, topic-of-the-hour phase of the Little Blue Books. In general, this is not worthwhile. Sometimes it is all right to put in a book that will stay for perhaps a year and then drop out. I refer to such dated items as the *1926 Price Range of Stocks, 1927 Directory of Radio Stations, 1924 Republican and Democratic Platforms,* and the like. The fad of crossword puzzling brought a couple of crossword puzzle books into the list, but these will stay. Their sale is nothing like what it was during the height of the craze, but it is good enough to be worth devoting a number or so to it. When the Ku Klux Klan finally fades into oblivion, it may be that the two books on the Klan will go into The Morgue. Meanwhile, there is enough interest to sustain them. And there is no reason why *The Best Jokes of 1926* should not sell for years to come, like the O'Brien short-story anthologies.

I am sorry that such a book as Dr. Isaac Goldberg's *Guide to Cervantes* should have had to go to The Morgue. But even this tells its helpful story. I can put alongside it Goldberg's *Dante: An Esthetic View,* and Julius Moritzen's *Significance of Georg Brandes* and also his *August Strindberg: Literary Enigma,* all of them now in The Morgue, and say to you that this again proves the evolution of the Little Blue Books into a general series of wide appeal. Why is it that Dante's *Inferno* is a good seller, while an introduction to Dante as a whole goes begging? There is only one answer. The reading public is willing to accept guides to anything except reading, speaking generally. People would rather read a famous book by Dante than read about him. They will accept a tabulation of good books, like John Cowper Powys' *One Hundred Best Books,* but they do not care for the significance of Georg Brandes or anyone else when it is written like a thesis for a collegiate degree.

I am sorry, just as I know many who read this candid account will be sorry, that the story, in some of its aspects, is not different from the truth. I would like more than I can say to have kept many of these books out of The Morgue. I wish I could keep them before even that small portion of the public that would like to buy one of them now and then. But I am not playing hit or miss, like some playful god – like, at a venture, the Setebos fancied by Caliban in Browning's poetic description of theology on the island! I am not pulling in this title and taking another out just because I think I should. It is all a matter of figures, as the Efficiency Expert would say if I had one. The books are wanted or they are not wanted—it is quite simple.

As for general conclusions from The Morgue, it can all be summarized by simply saying that the reading public, viewed as a whole, wants books that are not too esoteric, not too high-hat, not too refined and highbrow. People as a mass want books for everyday appeal and value, which does not at all mean that they want badly-written books, or books that deal insincerely or half-heartedly with the subject treated.

The worst classes of books, from my point of view, as a publisher in mass quantities, are poetry, literary criticism, biographies of less than international figures and personalities that are known by people of special education or limited interests, compilations of any sort except fiction or humor and works of the better known masters, and the large group of books usually called belles-lettres for want of a better name. On the whole, I avoid both the familiar and the formal essay, unless the subject is of wide appeal. Books of orations and speeches are not desirable as a class, though I have succeeded very well with a large group of debates. The printed drama as a group is decidedly not in demand.

If I could have given myself, when I began the Little Blue Books, advice that I now might offer out of my nine years' experience, I would have said something like this: "Whenever you consider a book for publication, pick out twenty-five imaginary readers for it from all levels of life. Pick out a college professor, a scientist, a college student, a highschool boy and a highschool girl, a day laborer, a factory worker, a stenographer, a housewife, a school teacher, a hobo, a chorus girl, an editor, a doctor, a lawyer, a soda-fountain clerk, a waitress, a Pullman porter, a millionaire, a salesman, a bootblack, an undertaker, a grocery man, a preacher, and a tired business man – and put yourself in the place of each one in turn, and ask yourself candidly whether such a person would buy the book for the price you are selling it if he had the chance. If fifteen out of the twenty-five would probably buy the book, then I would recommend putting it into the Little Blue Books. If less than fifteen would be likely to buy it at some time or other, its success as a Little Blue Book would be doubtful. If less than ten would buy it, its failure would be assured."

CHAPTER XI
AN EDITOR AND HIS WRITER

Peculiar Editorial Problems of the Little Blue Books

A s I look back at the history of the Little Blue Books, from those first two volumes of poetry – *Rubaiyat of Omar Khayyam* (No. 1) and Oscar Wilde's *Ballad of Reading Gaol* (No. 2) – to the list as it is now, totaling 1,260 different volumes, I am amazed at the panorama of experience spread out before, or rather behind, me. Nine years have contained a surprising number of things. When I began with two fairly well-known classics, and poetry at that, I had not the least inkling that my top number would be a book by my wife on a contemporary sociological situation, *Story of a Southern Lynching*. Nor had I any idea, either, that the next to the top number would be a reference volume such as *A Dictionary of Geographical Names*, compiled by Leo Markun. But those four volumes, the first two and the last two, numerically speaking, are an epitome of the wide range of editorial growth and change through which the Little Blue Books have carried me.

It was Frankenstein who created a monster and gave it life, whereupon it leaped beyond his dreams and terrified him. Sometimes I feel like that. Sometimes I am awed by contemplating how I started the Little Blue Books – pocket classics for the people – and how they leaped into the impressive conception of a University in Print, finally realized. Of course, the series is incomplete. I haven't been able to keep pace with it at all. I candidly admit that the series has grown like some mighty beast, now and then obeying my command, but just as often cavorting here and there seemingly of its own free will.

But what would you have in nine years? According to arithmetic, which is practical enough certainly, the average increase per year is 140 titles. That is an aggregate of 2,100,000 or so words. As a matter of fact, some years I added more than that, for many of the years, especially the first years, the expansion did not proceed to anywhere near that speed. I am not ashamed that I made mistakes. And I do not hesitate to be proud that I have behind me a record of real publishing achievement.

All of which is intended as a preamble to saying that there is nothing else quite like the Little Blue Books. I had newspaper experience before I tackled this pocket series idea. I cannot imagine what other background could have helped me at all. I was plowing a virgin field, and I knew that I had to hit stones and that I had to risk the harvest, good or bad. As I have emphasized in another place, there was only one principle to guide me in editing a series of this kind – a Little Blue Book would be bought only to be read.

Problems that arose in editing the Little Blue Books were unique. I had nothing to guide me except my own experience, and why shouldn't I confess that my own experience was precious little at times? I was getting that experience even as I struggled along. Occasionally it was costly. Often it was profitable. But I did not hesitate. There was never any backsliding, never any attempt to pass the buck, never any claim that my inspiration was infallible, never any admission that I was failing. For after all, as the present list of Little Blue Books shows, it was a magnificent success all around. Now the story can be told. Now I can tell, and I am doing it, exactly what nine years of publishing and editing these 1,260 Little Blue Books have taught me.

The series had not progressed very far – possibly there were 250 titles in print – when the first important editorial step had to be taken. Up to this point the series had been strictly made up of reprints of classics – and by that I mean books that had appeared in print before, most of them by writers already dead, most of them in the public domain, which is to say that there was no longer any copyright making them the exclusive property of any individual or corporation. The series had to start this way. There could not be any payment to authors, for special manuscripts for the series, until capital accumulated to justify such expenditure. But the success of that first 250 books, reprints though they were, opened the way for a new era of publishing pocket-sized books. It meant that writers could be hired to prepare manuscripts of exactly the right length, in exactly the right style, on exactly the right subjects, to embody the Little Blue Book idea. I am tempted into an aside about copyrights and the so-called public domain of literature. I sincerely beg the pardon of any readers whose sense of coherence and unity and all that pedantic ritual is outraged, but the story of the Little Blue Books contains so many interesting oases along the route that I cannot help being lured into bypaths. Many people have not the least idea what a copyright is or what it means. Most people stand in considerable awe of the majesty of the law anyway, and seem to have the strange notion that it is all beyond their puny understanding. I have frequently had the question put to me, for example, how it is that I am able to publish Shakespeare in the Little Blue Books without paying colossal royalties.

Again, many people have been under the impression, fostered largely by the beginning of the Little Blue Books, that the entire series, even today, is made up of reprints. Such people are always astounded when I tell them that fully three-fourths of the list is protected by copyright. They are incredulous when they are informed that a large part of the material in the Little Blue Books can be obtained in no other form. But that is the actual state of things – the copyright records and documents of the Little Blue Books occupy an important niche in the plant's huge vault. This sounds puerile, but I give you my word that it will be news to some of my readers.

Copyrights have a definite life. When they expire they may be renewed, but renewed only once. After that the work automatically becomes a part of the public domain, and may be published by anyone without payment of royalty. Unfortunately the United States copyright law is in many ways inefficient and unjust, but I cannot go into the technicalities of the law here. The general statement is enough to give an understanding of the situation. Shakespeare, Boccaccio, Irving, Poe, and so on, are in the public domain. It is rather funny, then, to have someone ask me how I can publish these works.

Affidavits for copyright registration are always made out by a girl in the office and this has given rise to some amusing incidents. I remember how one of the girls who had this among her duties, once asked me if Boccaccio was a citizen of the United States. I think she was intending to slip in a copyright on *The Falcon and Other Tales*, by Boccaccio of Decameron fame. At another time she, in an absent moment, handed me the form properly and correctly made out for *4,000 Most Essential English Words*, which has no author, but lo and behold! In lieu of an author she had drafted the book's subtitle into extra duty and entered, in the blank space for author, A Basic Literacy Test.

In contrast with such anecdotes is one I read somewhere about a plagiarist who tried to foist Bret Harte's *Luck of Roaring Camp* on an editor of a fiction magazine. The amateur pirate insisted the story was his own work, and when told that, due to some irony of fate, a gentleman by the name of Bret Harte had written it long before him, he retorted that it was true, but made no difference since the story was in the public domain. All of which adds to the merriment of life, but is not getting me on in my chronicle. The Little Blue Books, as I said, soon entered the field of including copyright works especially written or edited for the series. Immediately this necessitated a somewhat unusual editorial policy. Due to the strict mechanical requirements, which at first were confined to sixty-four, ninety-six, and 128 pages in the completed book, and later were standardized to sixty-four pages or occasionally thirty-two, it was impossible to consider unsolicited manuscripts in the manner of most publishing houses. In other words, I could not go into the general publishing field and pick out here and there a book or two from the great mass of freelance manuscript. It was impossible. It could not be thought of – manuscript already written was so much flotsam and jetsam as far as I was concerned, no matter how excellent.

Manuscripts for the Little Blue Books are now strictly standardized to 15,000 words each. This is the absolute mechanical requirement, and although it may and does vary a trifle, the margin of variation is very small. In the first place, a sixty-four page Little Blue Book must contain at least sixty pages of type matter or the man who buys it will feel cheated. This is a fact that always has to be kept in mind. After all, there is always that sales resistance to a *pamphlet,* and when I advertise that a Little Blue Book contains 15,000 words it simply cannot contain, with any frequency, only 10,000. In the second place, type is not infinitely elastic. If the manuscript for a Little Blue Book, when set in the usual style of eight point on an eight point slug, sixteen ems wide, runs beyond the bottom of page sixty-four, it has to be cut, and that is expensive. When you are producing a five-cent product expense must be reduced to a minimum. Hence, manuscripts are written strictly to order.

Of course I have had the accusation of *hack-writing* flung at me time and time again. The implication is silly, as any editor knows. Art is one thing, well enough, and literary craftsmanship is another. Whether a thing is written to order, or comes from *divine* inspiration, matters very little. The result is what counts. An editor can tell a good book when he sees one and he bothers his head not at all about how it came to be written if it meets his need. The folly of crying *hack-work* at anything done on order, and according to specifications, is easily shown. But the prize incident that comes to my mind is the slurring letter I once received that accused me of hiring an ordinary hack by the name of Francis Thompson to write a stupid essay on Percy Bysshe Shelley. That is No. 10 in the Little Blue Books. I would have been proud to hire Mr. Thompson – but the work had been done for some other editor before me, and it was my honor only to reprint it.

I do not pretend to imply that 1 am the only editor who corresponds with writers and tells them what he wants. That would be preposterous. All editors do this regularly, especially with writers from whom they can expect work to meet their requirements. It is even done with fiction, that standardized fiction that entertains the masses from week to week, and I see no objection to it as an editor. I do not use that kind of fiction, for with fiction I have other standards, but then, I am doing a different work. But I do say, flatly, that my particular method of eliciting work from writers by correspondence was induced by the requirements of the Little Blue Books and has peculiarities all its own.

The Little Blue Books are quite different from the publishing program of any publisher of clothbound *library* volumes, which arbitrarily includes from twenty or thirty to 100 or so new volumes every year. There is seldom a peak in the sales record of an individual Little Blue Book, and then a steady decline until the book is sold out and never reprinted. It is my intention, when I schedule a Little Blue Book for publication, that it shall remain in the list indefinitely. I am not clairvoyant, and many a Little Blue Book has had to be withdrawn, as my Morgue readily shows, but in general the life of a Little Blue Book is the life of the series itself. If it is a genuine Little Blue Book, filling all the requirements of the series, it stays for good. Thus, you can begin to see how the Little Blue Books have blazed their own trail, so to speak. They have made it necessary to impress upon writers these special requirements, and they have eliminated at once those writers whose work is creative along rather indefinite artistic lines. For example, I might not have published the stories of Sherwood Anderson if he had submitted them to me originally. But it fitted into my plans admirably to be able to make arrangements with Mr. Anderson's publishers for two volumes of his representative stories, after he became known. The same has been true of Ben Hecht, Stephen Leacock, Fannie Hurst, Theodore Dreiser, Wilbur Daniel Steele, and so forth. In a manner of speaking, the Little Blue Books have been a kind of periodical, each volume being an issue, of which the best-selling *back numbers* are continually kept in print and on sale. This illustrates rather well the necessity for general and constant appeal in considering a manuscript for publication, combined with the excellence and high literary standard that I have always set for my writers. The original works have been confined to the preparation of specially written biographies, brief histories, self-teaching educational volumes and, to a slight extent, volumes of literary criticism. Original works of fiction, poetry, and belles-lettres, not previously published, have not been sought.

From the first, then, my contact with writers has always been – when they have been working for the Little Blue Books – through extensive correspondence and frequently by discussions in personal interviews. One of the first writers to work for me, Charles J. Finger, I made all arrangements with in person. I remember when the Little Blue Books were still young

162

– it was along in April, 1923 – that I drove from Girard to Fayetteville, Arkansas, where Mr. Finger has his workshop, expressly to talk over the matter of Little Blue Book manuscripts with him. He had already done some books for me, and there was waiting for me, when I arrived on that trip, *Oscar Wilde in Outline*.

It was to introduce a number of classics that Charles J. Finger was specially needed at that time. He wrote the introduction for Burton's *Kasidah*, which later had to be consigned to The Morgue. Among his books still in the list are such unique Little Blue Book features as *Sailor Chanties and Cowboy Songs*, *A Book of Strange Murders*, *Great Pirates*, *Lost Civilizations*, *Historic Crimes and Criminals*, *Adventures of Baron Munchausen*, and so forth. Of his biographical and literary introductions, among the best liked are *Barnum and His Circus*, *Robin Hood and His Merry Men*, *Thoreau, the Man Who Escaped from the Herd*, *Mark Twain, the Philosopher Who Laughed at the World*, and so forth. Mr. Finger helped the Little Blue Books wonderfully in those early days. He was close at hand, which was necessary, because many a conference was imperative before these manuscripts could be properly prepared.

Murray Sheehan was another resident of Arkansas who wrote for me in the beginning. Some of these names, I take pride in pointing out, were but little known when they began to appear among the Little Blue Books, but have leaped into more prominence in recent years. A most remarkable case was Will Durant. Mr. Sheehan was especially helpful along practical lines, writing such books as *Hints on News Reporting*, *A History of Architecture*, *A History of Painting*, and so forth.

Anyone who has followed the Little Blue Books closely will have noticed that certain of my writers gained rather rapid prominence in the list and then ceased work as far as the Little Blue Books were concerned. I made use of a writer only as long as he could serve the purpose of the series itself. The requirements of the Little Blue Books, in different phases of their growth, have sapped several prolific writers dry. Names that loom large in the list have been seemingly spasmodic, because the Little Blue Books have been able to absorb all of a writer's work that would fit. Such names, besides the two already mentioned, are those of Leo Markun, Carroll Lane Fenton, William J. Fielding, Hereward Carrington, Theodore M. R. von Keler, Vance Randolph, Clement Wood, Lloyd E. Smith, Isaac Goldberg, Alexander Harvey, Julius Moritzen, James Oppenheim, Ralph Oppenheim, R. A. Power, Maynard Shipley, Miriam Allen deFord, Henry C. Vedder, Nelson Antrim Crawford, George Sylvester Viereck, Keene Wallis, Clarice Cunningham, Josephine Headen, and so forth. Each of these writers either wrote or edited several Little Blue Books – they were good workmen, within their limitations, and their work was needed.

Some of these people have written for me over a long period. William J. Fielding is a notable example – without doubt the most popular writer in the entire series. More of him in due course.

Of those still at work, Joseph McCabe is the outstanding king of them all. In the list I have given, you see at once the small army that the Little Blue Books have put to work, a veritable battery of busy typewriters. (Of them all, Joseph McCabe is the only one who prepared his manuscripts by hand, with pen and ink.) Nor is this all. There are two or three dozen names of writers who prepared from one to three or four books that I have not mentioned, among them such familiar ones as Floyd Dell, Ludwig Lewisohn, Pierre Loving, Thelma Spear, B. Russell Herts, and so forth. I haven't the space to discuss each of these writers at length. I put George Sylvester Viereck to work at a time when, because of the aftermath of the World War, he was finding it hard to get into the swing of things again. Prejudice has never meant anything to me if a writer can do the work I want the way I want it, particularly that prejudice which comes from difference of opinion. Julius Moritzen I accepted at his own valuation as the semi-official representative of Georg Brandes and Scandinavian literature in America. Henry C. Vedder, as a religionist, served very well to give the Bible and certain theological personalities places in the list. James Oppenheim took charge of psychology in his role of psycho-analyst. Keene Wallis did some admirable translations from the French; perhaps it will be remembered that he won the Blindman's Poetry prize for 1925 with his poem entitled *Coal Black Jesus*; in this same contest Clement Wood received honorable mention. Hereward Carrington was active chiefly in that demimonde between science and psychic paraphernalia, a field that I soon thought wise to abandon. And so on and on.

All of this work was arranged by correspondence. Strict specifications were given each writer, even to such prosaic particulars as the number of typewritten pages, margins, and so on. It has always surprised me to find out how few people who write for a living really know how to prepare manuscript properly. This is a difficulty all editors have, and it finally drove me to include in the Little Blue Books a complete set of directions: *How to Prepare Manuscripts*. Writers who failed to follow instructions had their manuscripts returned to them, and probably they did not get any more work to do for me. It is possible to write a biography in 15,000 words; several of my writers have proved it. Every subject the Little Blue Books have required has been fitted into this mechanical measure, or a multiple of it.

When illustrations were desirable, writers either made them for their own manuscripts, or drawings were made by a commercial artist. People are often surprised to find Little Blue Books generously illustrated. It is expensive, of course, but where it has been necessary it has always been done. Even regarding the illustrations, careful instructions were always given.

Hundreds of unsolicited manuscripts have been received. That is inevitable. But I can truthfully say that I never received one that was ready, without correspondence, to go into the series of Little Blue Books. The work has all been done on assignment. Instead of fitting the book to the manuscript, making each volume conform to the nature of the copy, with me it has been a problem simply of fitting the manuscript to the book.

One scientist who did a lot of work for me was Carroll Lane Fenton, a professor. He was sometimes assisted by his wife, who is a paleontologist. Mr. Fenton not only prepared various manuscripts about the earth, evolution, zoology, and so on, but he frequently did accurate scientific illustrations. He did much to popularize certain phases of science through the mass medium of the Little Blue Books. Later on, his work was carried to wider fields by Maynard Shipley, President of the Science League of America, and author of the recent book, *The War on Modern Science*. Mr. Shipley's work more directly linked science with a rational view of life, which especially fitted into my plans and my own beliefs. From this last I do not want it assumed that the Little Blue Books are any sort of engine for propaganda. True, it has been my effort to give the facts and the truth about things, in the light of modern discoveries and from intelligent viewpoints. But the wide variety of the material in the series defeats any accusations of special and limited propaganda. The Little Blue Books are representative: that much has been achieved beyond the question of a doubt.

As far as I am aware, the fact that the Little Blue Books have included such works as Maynard Shipley's *Sources of Bible Myths and Legends* or his *Evolution vs. Dogma* has never been any handicap to their popularity. Once in a while some fanatic will take the trouble to write me that he has burned his supply of Little Blue Books because he happened to see some anti-religious work in the list. This sort of wild-eyed activity, however, no publisher should take seriously. I have never given any of my writers any curbing as to saying exactly what they believe, as long as they err on the side of being too scientifically frank or too rationally candid.

As a matter of record, my instructions to authors have now and again included admonitions to beware of bunk. I have always urged my writers to give the facts, and at the same time to avoid carefully empty wordiness and blatant poppycock of one kind or another.

I shall always point with pride to the story of philosophy as told in a dozen Little Blue Books by Will Durant. This work went on, as a matter of fact, subsidized by the support of Little Blue Book readers. It was the pocket classics that made this continuous introduction to the world's great philosophers possible. That it should, when issued as a clothbound five-dollar book, become the best-selling non-fiction book in America is no more than just.

Beyond a doubt, as far as the Little Blue Books themselves are concerned, those bearing the name of William J. Fielding are far and away the best sellers. This is partly because of the immense interest his subjects are sure to arouse in any prospective reader, and also, in all fairness, partly due to the well-known name of the author. His larger books in recent years have included such as these: *The Caveman Within Us*, *Sanity in Sex*, and *Sex and the Love-Life*. His first Little Blue Book was *Psycho-Analysis: Key to Human Behavior*. This was rapidly followed by others along psychological lines, especially his *Puzzle of Personality*.

It soon became clear that there was a greater and still more important work for which Mr. Fielding was eminently fitted. Every intelligent and progressive person believes that honest information about love and sex should be available to everyone. This information should be accurate and authentic. By this is not meant anything obscene, any pornography, or stuff of that sort. Just the facts, told in a way everyone can understand, without concealment, with nothing of false modesty, so as never to be in any way misleading. I had tried out Margaret Sanger's *What Every Girl Should Know* in the Little Blue Books. The demand for this hook showed beyond any argument that the Little Blue Books were the medium that should give information about sex and its place in life to the public at large.

Taboo has played no part in the job of editing the Little Blue Books, except as it may have kept bunk and hypocrisy out of the list. The taboo against sex is being rapidly lifted in these more enlightened days, and the next few years will see an even more intelligent attitude toward it, but when William J. Fielding first undertook the task of preparing a Rational Sex Series for the Little Blue Books, we were still in the fringe of the dark ages. It was all right to speak of love, but the word *sex* was never used in the most polite parlors of our great American homes. A few magazines still censor some of the Fielding books from my national advertising, but I am sure the general public has never been anything but grateful to have these always available in the complete catalogue of 1,260 titles.

First of all, Fielding followed Mrs. Sanger's admirable lead, with *What Every Boy Should Know*, and so on for every young woman, young man, married woman, and married man. If there is anyone who winces at the candid manner of these titles, or of *Woman's Sexual Life* and its companion volumes on man, the child, and homosexuality, I challenge him to read the books themselves. For a time the Canadian Government prohibited the importation of these books into Canada, under the impression that they must be disguised obscenity. Finally I was enabled, through the kindness of a Canadian citizen who prefers to remain anonymous, to get in direct touch with the authorities, and when the books were properly examined the ban was immediately lifted. I cite this as but one indication of the honesty, the straightforwardness, the health and sanity of these rational booklets of sex information. I know that many a publisher would have shied like an unbroken colt at one of Mr. Fielding's really courageous and genuinely helpful *sex* books. I refer to . I know, too, that many a writer would have insisted on hiding behind a pseudonym – and yet, for what earthly, sensible, or even extraordinary reason? This is life. It is nothing to be ashamed of. It is the way the world is and the way we are; knowledge can only help, and never hinder.

Mr. Fielding is one of my indispensable writers. He is still carrying on, just now completing a new series on woman down through all history. The first of this new group is already in print: *Woman, the Eternal Primitive*.

My story runs ever longer than I wish, but there is so much more to tell than it has ever seemed. Years fly swiftly, crammed as they are with events and progress. One who has stood by me from early days is Isaac Goldberg, the affable critic who lives in Roxbury, MS, a part of Boston. Coldberg did his best work for the Little Blue Books in two volumes of the self-help group, *How to Enjoy Music* and *How to Enjoy Reading*. He has done much other work, some of it literary criticism, some vitally concerned with music, notably his recent *Jazz: What It Is and How to Understand It*. To regular followers of my publications, Goldberg is best known for his book review column in my *Weekly*.

Some of Goldberg's Little Blue Books, too, grew into larger clothbound volumes, notably his *Havelock Ellis* and his *The Man Mencken*. Thus have the Little Blue Books frequently paved the way for more conventional library volumes – paved the way in two separate capacities: first, by enabling the author to publish his work before the complete material for the larger book is ready and, second, by testing out the appeal of the material to the populace. Naturally, I do not offer the Little Blue Books as a testing ground for miscellaneous writers. I publish only those manuscripts that seem to me, as I am influenced by the policy of the moment, to fit snugly into the series.

Versatile Clement Wood gave the pocket series much of his effort at a time when it was in need of a wide range of new subjects. Mr. Wood is a facile worker – at times he seems to sacrifice accuracy for speed, so rapid is his production. It was Clement Wood who edited a variety of collections from Mother Goose rhymes to limericks and Broadway wisecracks. He did several volumes on women and famous lovers, as *Great Women of Antiquity* and *Cleopatra*. He did a booklet on *The Stone Age*, one on philology, a dictionary of slang, a history of the Jews, a brochure on Torquemada, the crossword puzzle books, and so forth. His industry was due to my need, and the scope of his books show how readily a writer may adapt his output to specific requirements. I point this out principally to refute the contentions of those who cry *hack* at every edict of an editor's pen. Clement Wood wrote a biographical and critical study of Amy Lowell that won the praise of as discerning a critic as Isaac Goldberg; yet the same man could, under the Little Blue Book regimen, turn out a booklet of mathematical oddities.

I sometimes wonder if inspiration and working according to specifications are so incompatible. Of course, such practical Little Blue Books are not works of art, but they are certainly good craftsmanship. Take, for example, the books that Leo Markun did for me. This young chap over in Indianapolis undertook to cover the many phases of practical psychology – memory, laughter, fear, and so on – after he had also proved his versatility. He worked strictly according to order. Yet his books are eminently readable and deservedly popular. If I had waited for the writer to receive the inspiration, the books would be still unwritten.

The main thing was always to find the writer, unknown or not made little difference, who could do the work well. That is why I had no hesitancy in letting Lloyd E. Smith prepare an entire series of self-teaching volumes on English grammar, spelling, vocabulary, and so forth. Mr. Smith even undertook the arduous task of compiling for the Little Blue Books an entirely original dictionary of synonyms, which was devoured hungrily by crossword puzzle fans during the height of that word-mania. This book of synonyms is still an excellent seller. Though it may seem impossible to offer such handy books of reference for five cents apiece, nevertheless, due to the cooperation of this same Lloyd E. Smith, it has been done – including *4,000 Words Often Mispronounced* and *How to Pronounce 4,000 Proper Names*. Good work, accuracy, and a thorough understanding of the requirements, mechanical as well as editorial, are the elements that have made assignment-work of this kind feasible.

But my crowning achievement in finding a writer and putting him to work came to pass when I met the famous British scholar, Joseph McCabe. I may say that this man is British only because he happens to reside in England. His scholarship and his outlook are as cosmopolitan and timeless as it is humanly possible for them to be. He has educated himself in many lands and through many languages; as he wrote in one of his books, nothing is alien to him when he travels. He combines a mature deliberation and judgment with the energy and fire of youth. He feels more fit, he says, at sixty-one than he remembers he did at twenty. Joseph McCabe was in the United States debating and lecturing in the winter of 1925-1926. I already knew of the man – for who has not heard of or read his *My Twelve Years in a Monastery*? Even at that time I had already included in the pocket series his debate with Arthur Conan Doyle on spiritualism, in which Mr. McCabe, of course, took the negative. When I was informed that he was accepting my invitation to come to Girard, my enthusiasm mounted until, after he had come and was gone, there was a contract for no less than fifty Little Blue Books, to be written strictly according to specifications. The work was to take a year; the books were to comprise a complete, thoroughly candid, humanistic and rationalistic history of religious controversy.

Joseph McCabe's fifty-volume story of religious controversy was completed, closely following the original outline discussed and drawn up when he was with me in Girard. Apart from this, he also did a personal interview with Luther Burbank, following the horticulturist's declaration of agnosticism, and a volume giving vital facts about the classics viewed as a whole.

This book about the classics, by the way, grew out of an interesting experience with the American reading public. Some years ago I put into the series, in two volumes of the Little Blue Books, Albert Mordell's *Dante and Other Waning Classics*. It soon developed that this was a failure. People did not care anything about Dante and any companion classics, on the wane or not. The title of these two books, volumes I and II, was changed to *Facts You Should Know About the Classics*. The sales record jumped from less than 1,000 copies a year in 1925 to over 15,000 copies in 1926. Such is the wizardry of titling – a bad seller was made a good seller, and it was discovered that the public wanted a book such as the new title implied. Therefore I assigned to Joseph McCabe the task of writing a sixty-four page, one-volume work (works in more than one volume, as I have remarked elsewhere, are not feasible in the series) to be called *Facts You Should Know About the Classics* and the Mordell volumes have been withdrawn.

But this work done, what next? Here was a man who began to think about life and the whys and wherefores of things when he was a monk in a monastery, known as the Very Reverend Father Antony. Slowly but surely he came to a rationalistic and substantially an agnostic viewpoint, though he dislikes labels so much that it is really unfair to classify him. He is certainly a thoroughly debunked, en-lightened, and civilized human being. He harbors no bitterness for the loss of his youth within monastic walls. In fact, his tolerance of modern youth and his sincere sympathy with youthful hopes and interests is one of the most invigorating and refreshing things to be found in his books. Finally he left the Catholic Church, giving a true account of his experiences in the autobiographical chronicle of his monastery years that I have already mentioned.

The process of education and the acquisition of knowledge did not stop there. Joseph McCabe has traveled all over the world, and I do not hesitate to acclaim him as the greatest scholar now living. If the Little Blue Books have done nothing else, they deserve a great deal of honest credit for finding such a scholar as McCabe and putting him steadily to work so that much of his learning and experience may be offered to the general public. It is strange how things happen, but due in a large measure, perhaps, to the prejudice against McCabe because of his apostasy in the eyes of orthodox believers, this eminent scholar was slipping into obscurity. It was Joseph McCabe who was engaged to prepare the *Outline of Science*, but he had it taken away from him and it was turned over to Professor J. Arthur Thomson. I suppose the publishers were afraid of Mr. McCabe's unsavory – to their nostrils – reputation.

Here was a man who had written the complicated story of the evolution of mind, a man who had made an excellent English translation of Ernst Haeckel's Riddle of the Universe, a man who knew Haeckel and

Huxley personally, a man who wrote outstanding biographies of Abelard and of Talleyrand, a man who had followed the lure of knowledge around the world and through the labyrinths of foreign tongues, a man who had worked to some extent in books popularizing science – a man who, in short, had done many amazingly wonderful things, but who had never been given a real chance to do his utmost. I have McCabe's own word for it that the task of writing those fifty Little Blue Books put new life and zest into him. I cite from one of his enthusiastic letters:

"I am feeling better than ever and rejoice in the big work before me. Have had a splendid holiday across Mexico and Cuba – and learned much."

The preceding was on his return to London, dated April 14, 1926. Much later (January 17, 1927), when nearing the end of the Little Blue Book contract, he wrote:

"Life will seem quite blank when I have completed my fascinating task."

Again, on February 11, with two more books to write:

"This big job has been quite a pleasure to me and I am glad you appreciate the work. I feel on my part that you are doing more good – broader work and more of it – than all the heterodox associations put together, and I am proud to be so much in it."

Commenting on a report of the success of the books then in print, he wrote on February 18:

"I have your letter in which you tell me, to my pleasure, that the books are going satisfactorily. I have been anxious that you should not lose, as one has a chance of doing on a big and bold enterprise like that. I think we may say that between us we have done the finest thing for advanced thought that has been done for many a year. I am inclined to think that the value of the work will be gradually realized and the sale go up."

And on August 13: "I continue to have better health than I ever had before and am quite reconciled to life." I cannot help feeling proud of an enterprise like the University in Print, which has literally brought to life and busy activity a scholar such as this man McCabe. Through the Little

Blue Books he has reached a wider distribution than ever was possible from the lecture platform or in any other medium of publication. Further, it is all newly-written work, copyright material, and I assure you that it all follows the best Little Blue Book tradition – if a series can be said to have a tradition after nine short years of actual existence.

If I ever did a courageous thing in making a publishing venture, I would rather the McCabe series should be cited than any other. Some people consider it a mark of editorial courage. It is daring, they say, to offer so much *propaganda* (their word) against established theology and dogma and ritual. Perhaps it is. But it is the only honest thing to do. If it is courage, it is the courage of conviction. I have never seen any reason why the Little Blue Books should restrict their program of education because of this and that taboo. The standard I set was that of an enlightened and civilized minority, but the immense circulation of the McCabe books – and *Self-Contradictions of the Bible*, merely an unsigned compilation, is a real best seller – and others along similar lines demonstrates powerfully that the general public is curious and has a strong desire to satisfy that curiosity. If people want the truth, I believe in giving it to them. I tried them by offering the truth – I am happy to say that they have been willing to pay for it. Not much, but as I pointed out in other places, Little Blue Books are bought only to be read.

The culmination of the revival of Joseph McCabe has come with his newest and most comprehensive work, *The Key to Culture* – a series of forty 30,000-word essays comprising all the knowledge everyone should have as a foundation for general culture. This is still in process, but it is an important forward step in the great task of humanizing knowledge for the masses. Here, at last, and due to the Little Blue Books and their commercial success, is the full result of a scholarship matured and perfected through forty years of continuous study. I can do no better than let this effectively close this chapter

173

CHAPTER XII
HOW THE LITTLE BLUE
BOOKS ARE PRODUCED

The Facts About Mass Production

The question people ask most frequently about the Little Blue Books is this: "How can you turn them out in such large quantities and for such a low price as five cents apiece delivered anywhere in the world?" Of course, the two words Mass Production tell the whole secret, but many people would no doubt like to know the facts behind this production of literature in mass quantities – just how many books are produced, and how it is done. It is easy enough to mumble Mass Production in reply to this persistent inquiry, but how? Sooner or later I have always known that I would find an opportunity to answer the question in detail. In a book telling the whole story of the Little Blue Books, a chapter on production surely finds its proper place.

Usually there is little romance attached to the manufacture of a product. In spite of the fact that poets have attempted to find souls in machines (there is even a movie called "Metropolis" that makes capital of marvelous machinery), few people ever become greatly excited about it. Machinery is dirty – it is always greasy, for one thing – and it is terribly noisy. But printing is something else again. From Gutenberg on down, the printer's craft has had a glamour about it. When the first types were made and the first books produced it was thought wonderful that several hundred copies of a book could be made without immense labor. Nowadays, viewing the gigantic presses that turn out a modern metropolitan newspaper, one

175

looks back at the early methods thinking what a lot of work printing used to be. Certainly it is a far cry from the hand-printed books of days gone by to an output of pocket-sized classics running to as many as 80,000 books in one eight-hour day — the utmost capacity of my plant. Yet this can be tripled, if necessary, by running three 8-hour shifts — with no increase in equipment.

The production of the Little Blue Books began, however, like the acorn and grew into the oak. When I look back at the laborious method of turning out those first few books — in editions of 3,000 each, and some of them running to over 100 pages — I sigh rather heavily and reflect that in a mechanical sense the world, and the various units that make it up, certainly do progress.

The first books sold for twenty-five cents. Getting the price down to five cents per book was a matter of increasing production, after installation of the latest machinery, and of increasing the sale of the books enough to support production on a large scale. The sale of the books belongs under the last three chapters, and is told there with all its details.

A Little Blue Book, when finished, measures $3^1/_2$ x 5 inches. The standard size contains sixty-four pages, the type measuring sixteen ems wide by twenty-five ems deep (including the folios or page numbers). The first books were printed on a 12 x 18 inch job press, in signatures of sixteen pages at a time. This meant that only eight pages were printed at an impression, and when one side was completed this had to be backed up making a sheet or signature containing sixteen pages. Thus it took four such signatures to make a sixty-four page book, or eight impressions for each book, not counting the cover. An edition of 3,000 thus meant 24,000 impressions — and some of the books had more than sixty-four pages. This press could turn out a thousand impressions an hour at its best — it thus required three working days of eight hours each to complete the printing of one book alone — still without its cover.

I have been idealistic even in these computations of the printing of the first books. I have made no allowance for the time taken to change the forms, or to make ready on each form — preparing the type so that it will print evenly and with a clear impression all over the sheet. This would certainly, on the average, increase the press time by another half day for each sixty-four page book in an edition of 3,000. It took another half day to print the cover. Then each of the four signatures and the cover all had to be folded by hand – an extremely tedious process – and stitched one at a time with two staples in each book on a foot-power stitcher of an old type. Then followed the trimming and the book was done.

It is easy to understand, considering these particulars, why the first Little Blue Books sold for twenty-five cents apiece. They were not Little Blue Books either – that is, they were not known as such, for the name by which the series is now internationally known came into being something like two years after the first books were printed. These first books had covers of all colors – red, brown, green, yellow. The series was variously called the Pocket Classics, the People's Classics, the Pocket Series, and so forth, for the first two years or so.

One of the first numbers of the Pocket Series, in the days when it was printed so laboriously, was *The Trial and Death of Socrates* – made up of verbatim Platonic dialogues, with no attempt at editing and without any explanatory introduction – totaling no less than 160 pages. Early readers of these books may remember this title. It was later supplanted by a specially prepared edition with the same title.

The first books were always printed from linotype slugs. Old Nick, the czar of the linotype, set some of those first titles. Nick, which is short for Mr. Nichols, still operates the linotype keyboard – he has been an operator for the past thirty years, or close to it, and turns out an astonishingly clean galley of slugs in record time. It was his chief task to set the first Little Blue Books, until the series began to grow too fast for even the two linotypes in the Girard plant, and the setting of the Little Blue Books began to be done on contract in Kansas City, MO.

Something like 500 titles in the Little Blue Books were in linotype slugs at one time, stored away on galleys in the Girard composing-room. The weight of the metal was tremendous. It was awkward to handle those linotype pages whenever a new printing of a particular title was required. Even with the utmost care, pied pages and transposed lines would occur, and not always be caught on the press proof. Occasionally a line would be lost entirely. Any publisher knows the handicap if he has had occasion to send a book in linotype slugs to press for the second or third time. And some of these Little Blue Books in linotype slugs went to press as many as ten or twelve times. Then the type would wear out and the book would have to be reset.

Even the covers of the Little Blue Books were standing in type at first. Some of them were set by hand every time a new edition went to press. The type was larger than the linotype could produce. Now each title has a cover plate, cast in a nickeltype, mounted on a wood-base, ready to go into the form that prints the covers sixty-four at a time. This is made at the same lime the Little Blue Book is electrotyped.

Soon the books were graduated, however, from the job press to a flat-bed press that would print signatures of sixty-four pages each – thirty-two pages at a time, then back up. This was a considerable advance, and this press is still in the shop and is now called, affectionately and not at all contemptuously, the Pony. The series now contains a few books of only thirty-two pages, and the Pony still serves by printing these smaller books. The Pony is able to turn out about 1,500 impressions an hour. In number of impressions it is faster than the new Perfector – but the Perfector prints four books at a time, complete.

The series grew by leaps and bounds. Soon two new flat-bed presses were added, capable of printing sixty-four pages at a time, or signatures of 128 pages when necessary. But these double signatures were cut in half to be folded. At about this time the special folders were installed, of which the plant now has four. These folders readily handle, when required, the capacity output of 80,000 Little Blue Books in one day.

So far the Little Blue Books were printed singly, making them rather small to handle and trim. This caused bungling at times, and I had to consider the problem of how to eliminate some of the handling. The solution was simple enough, but it revolutionized the production of Little Blue Books. The price was dropped to ten cents apiece as a direct consequence of the innovation.

From that time on the Little Blue Books were printed, folded, stitched and trimmed in pairs – one book above another, two at a time all through the shop. Pick up two of your Little Blue Books – any two with the same number of pages – and place one directly above the other, so that one title is on top and the other just below it. The cut that separates the two books is the last cut made in manufacture – we call it guillotining. A single knife slices the books apart, whereupon they are packed in corrugated cardboard boxes and sent to the warehouse.

Pairing the Little Blue Books for production purposes was possible only when there were enough titles to justify it. Nearly 500 titles were in print when the innovation was made. The same press-work, folding and stitching labor, and handling for trimming and the other processes, thus sufficed for two books instead of one. At this time it appeared to be advisable to standardize new books as far as possible at a maximum length of sixty-four pages each. All sixty-four page books could thus be readily paired.

A sixty-four page Little Blue Book, with its companion that follows it like a Siamese twin all through its manufacture until the final severing, requires one sheet of paper 29 x 42 inches in size. This sheet thus represents two books, and it is one signature. On the three smaller presses – not including the Pony – this means two impressions for every two books: the printing of one side and then the backing up or the printing of the other side, making 128 pages in all, sixty-four pages to each book. A 128-page book, of which there are still several in the list, requires two such signatures and thus increases the cost of manufacture by about one-half. The 96-page books, of which there are still a few, require two signatures – one of sixty-four pages and one of thirty-two. The labor is the same as for 128 pages.

The printer's arrangement of the pages for two sixty-four page books, so that when the sheet is folded the pages will follow in proper numerical order, is as follows. I put these data in for the benefit of many of my readers, to whom printing books is much of a mystery – as I am made fully aware by the many visitors who view the plant and its work in Girard.

One Side, with Page 1								Other Side							
6ᔭ	9I	ᘔI	8ᔭ	ᙍᙍ	ᘔᙍ	I	ᔭ9	ᙍ9	ᘔ	ᙍI	ᔭᙍ	ᘫᔭ	8I	Iᙍ	0ᙍ
6ᔭ	9I	ᘔI	8ᔭ	ᙍᙍ	ᘔᙍ	I	ᔭ9	ᙍ9	ᘔ	ᙍI	ᔭᙍ	ᘫᔭ	8I	Iᙍ	0ᙍ
56	9	24	41	40	25	8	57	58	7	26	39	42	23	10	55
56	9	24	41	40	25	8	57	58	7	26	39	42	23	10	55
ᙍᙍ	ᘔI	Iᘔ	ᔭᔭ	ᘫᙍ	8ᘔ	ᙍ	09	6ᙍ	9	ᘫᘔ	8ᙍ	ᙍᔭ	ᘔᘔ	II	ᔭᙍ
ᙍᙍ	ᘔI	Iᘔ	ᔭᔭ	ᘫᙍ	8ᘔ	ᙍ	09	6ᙍ	9	ᘫᘔ	8ᙍ	ᙍᔭ	ᘔᘔ	II	ᔭᙍ
52	13	20	45	36	29	4	61	62	3	30	35	46	19	14	51
52	13	20	45	36	29	4	61	62	3	30	35	46	19	14	51

Later, partly to offset the additional expense of the desirable 96-page and 128-page books, and also because many titles did not lend themselves readily to a book as long as sixty-four pages, a small number of thirty-two page Little Blue Books were added. These are printed on the Pony press, each pair of thirty-two page books requiring a single signature of sixty-four pages.

The covers for the Little Blue Books, all on a standard blue stock of stiff cardboard, are paired to correspond with the books as they are printed. A run of sixty-four covers at a time, or thirty-two paired combinations, is made on one of the smaller presses, known in the shop as the North press or the Miehle. Knives are inserted so that as the large sheet of cover stock is fed through the press, just after it is printed it is automatically cut into strips of eight covers each. These strips are later folded on a special folding-machine, which puts a single crease down the middle where the book is to be stitched and at the same time cuts the strip into its four pairs. These folded pairs are packed away in boxes until the bindery is ready for them.

It is essential that in running covers the various pairs exactly match the pairs of books being printed. Due to the obvious fact that no two Little Blue Books sell at exactly the same rate, it is impossible to decide how the books shall be paired very far in advance. The pairs are determined by a stock report of those books of which ten boxes (a sixty-four page book packs about 500 in a box) or less are shown on the inventory. So far as possible, those books are paired together that have approximately _ though never quite _ the same sales record. Since the printings vary, ranging from 10,000 to 30,000 books at a lime, depending on a book's popularity, this attention to pairing is imperative.

It is also necessary always to pair two sixty-four page books, two thirty-two page books, or two 128-page books. Unless this is done the books cannot be printed or otherwise banded together.

The next innovation was double—it came with the setting up of the huge Perfector (Miehle) press that prints both sides of a sheet at a time. The one in Girard was the first of its kind west of the Mississippi, if not west of Chicago. It prints two pairs of Little Blue Books, making four complete books at every double revolution of the cylinders. The output is 40,000 Little Blue Books every eight hours.

By this time all the other presses had been equipped with automatic feeders. Those on all the smaller presses are of the buckling type, which is a system of knobs or rollers pushing up each sheet as it is ready, and shoving it into the grasp of metal fingers that slide it into place against the cylinder, whereupon it is whirled around, printed, and slides onto long metal fingers that somersault it through the air to the printed stack at the other end of the press. Friction is the basic principle of these feeders. The Perfector press is equipped with an air-suction feeder, one of the latest models. Here the top sheet of the pile of stock is lifted by suction cups and shoved into place for going down against the first cylinder. Vacuum is the basic principle of this feeder.

The two flat beds of the Perfector work with a shuttle-motion opposite each other, each having its own cylinder. The unprinted sheet is whirled around the first cylinder, and one side of the sheet is printed. Then it goes onto the adjacent cylinder, is whirled around again, and the back of the sheet is printed. It will occur to everyone immediately that the ink from the first impression must still be wet when the sheet is backed up, and therefore what is known in printing as offset might result. However, this press, at the top of this second cylinder, has a special roller that dips into oil. As the printed sheet goes with its printed side against the tympan or backing paper fastened to the cylinder, it leaves an imperfect impression of its printing on that roller. To prevent this from rubbing off on the next sheet, this oil-roller places the thinnest possible film of oil on the tympan, which does not harm the next printed sheet and keeps the ink from offsetting.

On the three smaller presses, and also on the Pony, the stock has to be loaded from the warehouse platforms onto an elevator attached to the press. This elevator platform holds from 10,000 to 20,000 sheets at a time. A special hoisting motor then raises it so that the top sheet is in position under the automatic feeder.

But for the Perfector this handling of stock is eliminated. The loaded platform of stock from the warehouse, moved by one of the *iron men* or trucks that move platforms of everything around the large plant, can be wheeled right under the Perfector's feeder, where two steel bars are slipped under it and chains raise it into position. And though the oilier presses stack the printed sheets onto a raised table at the front end, where at intervals a lift of 500 sheets or so has to be removed by the pressman, the Perfector stacks an entire run of 10,000 sheets on a specially arranged platform at its front end, where the platform can be wheeled into the warehouse, when ready, by one of the trucks.

With this Perfector press able to print four Little Blue Books at a time, an even lower price level for the series was in view. This was finally experimented with – the famous five-cent price for each book – and meant the other innovation that the Perfector made necessary: electrotyping the Little Blue Books.

Linotype metal has a comparatively short life, besides the difficulty of handling that I described in the preceding pages. With the prospect of electrotyping, it was desirable also to reduce handling of the plates to a minimum – and I am very proud of the solution that is still in operation. The arrangement of the Little Blue Book plates has always been one of the most interesting and original aspects of their production in mass quantities.

A single plate for a page measuring only $3^1/_2$ x 5 inches would be awkwardly small. The solution was to gang the plates in fours – four plates for four pages grouped together in a horizontal row. Thus, if you will refer to the table of arrangement of pages for a sixty-four page book, given a page or two back, the four page numbers at the left of the top row represent the first solid electrotype plate. Each row thus contains two electrotype plates, and for a sixty-four page book there are sixteen plates in all – or thirty-two separate plates for the paired-combination of two sixty-four page books.

These electrotype plates are not made type-high (.918 inch). The type-surface is of copper, fastened to a lead base, the whole being about three-twentieths of an inch (11 points) in thickness. A special base is locked in the chase that goes on the press, or that is always on the Perfector, so arranged that when a Little Blue Book electrotype plate is put on it the whole is type-high and the plate can be locked on by flanges that grip and hold it in place. The thirty-two plates necessary to print a pair of sixty-four page Little Blue Books weigh eighty-eight pounds. The linotype slugs for the same two books would weigh about 160 pounds. The difference, entirely aside from the immense saving in handling and elimination of error, and besides the much longer life (four or five times that of linotype) of the plates, is immensely significant.

These electrotype plates are cast from type set in Kansas City, MO, and sent down to Girard by overnight freight. Page proofs of the Little Blue Books are always read by the editorial staff in Girard before any book is given an okay for being sent to the foundry. Each Little Blue Book is read, on the average, four times in order to make it as free from error as possible. In the case of originally prepared manuscript, the author is also asked to read the proof.

To set that first 500 books in type and have electrotypes made was a colossal task, indeed. But it was done, and now the entire list of 1,260 different books is in plate form stored in three huge vaults, one above the other from the basement to the second floor, in the Girard plant. These vaults are fireproof with special automatically locking fire doors. When you reflect that it takes sixteen plates of four pages each for every sixty-four page Little Blue Book, you will realize that these vaults contain in excess of 20,000 separate plates. The plates of all withdrawn Little Blue Books are also on file – sometime, you know, it may be desirable to issue them again.

Little Blue Books are printed on a fair grade of book paper. The stock is commensurate in quality with the selling price of the books. It is shipped to Girard direct from the mills in carload lots, ranging from twenty-five to thirty-five tons to a car. It comes all ready in the proper sizes for the Perfector and other presses and is stored in the warehouse, stacked flat on platforms. These platforms are wheeled in to the hungry presses on the trucks before mentioned. Usually a dozen stacks are kept in the pressroom, especially in winter, to be dry and warmed so as to keep static electricity down to a minimum. Static, by the way, which causes sheets to balk at the feeder, to run crookedly down to the cylinder, and so on, making all kinds of grief, is one of a publisher's annoying problems. All the presses and other machinery are electrically driven, by power supplied from the municipal power plant in Girard. Even the automatic letter opener in the front office runs by electricity.

From the presses the printed stacks of paper go to the bindery, where the automatic folders I have already mentioned proceed to fold each signature of two books to make them ready for stitching. It takes five folds to complete the folding of a pair of sixty-four page books. The signature now looks like two books, one above the other, without covers, unstitched and untrimmed.

The boxes of folded signatures and boxes of corresponding folded covers are now placed alongside the stitchers – of which there are two. For a sixty-four page book it takes three girls to operate the stitcher – one feeds the signature on the endless chain, another feeds the cover to match, both are jogged automatically so as to be even and are then stitched with two wire staples in each book, and the third girl receives the stitched book and packs it again into boxes.

The boxes of stitched books now go to the trimmers, of which there are also two. In stacks of sixteen these stitched books, still paired, go into place under the knives – a stack of sixteen on each side. With the trimmers in use here, two operations are necessary – the books are first trimmed on the outside edges and then, being turned around on the block by a special handle, they are trimmed on the ends. The operator packs the trimmed books into boxes once more. Now the books are ready to be guillotined.

One cutter only is necessary to handle the entire output at this final stage of the manufacture of Little Blue Books. In stacks of sixteen, the books are placed parallel under the long knife, there being room for twelve such stacks. When the knife comes down, motor-driven, it cuts the book exactly in half at one operation. The books are then packed in *house boxes*, each box being numbered to indicate the book it contains, and the boxes are stacked on platforms ready to go into the warehouse and be put away on the shelves. The place of each box as it is put away is recorded on the inventory cards, so that a box of any desired number can be located in a moment. Each house box contains about 500 books; for an edition of 10,000, therefore, about twenty boxes are required for storage. This varies for thirty-two page books, which average 800 books to the box; ninety-six page books average 350 to the box, and 128-page books average 250.

At any time, with a list of 1,260 titles, the warehouse inventory shows an average total stock of between 7,000,000 and 12,000,000 books. The lowest level in times of active distribution has been 6,000,000 books – or an average stock of 5,000 copies of each title. This would last only six months on the principle that a successful Little Blue Book must have a sales record of 10,000 copies annually – and the best sellers run to as many as 30,000, 50,000 and even 70,000 copies sold in a year. The necessity for a routine printing procedure to keep all the books in stock is thus clearly evident. The minimum edition or printing of a Little Blue Book is set at 10,000 copies. The maximum is limited to 30,000 copies at one printing. Some are printed in quantities of 20,000 copies. The reason for this is the limit of warehouse space, plus the necessity of constant rotation in printing the editions in order to keep all the books in stock. Naturally, it would be cheaper to print editions of 50,000 copies and store them away, but the growth of the series has been so extraordinarily rapid that facilities have not grown sufficiently to take care of more than the average printing of 10,000 books at a time. There are always about 300 books with a stock of less than 5,000 copies – some of the fairly slow sellers – so that there are always books ready for new printing. Thus the presses have always been kept in operation.

The total number of Little Blue Books produced and sold is taken up and analyzed in the first six chapters. The average printing, distributing it evenly over the nine years from 1919-1927 inclusive, has been close to 13,000,000 books annually. At first, of course, the figure was but a fraction of this, and at maximum capacity it has run to over 25,000,000 books in one year.

The waste from the trimmers and other machines is, of course, baled and sold for waste paper, by the carload. It is worth while to mention, in passing, that the only serious accident during the entire nine year record of Little Blue Book production occurred with this motor-driven baler – the young man operating it got his finger caught in the tightening wire and lost the first two joints of the second finger on his left hand. He is now an apprentice in my composing room.

Summarizing, the machinery ready for a maximum output of 80,000 completed Little Blue Books per day of eight working hours, includes one Perfector press, three smaller presses, and the Pony press, four folders, two stitchers, two trimmers, and one guillotine. There is also one folding machine for folding covers. Occasionally covers are run two up or four up on a job press – especially for a rush printing – and the two smaller cover folders stand ready to fold these special rims. There are four job presses – one 12 x 18 and three 10 x 15, all with automatic suction-feeders – for printing special runs of covers, order blanks, office forms, circulars, and so forth There are two special folders to handle the output of these presses. There is also a perforator, for office forms, and a foot-power stapler if desired. There is also a motor-driven extra cutter for preparing special stock, and a motor-driven sharpener to sharpen the various knives used in manufacturing the books. For waste paper there is the baler.

For maximum production, the total number of employees runs about as follows: for the pressroom, eight, for the bindery, sixteen, for the baler and warehouse, five to seven. The latter includes the labor of wheeling stock into the pressroom, printed stacks to the bindery, shelving books for inventory, and so forth. Besides this, for changing the presses and for such composition as may be necessary, there are two linotypes, with operators, and a foreman and two assistants in the composing-room.

I have not described my three publications – the *Monthly*, *Quarterly* and the *Weekly*. For the latter, to mention it for the sake of completeness, there is a rotary press capable of printing from four to sixteen newspaper-sized pages. There are also the necessary equipment and machinery for putting from four to eight pages to bed, making steam-heat-hardened mats, casting rotary stereotype plates, and so forth. The *Haldeman-Julius Weekly* is printed in the same manner as the famous *Appeal to Reason*, of which it took the place when I bought the old Appeal plant. So thoroughly did the Appeal, as it was intimately known, fasten its name upon the town of Girard that even now the Haldeman-Julius plant is always spoken of by the townspeople, and even by many of the employees, as *the Appeal*.

CHAPTER XIII
FOLLOWING A NEW TITLE
FROM COPY TO CUSTOMER

How a Little Blue Book Gets from Author to Reader

U ndoubtedly the best way to understand the whole process of getting a Little Blue Hook into print, on sale, and sold, is to follow one of the titles added during the big year of 1926 through the entire process of its creation and manufacture, advertising and delivery. There are certain aspects of the process that cannot be told in any better way than this. And this will insure a unified and continuous narrative of all that goes into the making of each Little Blue Book – following it from its inception and assignment, and its birth on the author's typewriter (assuming for this purpose that it is a book especially prepared for the series), to the home of the ultimate reader who has seen it advertised and has included a copy of it in his order.

I put down the year 1926 as the banner year of Little Blue Book growth. The list leaped in that year from slightly over 900 to more than 1,200 titles, and there began a drastic policy of replacing almost 200 books scheduled for The Morgue with new and more popular books. For various mechanical reasons – one of them being the fact that a larger list becomes increasingly unwieldy and expensive to handle – the list has become fairly established at the total of 1,260 different titles. The rather odd number is due to the capacity of the order-filling departments. But the limit is also approximately that of the capacity of the present equipment to keep in stock. Occasionally, as some old title and very slow seller sells out or nearly sells out, new titles will be added as replacements of old numbers. Public taste is always changing, and must be met and satisfied.

The idea for a new title is born from the union of several contributing factors. Possibly a series – as on English grammar and syntax – has been planned and there are still a few titles needed to round out the series. Perhaps a sudden and unforeseen popularity of some isolated book – as the *Book of Riddles*, for example, gave rise to books of puzzles, brainteasers, and more riddles, one of which, a book of tongue-twisters, is in the process of preparation even now – possibly the popularity of some such books as this riddle book will indicate that a number of similar books are needed. Perhaps there is just a sudden and unaccountable *inspiration*, or spontaneous idea, for a new title – as happened when I impulsively decided to add two books, one on Fascism and one on Mussolini, and promptly wrote to Miriam Alien de Ford to do the job. It just seemed as though those two books ought to be successful Little Blue Books; and so far, I am happy to say, they have been.

Then again, some regular contributor to the series may have ideas of his own. He is not in touch with the sales end of the Little Blue Book organization, and he is probably not familiar with the broad lines of the growth of the series, but he sends in a batch of ideas, jotted down for ready reference. Out of this list of ideas submitted by a writer, new titles are frequently born. Just as civilization has advanced the most rapidly where there has been a clash of cultures, so the Little Blue Books have increased where the ideas of several people have mingled and multiplied.

Thus, either the idea emanates from the Girard editorial sanctum, so to say, or it is an idea approved and perhaps somewhat modified in that pregnant retreat. For it is here, not behind closed doors and without secrecy or ceremony – though in fancifully facetious moments I sometimes like to think of the birth of a new Little Blue Book idea being heralded with tom-toms or at least with oboes and viols! – that every Little Blue Book has had its real beginning. The title fairly well decided upon – it may still be changed when the manuscript arrives, before it is set in type – the author is selected to do the job, unless it is an idea that some author has

190

submitted, when, of course, he is given the chance to write an acceptable manuscript for it.

I like my authors to be prompt. Few of those who have contributed to the Little Blue Books have taken longer than two months to deliver a manuscript assigned to them to prepare. For one reason, the books any single writer has done have nearly always been on subjects he is familiar with already, reducing the labor of research. As discussed in the chapter entitled "An Editor and His Writers," the author is given very specific instructions. When the manuscript is ready, prepared according to specifications, it is sent to me in Girard. I read it – at once. I cannot understand editors who keep authors waiting for decisions on manuscripts – especially those within the Little Blue Book limit of 15,000 words. Long book manuscripts are another matter, but work of this kind and length should require no more than a week for a decision. I often read a manuscript during the evening of the day it is received – and if it is acceptable a check for it goes to the author by the first mail the following day. This has been an unbreakable rule of mine for work done on assignment. I have had the pleasure of having some of my authors express personal appreciation of this promptness of payment. And I know from my own freelance days that it is a method of payment that, in effect, doubles the actual amount of the check in the eyes of the grateful and appreciative recipient of it. The rate of payment, incidentally, has been decided in the correspondence that assigned the manuscript. It is governed, of course, by the author's experience, prominence, and so forth.

Having been accepted and paid for, the manuscript is scheduled for publication. First of all, it is given a number. Before the series reached its top number, this simply meant giving the manuscript the next highest number available. This is recorded in a card index, with the number, name of the author, title of the book, and the number of pages the book is to contain. This last information is so that the cover may be printed far in advance of the book itself, and paired off with another title with the same number of pages. Now that new titles are replacements only, the number has to be determined by the stock report, and it is the one of some book destined for The Morgue.

Before being sent to the typesetters in Kansas City, MO, the manuscript is carefully edited. I often do most of this when I read the manuscript the first time editorially. Matters of style are indicated, the position of illustrations is indicated if the author has not already done it, the type, copyright notice, and so forth, are written on the copy. Usually, a Little Blue Book is set in eight-point type cast on an eight-point slug, which makes thirty-five lines to the standard Little Blue Book page. Sometimes, when it is very desirable to get in more words, it is set eight-point on a seven-point slug, which makes forty lines to the page. Quoted matter is marked to be set seven-point, and likewise any footnotes. A long index is usually set five and a half-point, two columns to the page.

The copy is set in Kansas City, on contract, and the galley proofs are read and corrected there. The book is then paged, being made up with title page first, then copyright notice and Table of Contents. The first page of the text is on either page three or page five. Running heads repeating the title are at the top of each page, though sometimes this heading varies and indicates each separate story in a collection of short tales. The book is proofread once and sent back for revise, or correction. Then the proof is sent to the author, as an extra precaution, and when it comes back the author's corrections are checked and the book is given a final reading before being given an okay. When at last okay, it is sent back to Kansas City and the type is delivered in the foundry for the casting of the electrotype plates described in the chapter entitled "How the Little Blue Books Are Produced."

The plates for the new Little Blue Book arrive in Girard by freight or by express if it is a rush. It is promptly scheduled for printing, and no doubt the covers are ready waiting for it. In the regular routine it is printed, goes through the bindery, and is ready for the warehouse. Each box in which this title is packed has the number on it – everything relating to this book throughout the plant is done entirely by its number – and as it is shelved, a boy records it on its inventory card. When the order departments need new supplies of the book it can be readily found and promptly put in place.

When the new book is first placed in stock, several copies of it are brought to the office. Everyone in charge of a department gets a copy, including each of the proofreaders – and fifty complimentary copies are sent to the author, if it is a book written specially for the series. If the book is to be copyrighted (as all the new books are), the proper form and affidavit are made out; I sign the latter before a Notary in the approved manner, and it goes to Washington, DC with two copies of the book, for recording in the federal archives.

Meanwhile, from the time the proof has been given an okay, plans have been under way to list the new book in the catalogue and in the advertising. Little Blue Book enthusiasts scan each new advertisement, I am told, with all the fervor of astronomers scouring the heavens for new stars or comets. When a new title appears, these Little Blue Book fans spot it, I gather, with a cry of "Eureka!"

But the new title is given a classification before it can be listed. This classification may vary from the one in the catalogue, for several systems of classification are in use. Sometimes the sorting is done rather pedantically – Fiction, Biography, History, Science, and so forth. At other times it is done more loosely – Murder, Women, Love, Mystery, Health, Jokes, Fun, Entertainment, and so forth. It all depends on the audience for which the advertising is intended. In general, the looser and more general classifications have had the better sales record. Single-word classifications are now thought best in the national advertising. This is all described in the chapter entitled "An Editor Turns to Advertising." (I simply must keep some order in this narrative, which is very much like an untamable leopard and *will* run away with me!)

Soon the Little Blue Book is being ordered. Its number is found listed among others that the customers want to read (the minimum order being for twenty books, or one dollar). By this time, if everything has gone smoothly as it should, the new book should have been completed and is in stock.

The number only is necessary when ordering a Little Blue Book. Each book is identified by its number everywhere in the plant. The orders are filled by the numbers. If titles only are sent, prompt filling of the order is impossible because it must be set aside for a special clerk to look the numbers up and write them on the order. Now and then there is a little confusion when a new title replaces an old title with the same number – especially when someone orders from an old advertisement or catalogue. This is usually adjusted, however, and frequently it is caught by the checkers before the books are sent out. Or occasionally a typographical error slips in and a book is listed with the wrong number. But this is fortunately rare, and the system of identification by numbers works out, on the whole, extremely well.

The orders arrive in Girard at a varying rate. The average has been, in the past three years, about 2,500 orders per day, being much less in summer and going to a fairly constant average of 4,000 in the winter. This mail is opened several times a day – each letter being slit by an automatic mail-opener that slices a tiny strip from one edge of the envelope.

Girls sort the orders into pigeon-holes by states, and the mail is finally opened as arranged by states. This is for convenience in zoning the parcel post labels later on. Pairs of girls work together in opening the mail, each pair having an adding-machine. They sit on opposite sides of a desk, with a specially constructed box between them that has separate compartments for checks, money orders, bills, specie, one-cent stamps, two-cent stamps, and other stamps.

As each letter is opened one girl carefully notes the amount of the remittance enclosed, tossing all the other contents of the envelope, as well as the envelope itself, to her partner. The contents, plus the envelope (which may be useful in checking carelessly written addresses, or for identifying orders that contain no name or address inside the envelope, as frequently happens), are placed on a file by the second girl. The first girl calls out the amount of the remittance, indicating its nature, as X if it is a check, P.O. if it is a money order, cash, or stamps. Thus if a man sends a dollar bill, the girl calls: "One dollar cash." If it is a check for $1.10, she says: "One dollar ten cents X." If it is stamps, she says: "Forty-two cents stamps."

The second girl verifies this amount with that in the order or letter. If it agrees she writes the amount and character of the remittance in red pencil on the order or letter; if there is a discrepancy it is checked up at once. At the same time the amount is recorded by the first girl on her adding-machine. The total of each file of orders is thus secured, and the adding-machine slip pinned to the full file, to be checked upstairs in the clerical department before the orders are sorted into departments. C. O. D. orders and general inquiries are placed on separate files, as the mail is opened. If no remittance is enclosed, it is so written on the order.

Finishing her share of the mail, the first girl totals her adding-machine. Then the contents of the box – checks, money orders, cash, and stamps – are carefully counted and checked. If no mistake has been made, this agrees with the adding-machine total. If there is a mistake, it is searched for until found. Then the various receipts are prepared for deposit in the bank, and the group of mail-openers starts on the next mail. There are usually four such openings every day. In busy times eight girls work all day opening the mail. Upstairs in the clerical department, the mail is further sorted into orders for Little Blue Books, clothbound books (a small list advertised on circulars in outgoing packages), the publications, and foreign orders. The latter are given separate clerical files for handling by the more experienced clerks. Trade or wholesale orders are also separated and sent down to the Trade Department.

The Little Blue Book orders are then carefully checked – the number of books ordered is counted and checked with the remittance. Discrepancies are set aside for handling by the head of the department. Each order having been checked, and the orders being grouped in files of twenty-five orders each, typists prepare a combination parcel post label and receipt. Then the orders are *zoned*, as the girls say – the parcel post zone being indicated for the guidance of the stamping clerk when the package is mailed. On the order is marked to go by express, freight, and so forth, as may have been requested. A clerical force of from fifteen to forty girls, depending on the amount of business, is required for this part of the labor.

The files of orders are sent down to the Order Filling Booths, where girls take the files and start their endless promenades from number to number. These booths contain 650 pigeon-holes each, and each such hole will hold about thirty Little Blue Books, depending on the number of pages. It thus takes two booths for each complete order-filling section. These are arranged in numerical order, with guide numbers at the top of each row, so that the girls walk from number 1 around to 1260 to fill an order. It is helpful if customers list their orders in numerical sequence.

Specially detailed girls known as *case-fillers* see to it that the pigeon-holes of Little Blue Books are always full. They get their extra supplies from the house boxes, which are arranged likewise in numerical order on large shelves just outside the booths. These empty house-boxes, in turn are replaced with full boxes by ever-watchful boys.

Other girls act as checkers, sitting at long tables where each order, after it is gathered, is checked for error or omission. Each checker initials the order when O.K., fastens the parcel post label to the books, and it goes in oblong flat boxes, with other orders, to the packers. The checkers alternate with the girls who walk about filling orders, in about two-hour shifts, so that they first walk and then sit down, thus keeping them from tiring too much.

Little Blue Books are substantially packed in specially manufactured corrugated pasteboard cartons, which are ready in sizes suitable for twenty, twenty-five, thirty, forty, fifty, eighty, 100, 200, 400, 500, and 1,000 Little Blue Books, respectively. These cartons are sealed with strong gummed tape – it is permissible for mail-order houses to seal parcel post packages if they guarantee the contents to be as indicated on the label, and also if the parcel bears the notation: "May be opened for postal inspection if necessary." This makes a thoroughly sturdy package and makes sure that all shipments of Little Blue Books arrive in good condition. It is also a swifter and more efficient method of packing than the old-fashioned way of wrapping-paper and twine.

The sealed cartons, with the labels glued on, then go to the mailers. Here they are weighed and stamped according to the zone indicated on the label, and those to go by express drop down a special chute where an express agent picks them up at regular intervals. The stamped parcels go into United States mail sacks, and are carried to the post office by truck four times a day. Efficient train service from Girard means that the books are soon on the way to the customer and, received in good condition, the Little Blue Books are ready to be read.

The order-filling, packing, and stamping girls vary in number according

196

to the press of business. The minimum, at times of lowest ebb, is ten girls. The maximum has been rather flexible – once in a while the number of girls desired is not available – but it has been as many as forty-five girls, working in four sets of two booths each.

Of course, with the volume of orders constantly being handled, there are errors and misunderstandings, and consequently complaints. But the complaints are all handled by one girl in charge of the Complaint Desk.

As soon as the inventory of a Little Blue Book shows less than ten boxes in the warehouse, it is reported to the front office and a new printing of the book, if it is selling its quota, is scheduled. If the book is falling behind its quota it is sent to The Hospital, as described in the chapter on "Rejuvenating the Classics."

Such is the routine from day to day. Orders come in from everywhere – from China, Japan, India, Australia, New Zealand, all the countries of South America, from the West Indies, Central America, Mexico, and thousands from Canada, and also from all over Europe, and from Siam, Iraq (Mesopotamia), Egypt, South Africa, and so forth – in short, wherever English periodicals may be sent and read. One order, of which I have always been especially proud, recently came from way up North, on Alaska Red River, a tributary of the Yukon in the Arctic Circle – where there was only one mail service a year. The customer wanted a supply of reading to last from one year to the next.

There is more than a little romance in the daily mail. It must keep any mail-order business from becoming dull. Aside from manuscript and regular routine correspondence, there are all kinds of unsolicited communications – freely offered suggestions and advice, pleas for financial aid or donations of books, urgent inducements to invest in a new patent flywheel or some other *patent* whatever-you-may-care-to-call-it – sent in, by the way, complete with blue prints – confidential letters from fanatics who have found the secret of the universe or a panacea for all human ills, people who have always wanted to write a book or who have written one and are still seeking to get it published, pencil-written screeds and laboriously penned hopeless manuscripts, and so on. I have been invited to join scores of societies, associations, and clubs; I have been asked to be an

197

honorary member of this or a contributing editor to that. People want my advice on the books their children should read, or they want me to quote chapter, page, and verse for them on data for some debate or other. But I have passed up many such chances to become rich in a single night, or to be an everlasting benefactor to mankind, or to learn the deep, dark, hidden secret that rules this gigantic universe. I have never lost any sleep over these opportunities I have missed, for the next mail, along with a generous batch of orders for Little Blue Books, is sure to bring others to keep me and my assistants from being bored with nothing but nickels and numbers of titles wanted.

CHAPTER XIV
BUSINESS MAN
OR PHILANTHROPIST

Is the Policy of the Little Blue Books Commercially Sound?

Philanthropy is a word that has been gratuitously applied to the Little Blue Books so many times that it has come to be almost an accusation. One thinks of philanthropy as applied to hospitals, with thankfulness, and sometimes as thankfully when applied to libraries, but it becomes more of a gesture and less of a benefit when it takes the form of statues, bronze plates, and other bric-a-brac. To label the Little Blue Books with philanthropy, then, may be a doubtful compliment. Though it may indicate the generosity of the sponsor, it also suggests that the power of money alone supports the existence of the enterprise, and that is scarcely complimentary to the perspicacity and generalship that may be behind it all. It is an axiom that money can do anything, and people have ceased to be very much surprised by what money does. If they are impressed it is not because it is exceptional that money has such power, but because they are forcibly reminded of all that money may do if it can be obtained in sufficient quantity. I insist that I am a business man and not a philanthropist. I invested my capital in the Little Blue Book idea because I thought it was a sound business venture. It was my belief that the American reading public would support a series of this sort, and I gambled on that belief – gambled, that is to say, after carefully weighing the chances and deciding that there was likely to be more than an even break.

Perhaps the notion that philanthropy was backing the Little Blue Book arose when the series was given the idealistic name of a University in Print. For a five-cent series of pocket-sized booklets to aspire to be a University in Print is unheard of in modern business annals. It is visionary, say the skeptics, and surely it is folly, say the statistical business physicians who keep their fingers on the commercial pulse.

The only thing anyone thought could be sold to the public in mass quantities, in the way of reading matter, was a magazine or a newspaper, and particularly a sensational sheet with screaming headlines, or a tabloid with kindergarten pictures. So said the intellectual skeptics, It was even contended that you could sell chewing gum in mass quantities, but you could hardly expect the buyers of it to read even what is said on the wrappers. The Ask-Me-Another craze showed how few people who smoked thousands of cigarettes really had noticed whose picture was on the government tax stamp affixed to every package. But one is privileged to wonder, is he not, how significant all of these observations may be? By openly advocating a University in Print – not at a hundred dollars or so, but at five cents as a basic price per unit – I can understand that I did lay myself liable to the charge of philanthropy. But in this book there are figures, and tabulations of sales, and anyone can see for himself that I did not have to be a philanthropist – that, to put it very bluntly, I was as interested in making a profit as Henry Ford.

I use the word philanthropist in its most prosaic sense – as implying someone who gives for the sake of charity. He gives expecting nothing in return unless it be the plaudits of the multitude. The philanthropist is a lover of mankind because there is a vicarious notoriety in it. It is the next best thing to being a monarch or a general or a manufacturer of automobiles. But philanthropy may also have a figurative implication – it might be applied, I daresay, to an enterprise that is commercially sound and yet is genuinely valuable and beneficial.

So though I reject the name of philanthropist, and prefer being regarded as a business man, I hasten to explain that I would not do *anything for money*. I am glad that my profits have not come from the manufacture of munitions of war, for example. I am glad, in other words, that I have been able to use good business toward the improvement instead of the exploitation of the masses.

There were series of dime and nickel books before the Little Blue Books. Among others, there were the dime novels – many of which, by the way, were not as scarlet as they have been painted. But *dime novel* is universally accepted to mean something trashy and perhaps contaminating. "Little Blue Book," on the other hand, represents a standard – just because a book would sell in large quantities at five cents was never a sufficient reason for putting it into my series.

There is a difference between making money from the wide sale of a bad book and making a profit from the popularity of a good book. The difference is gratifying. It is one of those virtues that are their own reward. I see no reason why a man should not be proud of doing such a thing, and I see no reason why he should not insist that it is good business and not charity.

Certain denizens of an intellectual demimonde fling the word *popular* at this and that as though it were always a condemning epithet. What nearly everyone wants or nearly everyone is doing is, perforce, they contend, empty and worthless – flat and stale, though profitable. This is no true judgment. No sweeping generalization can be a true judgment

The Little Blue Books have gradually become popularized and are becoming more so yearly. I admit this, because it was the aim of the series in the first place, and because I see nothing derogatory in it. Early experimentation was to a large extent finding out what the reading public wanted most at a low price in the way of good reading. My fundamental contention was that the public would buy good reading if it was made available in a convenient form at a fraction of a dollar. This was borne out, and is still borne out, by the results. Necessarily, there has been a large number of books – part of the world's best literature, certainly – which have not had a wide popular appeal. This could not be expected. Even the proverbial well-read man has not read all of the good books, for there are plenty that will not appeal even to him. Tastes differ; some books are by their nature of wide appeal, while others are limited. The very fact that I did not keep unpopular books in the series, when it was found they were

201

not selling, is really sufficient evidence that I am not a philanthropist.

But with the ideals that have always been behind the Little Blue Books, the series, though growing more popular year by year, has never been degraded. Do you consider joke books degrading? A sense of humor is hardly lowbrow, and even the broadest joke the most intelligent of us may laugh at, for there is really nothing contaminating in the laughter that makes the whole world kin. Life needs more laughter. Joke books do not distort the truth, do not mislead their readers, do not misrepresent life – except, with the license of comedy, to make existence more endurable.

Profitable ventures among the cheap paper-backs have been manuals of fortune-telling, palmistry, astrology, and other forms of fanciful character-reading, so called. People will buy such books, I gather. But the books are deliberately misleading. Though ostensibly for entertainment and good fun, they induce the credulous to believe that there is something in them. What do you find in the Little Blue Books? Instead of solemn compendiums of this false knowledge, there are books that expose the frauds and show the falsity of all such systems, books written, too, with a sense of humor and good fun that makes them at the same time popular and honest.

I have dropped profitable books from the series because they did not come up to the standard set for the Little Blue Books. Such books got into the series in the early days – especially several on improving the mind, doctoring up the personality, and giving a rosy glow to the daily humdrum of life. These books were liars. They played falsely upon the imagination. Because of the great rush of the first days of the series – the necessity to get a large number of books into the series – some bad books, but lightly scrutinized, got into the list. This improvement group proved immensely popular – but later, in calm deliberation and determination to keep to a definite high standard, the books were killed. They went into The Morgue. This, if you wish, is idealism, or philanthropy in its figurative sense. But if you contend that it is not also good business, I retort by asking you, then, what is the worth of a good will built upon a maintained standard of truth-telling, sham-smashing, and a debunking policy that knows no favoritism or evasion?

I say again that this is good business. It is commercially sound because the reading public of America has shown that it will buy the truth if it can get it. It will buy good reading and the facts about life as it is, along with its fun and entertainment – with its jokes and its puzzles and its games, this reading public will buy Shakespeare, psychology, authoritative manuals of health, significant debates, science, the best fiction in the world's literature, self-educating books, some poetry, and the best thoughts of the world's greatest thinkers.

You can point out that this reading public will also buy bad books galore, that it is not really capable of exercising judgment or discrimination. I am not so sure of this. At any rate, it is the publishers who exercise the discrimination, and a man who must read willy-nilly will buy, after all, only such books as are on the market and within reach of his purse. But given a chance, these readers will buy good books, and by reading them they will acquire a better taste and learn to tell the difference between a good book and a bad one.

If I claim credit for anything, aside from establishing a commercially sound series of five-cent books, it is that this series, which has lived up to its aim of a University in Print, has done much to improve the reading taste of the American public. As I point out to some of the better-known writers today, if some of their best work appears in the Little Blue Books, a wider market for their other work is created. A man who reads one or two of the stories of Wilbur Daniel Steele, or some of the humor of Stephen Leacock, in the Little Blue Books, will be on the watch for other work, published elsewhere, by these same writers. I take a great deal of pleasure, personal deference aside, in introducing such names as Fannie Hurst, Theodore Dreiser, Ben Hecht, E. W. Howe, Will Durant, Joseph McCabe, William J. Fielding, Isaac Goldberg, Manuel Komroff, James Oppenheim, Sherwood Anderson, Max Beerbohm, John Cowper Powys, Clarence Darrow, Upton Sinclair, and so on, to mention some of the contemporary names, to a new audience through the Little Blue Books. Incidentally, this is probably the best place to demolish another astonishingly prevalent misconception of the purpose of the Little Blue Books. The charge is sometimes brought against me that I am trying to injure the cloth-bound book business by putting out these paperbound *jitney clas-*

sics. This is absurd. In the first place, a Little Blue Book by its very nature, though substantial and durable, cannot supersede a clothbound book. It has never been my intention to have it do so. Frequently, by circularizing buyers of Little Blue Books, I sell large quantities of clothbound books of other publishers – for I issue no clothbound books whatever myself.

The aim and field of the Little Blue Books are distinct from any other. Far from being competitors, the Little Blue Books are really tiny missionaries, spreading a taste for good literature and inducing a desire for better reading. The average man, the potential book-buyer of tomorrow, has but little spare cash to spend for books. The chances are he will not spend it at all unless he can he sure of getting what he wants. Perhaps he reads the reviews, but many times he does not. Even if he does, they do not tell him all he wants to know. But by making a selection from a series such as the Little Blue Books, he can nibble and sip at small cost, and thereby learn what he wants to read – and perchance find out that good books are not really dull after all, which is something, I wager that he never learned in school.

CHAPTER XV
AN EDITOR TURNS
TO ADVERTISING

How the Little Blue Books Have Been Advertised and Sold

Some people think it strange that I have always been my own advertising manager. But the enterprise of the Little Blue Books does have the peculiarity that production and selling are closely linked with editing the books. The phases are so closely interwoven with each other that it is really impossible to separate them. As an editor I could do my work best only by knowing the situation from the point of view of the advertiser; as an advertiser I could act to best advantage because I was also the publisher.

Though I have always been ready to consider good suggestions from others, the advertising of the Little Blue Books has been to a large extent dependent upon my experience in editing and publishing them. In another chapter I give a clear exposition of the date-lines sales policy in advertising the series, and why that policy has served its usefulness and is already discarded. That sales policy, however, as I pointed out, was a direct outcome of the publishing circumstances and conditions.

In national advertising several general principles characterize my policy. Of national advertisers using full-page space in magazines and newspapers, I am the only one who utilizes literally every agate line. My advertising has less *white space*, and consequently more type, than any other I can remember. Much of my advertising, since it carries a large list of Little Blue Book titles, is almost solid type. Though this is contrary to the dictates of some of the best advertising experts, all I can say is that it has done the work.

At the start of this discussion of advertising I should perhaps explain that advertising is measured in *agate lines*. An agate line is the amount of space required for a line of agate ($5\frac{1}{2}$ point) type a column wide. A newspaper or magazine page is divided customarily into a specified number of columns, a certain number of agate lines in each column. Agate lines run fourteen to the inch, so that an advertisement a column wide and ten inches deep would measure 140 agate lines. An agate line is the unit of measurement, and the advertiser must pay for it even though the space is not occupied by type, if the space is divided off from the rest of the page or paper as part of his advertisement.

Another consideration in Little Blue Book advertising has been that in printing the list of titles it has been necessary to confine each title to one agate line, if possible. This requirement has often made it necessary to alter the title, and it has always made it necessary to include all possible description – what would be the blurb for a larger and more expensive book – in that one agate line of space. I have discussed all this in the chapters entitled "Rejuvenating the Classics," "The Hospital," and "The Morgue." The Little Blue Book business, too, is fully ninety-five percent a mail-order business. A few scattered bookstores, and to some extent the five-and-ten-cent stores, handle assortments of Little Blue Books, but by far the greater part of the business is directly received from the customers themselves through the mails. This is another characteristic of the advertising – all of it urges the customer to order direct from Girard, enclosing his remittance with his order. The fact that the orders are received direct from the customers is important. It has enabled me to test the pulling power of all kinds of advertising mediums and methods, for all Little Blue Book advertising is *coupon advertising* – which means that it requires the customer to send direct to the Haldeman-Julius Publications, and the address given contains a key number, such as Department X-114. This *Dept.* or *key* number on the envelope or in the letter enclosed with the order tells at once what advertisement should receive credit for the business. It is much better than requesting the customer to *mention* the magazine or paper when ordering, and I have found that less than one person in a hundred omits the key number when addressing his order.

Key advertising is thus different from general advertising that has no direct returns. The advertisements of tobacco, cosmetics, chewing gum, automobiles, gasoline, machinery, and so on, which have no coupons (such as requests for samples), are published widely – and the only possible test is whether the business of the company as a whole, as compared with the advertising budget for previous years and the present year, shows a proportionate improvement. But the advertiser who uses no key cannot tell at all whether one magazine is better than another, or whether his billboards are doing any good whatever.

Even the advertising of most book publishers is unkeyed. The usual line is: *at all bookstores*, or *ask your bookseller*. If the book sells enough copies to pay all expenses including the advertising, with a margin of profit besides, the publisher balances his books with a smile. But he has no assurance that some of his space was not wasted. He does not know, for example, that he might have done even better had he stayed out of certain publications entirely and doubled his space in certain others. He has no way of knowing. The net result of the whole is the only figure available to him.

One might think it safe to assume that a magazine with a guaranteed circulation, with an advertising rate proportionate to that circulation, and with a sufficient number of regular advertisers to substantiate the stability and commercial worth of the publication, would be a good medium for advertising Little Blue Books. This is not at all a safe assumption to make. I would test such a magazine with keyed copy, and see how it compared with others of similar circulation and cost. If good, all right; if it failed, that would be the end.

Advertising is an *art*, not a science. That is to say, if it is successful it depends more upon a happy inspiration than upon a hard-and-fast rule of technique, all the advertising schools notwithstanding. If it were a science it would always work according to fixed laws. The expert could determine in advance, with graphs and formulas, just what the outcome would be – he could foretell whether the returns would vary as a parabola or would rotate like an ellipse. But, I am sorry to say, this cannot be done. Whenever I issue a piece of advertising copy, even to a medium that I know to be good, I await the result with an open mind. Often I am anxious; sometimes I am delighted, sometimes disappointed.

I have seen some of what I considered my best ideas fail when put to the test. I have been amazed to find others taking hold wonderfully. For example, two or three years ago I tested some copy headed: "An Agnostic Looks at Life," feeling that the time had come for general circulation of literature that advocated a liberal attitude toward religion. This failed. Now, recently, I am experimenting with Joseph McCabe's fifty Little Blue Books, discussing religion, with the headline: "The fascinating story of man's struggle to grasp the meaning of religion," and it looks as though this will be a success. And in the face of a failure to put across a Little Blue Book "Library of Love," as a set, I am having encouraging results from an endeavor to sell a high school "Educational Course," made up entirely of Little Blue Books, as a set. It is simply impossible to forecast what an advertisement will do.

It is a constant gamble – or, if you do not like that word, it is a constant repetition of experiment and change, and experiment again. It is not even true that the same piece of copy will do its work indefinitely; as a matter of fact, the results from one advertisement, without change in appearance, are never the same twice in succession. In this connection I should point out that I have never been able to afford – due to the low price of my product – advertising merely for *propaganda* purposes. For example, I could not spend money to run a standardized column-advertisement announcing new Little Blue Books, or to run copy that endeavored merely to get people's curiosity aroused about the Little Blue Books. Such methods double or treble the cost of the advertising necessary to put over a sale. I must sell, as I later explain, from the first insertion itself. That is one reason, perhaps, why I must always change the appearance of my advertisements, trying first this appeal and then that.

Many things must be taken into account when estimating the value of a magazine or paper. In the first place, if the periodical has a large circulation, how did it build up that circulation? A number of so-called mail-order periodicals have weekly or monthly circulations sometimes above the million mark – papers such as *Home Friend, Household Journal, Comfort, Home Circle, Gentlewoman,* and so forth – but are these magazines bought to be read? To a large extent, of course, the magazines will be at least hastily examined in the homes to which they go, for one reason because they go to rural districts and farms where little reading of any kind is available. But the circulation is built up with premiums – you get a dozen rose bushes and two or three magazines for a year, all for a half dollar or a dollar, as the case may be. The magazines contain comparatively little reading matter – on the whole they have been found undesirable mediums through which to sell Little Blue Books.

There are some magazines that base their advertising rate, not on the number of hundred thousands circulation, but on the *quality* of the circulation. If the magazine is read largely by families with incomes over eight or ten thousand dollars a year, or by people interested only in the more expensive products, this periodical can charge a rate commensurate with the quality of that circulation. Such magazines are *House and Decoration, New Yorker, Vanity Fair, Vogue,* and so forth. Due to the low price of Little Blue Books, and though many of the readers of these magazines might like to read the pocket series, these magazines cost too much for the business they get for such a low-priced product. I do not use them for Little Blue Book advertising, except possibly in very small space at different times, as a test.

There are a vast number of trade and class publications, of which the average reader has no idea. The tobacco world alone has several monthly periodicals devoted to it; so has the drug trade, the cosmetic and beauty shop business, hardware merchants, groceries, and all the rest. Even the filling stations have their own periodical. But these magazines are not read for general interest. Their appeal is based on the business or trade they represent. It is the same with union labor publications, or religious journals, or lodge papers. Their interest is so specialized that they do not divert a proper amount of attention to an advertisement of general reading such as the Little Blue Books. I have found them, on the whole, undesirable mediums.

In a group by themselves are the school and college papers. These run into the hundreds. They are nearly always unsound financially, and their advertising rate has no relation to their pulling power. I see no reason why vast national industries, with money to scatter promiscuously in advertising, should not help out these struggling student attempts. But I have found – either because the students are often penniless, or because their studies give them enough to read – that I cannot sell Little Blue Books to the school and university groups through their own periodicals. Though my audience is largely made up of modern youth, I reach these young people through the magazines they buy on the newsstands.

Of the more general magazines, printing an assortment of fiction and articles, the group known as women's magazines is the largest and boasts the largest circulation. I mean such magazines as *Pictorial Review, Ladies' Home Journal, Women's Home Companion, Delineator*, and so forth I have tested these at different times – or some of them – and I have always confirmed the early rule that women's magazines do not pay for Little Blue Book advertising.

Perhaps some of my readers will throw up their hands in amazement, protesting that women are known to be the largest part of the American reading public. Perhaps that is so. I have no precise figures to contradict this statement, but if it is true it must be because they buy their reading from other mediums than their own magazines. Of course, these women's magazines are largely addressed to the interests of the housewife and her household – and housewives have, on the average, little time to read much besides the one *home* magazine they may receive. Business women, who read many of the same general periodicals as men – like *Liberty, Judge, Collier's, Current History, Review of Reviews, Golden Book, Smart Set, Physical Culture, Cosmopolitan*, and so forth – perhaps are better buyers of books than housewives.

I do have one set of figures that is significant. In 1926 the Research Bureau of *Liberty* made an exhaustive test of Little Blue Books sold through their columns. This test – of 1,000 orders selected at random, confined only to twenty-five books each – showed that 79.8 percent of the books were ordered by men and only 20.2 percent were ordered by women. This ratio may be ten percent off, due to the fact that many women sign their names with initials only, and in this test only those orders that were obviously from women were counted as such. But the figures indicate that not more than 30 percent of the orders came from women. I think it fair to assume that *Liberty's* circulation represents a cross section of the multitude of American people, and if this is granted, it shows that more than twice as many men buy and read Little Blue Books as women. These are the only exact figures I have, but they strongly suggest why I have never been able to make the women's magazines pay.

In support of this arraignment of women as Little Blue Book readers, I can say that I have a fair list of books devoted exclusively to women's interests – beauty hints, how to dress, cosmetics, care of the baby, pin money, cooking, home helps, and so forth. But none of these books are sensational sellers, though most of them show a fair average. On the other hand, books *about* women – such as *Women of Antiquity*, *Women Who Lived for Love*, *Woman the Eternal Primitive*, and others like them – are very good sellers, probably because they are widely purchased and read by men. A new book is being added in 1928 – *100 Professions for Women* – which may indicate whether the professional interest is stronger in reading women than the home interest. It will be interesting to watch the record of this book. I am sorry that no figures are available for this discussion.

Unfortunately I have no figures whatever as to age. I have always had the feeling that Little Blue Book readers are largely young people. It is certain that a large number of them are of college age, or are in their early twenties – I gather this from letters I receive. But due to the fact that periodicals that appeal strongly to young people – as *Smart Set* and *Physical Culture* – are always good paying mediums, I know that young people form a large division in the army of Little Blue Book enthusiasts. I believe in the youth of America – these youngsters are wide awake, ready to learn, and urged on with real energy and ambition. They want to know all the facts – but it is a healthy sign that they want facts and not sordid misrepresentations or lurid products of the imagination.

How do I know whether an advertisement for Little Blue Books pays? I have already explained how the advertising is keyed, so that every order received can be credited to the proper advertisement. This keying is done

211

by one girl every day, as the orders are checked over. Special cards are provided, with the key number, name of the publication, copy used, space used, position given, and the cost. Entries on these cards are made twice daily – the morning receipts and the afternoon receipts. Thus I know not only how much the advertisement finally brings, but I know how long it pulls, how soon the receipts reach their peak, how soon the advertisement brings in its cost, and so on.

Good magazines pull for months after the advertisement has appeared. Orders are still received from advertising as far back as 1925 – in *Liberty*, for instance. But these dribblings do not materially help the advertisement's record, except that they show how long old magazines are perused.

In general, I am willing to spend from two to two and a half cents to sell a Little Blue Book – especially to get new names. If I have to spend less than two cents to sell each book, the medium is of exceptional pulling power. If I get $2,000 or more from an advertisement costing $1,000, I am satisfied. If I get $2,500 to $3,000 I am enthusiastic.

Here are some of the actual receipts from some particular advertisements:

Publication	Date	Space	Cost	Returns
N. Y. Times Book Review	10-30-27	2 Pages	$2,500	$4,348.89
Mid-Week Pictorial	9-15-27	2 Pages	300	924.56
N. Y. Daily News	1-30-27	1 Page	1,400	2,789.49
Physical Culture	Oct. 1927	1 Page	800	1,759.19
Smart Set	Nov. 1927	1 Page	850	1,888.35
Pathfinder	4-11-25	1 Page	1,000	2,763.66
Life	9-26-23	1 Page	650	1,215.23
Harper's Monthly	Oct. 1926	1 Page	200	382.15
Review of Reviews	Oct. 1925	1 Page	325	642.68
Golden Book	Oct. 1925	4 Pages	800	1,927.48
Liberty	1-9-26	2 Pages	5,000	13,321.31
Chicago Tribune	2-10-26	1 Page	1,300	2,884.36
Hearst's International	Feb. 1925	1 Page	1,000	2,369.12

Publication	Date	Space	Cost	Returns
The Nation	9-10-24	1 Page	150	349.29

To show how the returns from an advertisement steadily increase to a peak and then fall off, I am including a table of three insertions of two pages each in *Liberty*. This table shows the fluctuation of the receipts in an understandable way. It is worthy of note that the general trend of the receipts is the same, substantially, for all three.

Daily Returns form three *Liberty* Insertions
(Sundays Are Not Counted)

Date of Insertion	1st Day	2nd Day	3rd Day	4th Day	5th Day	6th Day	7th Day
Sept. 18, 1926	$13.74	$85.01	$447.38	$613.07	$849.06	$713.48	$1,042.48
(1st Day 9-13)							
Jan. 9, 1926	94.86	108.47	403.83	698.57	698.57	768.65	844.81
(1st Day 14)							
Jan. 30, 1926	55.43	90.61	452.65	666.36	699.84	233.40[1]	1,396.36
(1st Day 1-25)							

	8th Day	9th Day	10th Day	11-12th Day	13-15th Day	Final	Total
Sept. 18,1926	$319.82	$429.96	$344.11	$412.69	$904.62	(Dec. 6)	$10,050.39
Jan. 9,1926	356.23	526.11	612.75	920.64	805.52	(Mar. 6)	13,231.31
Jan. 30,1926	363.97	492.56	455.27	741.17	1,187.41	(Apr. 2)	12,051.46

[1]Saturday on which mail was opened only in the morning; what would have been the afternoon's mail is included in the next day's (Monday's) total.

In brief explanation of the figures in the foregoing table, I should add that an insertion in *Liberty*, if successful (and I have never had a failure in this magazine so far), will more than *pay out* (which means to bring in the cost of the advertisement or better) within the first three weeks of returns. The first returns begin almost always on Monday – the magazine is placed on the newsstands the previous Saturday, being dated the Saturday follow-ing. That is, *Liberty* for September 18, 1926, was placed on the newsstands September 11, and I had the first returns on the 13th. *Liberty* always *pulls* (brings returns) regularly for nearly ninety days and then drops down to from one to five dollars a day for another month or so, finally dwindling to a dollar or so every now and then.

Advertising in the newspapers has the same characteristics as that in the magazines. The emphasis in Little Blue Book copy – now that date-lines and sales inducements have been abandoned – is on two things: the estab-lished five-cent price, including postage to any address in the world, and the great scope of choice – 1,260 different titles. These two selling points, added to the reputation and general excellence of the series, are now do-ing all the work of selling the books to a wide and constantly increasing audience.

I can make the general statement, from a wide experience, that advertis-ing a mail-order product in small-city newspapers never pays. Only news-papers in the larger cities – New York, Boston, Philadelphia, Baltimore, Chicago, Los Angeles, and so forth – are good. Some papers in these larger cities are much better than others, not due so much, perhaps, to variations in the mentality of their readers as to a difference in purchasing power. An important factor is the reader-interest the newspaper has – and this is a matter of reputation. Is it bought because it is examined thoroughly from first page to last, or does it depend upon one or two features to build up its circulation?

I know that I have mentioned only two general considerations, and that even these cannot be applied like a blanket to all cases. The difference in pulling power between two papers in the same city is, after all, much more deep-rooted than either of these things. It would take an involved analysis to explain it. All that I know is that all papers are not alike, and I keep away from those in which I once wasted my money.

But it is an absolutely general rule that the small-city newspaper does not pay. This is because the rate is based upon two things – the actual circulation and the cost of running the advertisement. The latter includes typesetting, ink, paper, and so forth. But the circulation of the small-city paper is not sufficient to justify an advertising rate based upon that alone, so that per hundred readers, let us say, the cost is proportionately greater than it is to reach every hundred readers of a newspaper in one of the larger cities. The larger the paper, the lower the cost. For example, I have mailed copy from Girard late Saturday afternoon, every line of which had to be set – .totaling actually more than 1,300 lines of type – and have had the pleasure of seeing the complete advertisement inserted in the early morning editions of the *Chicago Tribune* for the very next Tuesday, and have received the first orders Wednesday afternoon! Chicago, you know, is 600 miles from Girard. The cost of rushing through that advertisement is really very large – a small-city newspaper could not afford it at a rate based upon circulation at so much per thousand as the *Chicago Tribune* figures it.

Newspaper advertising is more ephemeral than that in the magazines. By this I mean that it reaches its peak sooner, and falls off more rapidly. Newspapers are read soon after being delivered – at least on the evening of the day they are dated – and, except Sunday newspapers, which approach more nearly to the magazines, their readers act quickly on any mail-order advertising that appeals to them. To show this I am also putting in a table of three insertions of one full page each in the *Chicago Tribune*, which shows the fluctuation of newspaper receipts. Compare this with the table of *Liberty* – and then with the table of an insertion of two pages in *Review of Reviews*, a monthly of steady pulling power.

Daily Returns form three *Chicago Tribune* Insertions
(Sundays Are Not Counted)

Date of Insertion	1st Day	2nd Day	3rd Day	4th Day	5th Day	6th Day	7th Day
Feb. 10, 1926 (1st Day 2-11)	N/A	$202.19	$391.05	$177.80	$408.78	$118.62	$210.61
Jan. 14,1926 (1st Day 1-6)	11.31	962.08	491.67	258.32	221.54	154.23	161.19
Jan. 5, 1926 (1st Day 1-6)	14.76	350.76	448.35	332.65	295.77	53.71	153.49

	8th Day	9th Day	10th Day	11-12th Day	13-15th Day	Final	Total
Feb. 10,1926	$198.67	$100.21	$74.27	$135.55	$361.12	(Mar. 10)	$2,884.36
Jan. 14,1926	72.10	83.55	69.56	156.81	107.56	(Mar. 10)	3,788.62
Jan. 5,1926	98.35	81.73	141.12	54.41	105.30	(Mar. 10)	2,959.81

There are some interesting things to be noted about these three newspaper insertions. All represent copy for the sale that closed February 28, 1926 – threatening the withdrawal of certain titles, which were later withdrawn as had been advertised. The returns from Chicago usually start very slowly on the afternoon of the day following the insertion – for February 10 this small amount was not recorded. The big returns come in the first week, always – a newspaper is read very soon after its purchase or delivery, especially a weekday issue, but this was date-line copy and a number of people must have torn out the advertisement and set it aside until they were ready to order. The fact that all three of these insertions pulled rather steadily up to a week or so after the closing date of the sale shows this. It is also worthy of note that though two of these insertions were only nine days apart, both did very well indeed. Though some re-ordered who had responded to the insertion on the 5th, it is practically certain that a large number of those who answered the 14th advertisement had not noticed the one nine days before. Some, of course, were reminded of the previous advertisement, on which they had neglected or forgotten to act, and immediately took action when so forcibly reminded that these books must be bought immediately.

216

But many people do not notice much that comes under their eyes – they may have been in more of a hurry on the 5th than on the 14th – .so that in a paper with a large circulation it often pays to repeat frequently. Finally, note that the insertion of February 10, close to the closing date of the sale, kept much higher returns through a longer period – because the advertisement pulled from twenty-five to thirty-five days *less* than the previous insertions. Date-line copy always slumps to zero shortly after the closing date – its main disadvantage.

Daily Returns form *Review of Reviews* Insertion
(Sundays Are Not Counted)

October, 1925 Date of Insertion	1st Day	2nd Day	3rd Day	4th Day	5th Day	6th Day	7th Day
	$10.97	$4.65	$12.02	$8.08	$17.46	$11.44	[1]$7.95

8th Day	9th Day	10th Day	11-12th Day	13-15th Day	Final	Total
$14.00	$14.25	$9.82	$22.47	$33.04	(Jan. 1)	$518.68

[1]Saturday on which mail was opened only in the morning; what would have been the afternoon's mail is included in the next day's (Monday's) total.

It is interesting to observe that the *Review of Reviews*, being a monthly magazine, pulls much slower than *Liberty*, a weekly, or the *Chicago Tribune*, a daily. This magazine pulls fairly steadily for three months, paying out usually in the first thirty days. The difference in the way the returns come in is accounted for by the fact that a monthly magazine lies around on library table and lounge for weeks, where different members of the family pick it up and glance through its pages. It is filed away, too, more permanently in libraries, and even some individuals keep files of their favorite magazines. That is why some of my magazine advertising pulls – though it is in very small amounts – for a year, or even two years. It is therefore impossible ever to use a monthly publication if quick returns are desired – for quick results the newspapers are the only mediums. The closing date of monthly magazines, being far in advance of the date of the publication, is another handicap. They are valuable, but copy for them must be planned far in advance, and usually it is necessary to wait some time for full returns.

In general, I make but little change – sometimes no change at all – in the list of books advertised in magazines of the quality class, magazines usually classed as *low-brow*, high-class newspapers, and the tabloid newspapers. All of these supposedly vastly different audiences are given their choice of exactly the same books, at exactly the same price, under exactly the same conditions. To some extent, their selections from the same list do vary. In another place I compare these differences. But in general the appeal of the Little Blue Books is thoroughly democratic – they lure the nickels of the well-to-do as well as the nickels of those who have few to spare.

My newspaper campaigns are a unique feature of Little Blue Book advertising. Their success shows more than anything else that there is a real field for good reading at a price within reach of the average pocketbook. People like to taste, also; they will nibble at the classics and at college subjects if it will not cost them too much to make the experiment. The crowning achievement of Little Blue Book distribution, indeed, I regard as the success of selling them through the pages of the tabloids – the gum-chewers' ad-sheets, the most sensational papers printed anywhere. In these papers, I have successfully listed and sold Little Blue Books of acknowledged excellence – many of the same books bought by readers of *Harper's* and the *Atlantic Monthly*.

A complete list of the magazines that have printed Little Blue Book advertising would fill more than a page of this book. Some of them have proved good mediums for a time; others were tried for test purposes only. Several are used at long intervals; some are used regularly. They range all the way from *Police Gazette* to *Asia*, from the *Nation*, a liberal, to the *Pathfinder*, a conventional, from *Smart Set* and *True Confessions* to *Current History* and *Personality*, from the *Mid-Week Pictorial* to the *New York Graphic*, from *Hygeia* to *Physical Culture*, from *Harper's* to the *Writer's Digest*. Little Blue Books have been sold through the Capper Publications, the Fawcett Publications, the Newsstand Group, and the Macfadden Publications. They range from *Life, Judge,* and *College Humor* to the *Golden Book* and

Red Book. Wherever readers are found – there is a place for the Little Blue Books.

From my nine years of advertising in all kinds of periodicals and papers, I have built up a mailing list exceeding half a million names and addresses the world over. After each order has been filled, file clerks look up the name and address of the customer in these drawers of stencils. If the name is not already there, a metal stencil is stamped on a special machine, and this stencil is filed in its proper place by state and city. Filing by addresses is for the convenience of the postoffice department when large mailings are made from these lists. That is why, when there is a change of address, a customer must send both his old and his new address – for the stencil is filed by his address, and not alphabetically by his name.

These 500,000 names and addresses of book-buyers – only purchasers' names are stenciled, mere inquiries being answered and thrown away – are kept constantly up to date by a corps of clerks. All mailings of catalogues or circulars bear the line *return postage guaranteed*, so that if the address is wrong the piece of mail will be returned and the stencil can be removed from the files. In every mailing – and there are at last two each year – from ten to fifteen percent of the addresses have changed.

This list of names, by the way, pays for its upkeep by rental. Other publishers or mail-order organizations using direct-mail advertising rent the use of this list of names. I remember that Edward Bok, when seeking to give the widest possible publicity to his Peace Plan, used the entire list of Little Blue Book buyers. The circular letters, already in envelopes, sealed and stamped, were sent to Girard by express. Only the addresses were affixed here. This is the usual procedure, and the business from this rental of the mailing list pays for keeping it in shape, and it is always ready for my own use – a convenient list of people who have bought Little Blue Books and who are likely to be interested in new catalogues with new titles.

Though I am largely dependent upon direct returns from national advertising being large enough to be profitable in themselves, at the same time I count upon a large amount of re-orders, as every mail-order house does. In every outgoing parcel post package of Little Blue Books there is a small 32-page catalogue of the 1,260 Little Blue Books. From this catalogue alone thousands of dollars' worth of business accrues in the course of a year. For example, the little catalogue keyed as Dept. C-33, which was first sent out May, 1927, has brought in, to date, $20,630.55 worth of orders. These orders cost only the manufacturing cost of the catalogues; there was no mailing expense or other advertising expense whatever. The parcel post packages also contain *stuffing*, which is made up of circulars and advertising matter about my publications – *Weekly*, *Monthly*, and *Quarterly*, and Joseph McCabe's *Key to Culture* – and some advertisements of clothbound books of other publishers that I think will interest Little Blue Book readers.

A most interesting aspect of this stuffing is a small, inconspicuous $3^1/_2$ x 5-inch slip, on ordinary book paper in black ink only, with room for very little argument or persuasion of any kind. This slip has been inserted in Joseph McCabe's Little Blue Books, and merely calls attention to Joseph McCabe's new series, *The Key to Culture*. The amazing power of Mr. Mc-Cabe is shown by the fact that several people a day who read his Little Blue Books use this little slip, this tiny *stuffer*, to send in a subscription to *The Key to Culture*. This is selling a $5 article to a man who first buys something that costs only five cents. And just because of the influence of a man's name.

Another regular circular is a four-page $5^1/_2$ x $8^1/_2$-inch folder describing William J. Fielding's new clothbound book entitled *Sex and the Love-Life*. This is stuffed in all outgoing packages of Little Blue Books, and its only sales argument is a complete list of the contents of the book – and the price, $2.65. An average of twenty copies of this clothbound book are sold every day from this inexpensive circular – and to buyers of five-cent books. This speaks well for the influence of Mr. Fielding, and also for the sincere desire on the part of these readers to improve themselves by getting at the facts about life.

I constantly send out a $3^1/_2$ x 5-inch *coin-card*, advertising the *Haldeman-Julius Weekly* for ten weeks at ten cents. This coin card urges the reader to send back a dime and receive the *Weekly* for ten weeks. This card alone keeps the circulation of the Weekly at an average of 70,000 copies – making it an excellent medium to advertise not only Little Blue Books, but my

Monthly and *Quarterly* magazines. The *Monthly* costs $1.50 annually, and has been built up almost entirely through advertising in the *Weekly* to a circulation of 50,000 copies. The *Quarterly*, at $3 per year, has been similarly built up to 18,000 copies. Joseph McCabe's *Key to Culture* ($5 per 24 issues), through advertising in these publications and various circulars, has reached a subscription list of 7,000 (January 1, 1928).

Incidentally, I should point out that these publications of mine – especially the *Monthly* and the *Quarterly* – are not only valuable to me as advertising mediums for the Little Blue Books and for each other, but their editorial requirements constantly complement the editorial needs of the Little Blue Books. Manuscripts bought for Little Blue Books are run serially in the publications, thereby advertising the author, and manuscripts bought for the publications are frequently gathered together later for Little Blue Books. Some very successful books have been evolved through this mutually helpful method. I point out particularly how such authors as Joseph McCabe, William J. Fielding, Will Durant, and others, have been made well known to Little Blue Book readers by this policy. This also reduces the expense of manuscripts and helps to keep the selling price of Little Blue Books at five cents each.

At one time I utilized the space on the back covers of the Little Blue Books themselves for advertising. I could, as a matter of fact, sell this space for a tidy sum annually. But I took my own advertising off, and have allowed no other advertising on the Little Blue Books, for no other reason than that it cheapened the books without enough gain to offset this lowering of the quality of the product. Little Blue Book covers present an attractive if inexpensive appearance in their plain blue covers, except for the number and title and author on the front. I prefer not to mar this neat appearance, even though it might sell a few more books per year.

For catalogue distribution I depend almost solely upon the little catalogues stuffed in outgoing packages, and in yearly catalogues mailed to my list of buyers of the Little Blue Books. Although to some extent, when a new catalogue is ready, I advertise the publication of this new catalogue in magazines other than my own, I have found that the *general inquiry* form of advertising does not pay.

By general inquiry advertising, I mean that which does not solicit orders, but endeavors to arouse the interest of the reader so that he will write for a free sample, a free booklet, or a free catalogue. For something fairly expensive, like a large set of clothbound books, when the margin between manufacturing cost and selling price is large, this is all right, because it is not necessary to sell to so many different customers in order to make it pay.

But in selling Little Blue Books I must sell to a great many individuals, due to the low profit each separate order represents. If I depend on inquiries for catalogues, I have to do the work, in effect, twice – .first I have to interest the reader in a catalogue, and then, with the catalogue, I have to interest him in the books. It is better, I have found, to list some of the more attractive books in the original advertisement, and solicit orders directly on the merit of the product itself. If the reader also wants a free catalogue – well and good. But his attention is focused at once on the books, and his business is solicited without any intermediary correspondence.

Little Blue Books do well in this form of direct advertising because if a man knows what they are and does not buy them from their titles as listed he will not buy them at all – for I cannot afford to spend many pennies arguing him into a purchase that the lure of the product itself cannot consummate. My best policy has always been to print my catalogue – or as much of it as there may be room for – in the pages of the magazines and newspapers that carry my advertising.

A new form of Little Blue Book advertising is at present undergoing experimental exploitation. With so large a list it is possible to break the books up into a number of small, closely related groups of books. For example, Joseph McCabe has some fifty Little Blue Books giving a complete survey of religious controversy. These fifty books are being advertised, with promising returns, as a set – sold in unbroken lots of fifty, no choice being permitted. A series of fifty Little Blue Books giving the essentials of a high school education is being advertised and sold in the same way. This shows that different forms of appeal have their very separate values – people are buying these special sets, who may have up to the moment ignored general Little Blue Book advertising in which they could have picked out these

222

fifty titles or any fifty or less that they might have wanted.

A variation of this group advertising is also used when less than full-page copy is desired. I refer to advertisements of one column only, in a magazine, or even as small as 100 or seventy-five agate lines. I have even used as small an advertisement as thirty-five agate lines – listing a series of Little Blue Books on crime and criminals, with a choice of one book or more at five cents each plus a cent a book for postage. This is always to get new names from sources where it would not pay to run larger copy.

Some of the smaller advertisements have been headed: IMPROVE YOURSELF! These were usually in space of 75 agate lines, and are run in a wide variety of publications during spring and summer, when larger copy is likely not to pay out. I also use more sensational little ads, headed "I Want to Know About Love," with a list of the helpful Little Blue Books on sexual hygiene and love stories from the world's literature. These are the advertisements, usually in space of fifty agate lines each, which I now and then run in the mail-order publications. A list of from fifty to seventy Little Blue Books, though with abbreviated titles, can be set in small type in a space of fifty agate lines – giving a fair range of choice and making it possible for the advertisement to pay out on the two-to-one basis that I require.

Some of the results from such advertising are as follows:

Publication	Date	Space	Cost	Returns
Hygeia	Feb. 1927	1 column	$60	$128.58
Smart Set	July 1927	fifty lines	80	312.35
Psychology	Aug. 1927	fifty lines	25	123.49
Grit	May 1927	fifty lines	60	120.96
American Girl	Feb. 1927	1 column	40	96.77
Youth's Companion	Mar. 1927	100 lines	125	236.49

Frequently, of course, I have the advantage of being able to test a piece of new advertising copy in one of my publications – the *Weekly*, *Monthly*, or *Quarterly*, or even in all three. If it pays out in these publications I can be fairly certain that it will have a good chance of paying out elsewhere, especially in periodicals I know to be good mediums for Little Blue Books.

For if I have learned any one general truth from my experience in advertising Little Blue Books, it is that human nature is the same in all walks of life – which is nothing new. It is just that the Colonel's lady and Rosie O'Grady are really sisters under their skins, and so both of them buy approximately the same Little Blue Books. It may seem impossible that readers of the *Atlantic Monthly* should buy practically the same titles as readers of *Smart Set*, but it is nevertheless the truth. The desires and inclinations of all readers are much alike – they are limited chiefly by their ability to understand, by the range of their knowledge, and not by what they would like to read about if they can grasp it.

CHAPTER XVI

A COMPARISON OF

ADVERTISING MEDIUMS

Are Different Little Blue Books Sold Via Different Magazines?

I t is to their wide appeal that the Little Blue Books owe their success. By wide appeal I mean, of course, a series of books so selected and so distributed over a variety of subjects that the titles will lure orders from readers of *Harper's* as well as from readers of *Liberty* and *Pathfinder*. The same books are sold to all classes of readers – though there is a variation in the actual books selected, this variation is not as large as one might suppose. In most cases it is sound advertising to use the same copy in a group of publications of widely different tone and policy.

However, I have learned some interesting facts from my use of the same copy, in a variety of magazines and papers. I have learned, for example, that the *New York Times Book Review* is the only medium through which I can sell, in an appreciable quantity, the Little Blue Book edition of Charles Dickens' *Christmas Carol*. Don't ask me why – many of the results from Little Blue Book advertising are almost riddles. For this book does not sell at all, comparatively, to the readers of *Harper's* – and only mildly to readers of the *Nation*. The nearest competitor to the *Times* on this book is the *Smart Set*, with a sale of half as many.

Before I go into a lengthy discussion, I must explain the figures I shall use. I shall take up, in particular, the actual statistics secured from similar advertisements of 1927 in *Harper's, Nation, Smart Set, Pathfinder, N. Y.*

Times Book Review, *Liberty*, and *N. Y. Daily Graphic*. This offers a wide range. *Harper's* is a magazine of limited appeal – a rather conventional *quality*, thoroughly safe and reliable magazine. The *Nation* also has limited appeal – but it is liberal, decidedly progressive, and reaches a group of aggressively alert, somewhat radical readers. The *Smart Set* is a rather sensational young people's magazine, dealing in the confession type of short story, articles on love and marriage, and so on. The *Pathfinder* is a weekly news magazine, thoroughly conventional, going chiefly to small towns (less than 10,000 in population), with a circulation that is entirely mail order – no newsstand sales whatever. The *New York Times Book Review* is a feature section of the Sunday edition of the *N. Y. Times*, undoubtedly one of the world's greatest newspapers. The intellectual level of this review is high. *Liberty* is a national weekly *for everybody*, reaching a mass of middle class and laboring class readers, partly because it is a five-cent magazine, and partly because its editorial content is kept up to the minute, short and easy to read, and planned to attract the weary reader who is anxious to amuse himself in fleeting spare moments. The *New York Graphic* is a tabloid newspaper – read to a large extent in the subways of Manhattan, by thousands on their way to and from their work.

The question to be approached in this chapter is whether there are any wide differences in the books purchased by these seven groups of readers, and what these differences are. There are some, and they tell a story. But there are strong and significant similarities also – which will be demonstrated in due course.

The basis of the statistics has had to be given a common denominator, so to speak. The actual returns from the advertisements are necessarily widely divergent. But for the sake of comparison the figures used here represent the number of books ordered in a thousand orders. That is to say, if a thousand orders (of about twenty books each; or roughly 20,000 books in all) are received, and out of this group ninety people order Dickens' *Christmas Carol* – the 1,000 figure for this book is ninety. As a matter of fact, ninety people out of the thousand selected from the *N. Y. Times Book Review* returns did order this book; fifty people out of the thousand *Smart Set* readers also ordered it – but of the thousand orders received from the

Nation, only ten ordered it. These are round numbers, but they hold true, and are genuinely representative.

There is one possible explanation of the difference in the sales of this particular title. Readers of the *Nation*, being well educated and for the most part well read, are already familiar with the story. Readers of the *Smart Set* and *Times*, however, have merely heard of it (speaking in general), and are curious to read it. I cannot explain, however, the peculiar silence on the part of the readers of *Harper's*, who bought, for example, *Dr. Jekyll and Mr. Hyde* – to the extent of seventy orders out of a thousand.

One broad generalization can be made without any possibility of contradiction. High or low, rich or poor, read or unread, the interest in sex – the relationship between men and women, the attraction of male for female and vice versa – is universal. Rich man, poor man, beggar man, thief, doctor, lawyer, merchant, chief – all are fascinated by this subject. Whether the orders come from palatial residences or hovels, from cities or villages, from offices or homes, from colleges or prisons, the dominance of this subject is inevitable.

The interest in sex and love may express itself in different ways. The orders may be, indeed, for somewhat different books – but the impulse behind the orders, the motive for buying the books, is everywhere the same. Here are the figures, reduced to actual percentages, for the seven groups of orders to be analyzed here: *Harper's*, forty-one percent of the readers buy books on sex, love, marriage, or a related subject; *Nation*, sixty-one percent; *Smart Set*, seventy percent; *N. Y. Times*, fifty-four percent; *Graphic*, sixty-two percent; *Liberty*, seventy-one percent; *Pathfinder*, twenty-seven percent. In every case the proportion is more than a fourth; in all but two cases it is over half.

One of the amazing aspects of these percentages, to me, is the very low – comparatively speaking – sale of *sex books* to readers of the *Pathfinder*. Actually, these readers bought books of self-improvement and self-education – which is to say books helping them toward better English, better health, better understanding of themselves and others and their relation to the world – to the extent of thirty-one percent. The *N. Y. Times Book Review* also runs to thirty-one percent self-improvement books, but the

Times readers wanted to know about love and sex to twice the extent that *Pathfinder* readers did.

It is possible – no statistics are available, and I am merely offering a hypothesis – that readers of the *Pathfinder* are largely family groups, many of them perhaps elderly, living in small towns. Their interest in love and marriage has ceased to be intense, if I may put it that way. They show clearly that they are much more interested in educating themselves along lines other than phases of the relationship between male and female.

Viewing this interest in sex in more detail, though the dominance of the subject is paramount throughout all these mediums, the actual titles selected vary considerably, and are variously significant. For the sake of comparison I have before me lists of 100 best sellers for each of these seven magazines. In this list of 100 there are some sex books – a series by William J. Fielding – which are found in *all* seven lists. These are books that *everyone* wants, almost with exception:

Book Title	Copies Sold
What Married Women Should Know	260
What Married Men Should Know	220
What Young Women Should Know	200
Woman's Sex Life	200
Man's Sex Life	190
What Young Men Should Know	170

The figures indicate the average number of copies sold in each thousand orders. It is interesting to notice that the best seller of the group is *What Married Women Should Know*, and that the books for women outsell those for men. This holds true, in general, for all of my advertising. To some people this may indicate that women are more interested in securing authentic information of this kind than men. But in another place I have pointed out that from most indications men are the best buyers of Little Blue Books, and I rather think that men buy these books of facts for women as well as those addressed more particularly to themselves. I see no reason why both men and women should not read all of the books, and I am quite sure that this interest in the opposite sex explains the larger sale of the books for women.

As to whether men actually do buy more Little Blue Books than women, I have taken the trouble to find out. A careful tabulation of the orders received shows that seventy-one percent come from men and only twenty-nine percent from women. Elsewhere I have pointed out how women's magazines seldom pay out for Little Blue Books advertising, and I explained that this was probably the reason. The legend that women do most of the reading in America must be founded upon something apart from the Little Blue Books if it is to be something more than a legend. For these facts are indisputable – the Little Blue Books do depend on men for their greatest support. Mr. Fielding's *What Women Past Forty Should Know* is among the 100 best sellers for every magazine except the *Nation*, where it sold only sixty copies in a thousand orders. This seems to indicate that most of the readers of the *Nation* are men, for this is a book that men are not likely to be interested in. The average figure for this book in all the mediums is 100, which is hardly more than half the sale of any of the books listed above. It sold best in the *N. Y. Times*, 200 copies in 1,000 orders; next best in the *Graphic*, 130.

Gloria Goddard's *Confidential Chats With Wives* is a better seller than Dr. Wilfrid Lay's *Confidential Chats With Husbands*, in all the magazines except *Harper's*, where these two books were not advertised, in the ratio of ninety to seventy out of a thousand orders. They sold best in *Smart Set* (140 for Wives, 150 for Husbands) and *Liberty* (150 for Wives; 110 for Husbands).

Interest in marriage centered itself in the wide publicity now being given companionate marriage, as advocated by Judge Ben B. Lindsey. The book called *Judge Lindsey on Companionate Marriage* is among the 100 best sellers for *Harper's*, *N. Y. Times*, *Nation*, *Smart Set*, and *Liberty*. Its average sale was 160; its best sale was 300 in the *Nation*; its worst was 50 in the *Pathfinder*, though it sold only 60 in the *Graphic*. Readers of the last two publications can therefore be regarded as less abreast of the times in that they do not know about or do not care to know about companionate marriage. The sale of this book in the *Nation* shows clearly, too, that the readers of this progressive weekly are thoroughly wide-awake to what is going on in modern movements toward improving social welfare and individual happiness.

The book by my wife, Marcet Haldeman-Julius, called *Why I Believe in Companionate Marriage*, was also a best seller in the *Nation*, though not as good as the Lindsey book, selling only 110 copies in a thousand orders. The next best figure is 100 for *Harper's*. The worst is 20 for the *Graphic*, though *Smart Set* readers bought only 30 copies in every thousand orders when they bought 220 of the Lindsey book. The average for all seven magazines is 70. Thus I say again that it is never possible to predict what a book may do, or where it may sell the best.

Another book with interesting figures is Clement Wood's rather humorous book called *The Art of Kissing*, which sold an average of 170. The actual figures for each publication are: *Smart Set* – 350; *Harper's* – 200; *Nation* – 160; *Liberty* – 150; *Graphic* – 140; *Pathfinder* – 100; *N. Y. Times* – 80. The younger readers of *Smart Set* can explain that total, but how about staid and sober *Harper's*? And how is it that *Liberty* is fourth in the list? And *Pathfinder* actually displayed more interest in kissing than the *N. Y. Times*. Such are the vagaries of human inclinations. Mr. Wood's companion book, called *The Art of Courtship*, sold an average of only 60, as did also *Jokes and Clever Sayings About Kissing*. The latter book, by the way, went up to the phenomenal figure of 130 in the *Graphic*, practically equaling the sale of *The Art of Kissing*.

Fielding's *The Child's Sex Life* is among the 100 best sellers in only two publications: *Graphic* and *Smart Set*, each with ninety sales in a thousand orders. Dr. Reed's *What Expectant Mothers Should Know* is a best seller only in the *N. Y. Times* – 90, *Graphic* – 100, *Nation* – 80, and *Harpers* – 90. Freud on *Sleep and Sexual Dreams* leaps to prominence in startling fashion: N. Y. Times – 250; *Pathfinder* – 60; *Graphic* – 300; *Liberty* – 190; *Nation* – 150; *Smart Set* – 300; it was not advertised in *Harper's*. Havelock Ellis' *Love Rights of Women* is also interesting: *N. Y. Times* – 120; *Pathfinder* – 50; *Graphic* – 110; *Liberty* – 40; *Nation* – 130; *Harpers* – 110; *Smart Set* – 130.

The two books available on birth control – which is to say discussions of it pro and con, since specific contraceptive information is prohibited by law – show a wide-spread interest in the subject. A comparison is best shown by parallel figures, as follows:

Publication	Debate on Birth Control	Aspects of Birth Control
N. Y. Times	110	160
Pathfinder	30	50
N. Y. Graphic	120	350
Liberty	90	80
Nation	80	30
Smart Set	50	120
Harper's	Omitted	Omitted
Total Copies Sold	480	590

The *Nation* is the only periodical whose readers show a marked preference for the controversial side of the subject. The greater interest in the *aspects* is, I fear, due to a vain hope that the book may contain hints or at least some slightly veiled information, when it is obvious that a debate will not contain any details whatever.

The emphatic interest in sex, no matter what the phase, and regardless of the author of the work, is evidenced again by Theodore Dreiser's *America and the Sex Impulse*, certainly the best selling Little Blue Book of the trio he has in the list. This title, in fact, reaches some rather astonishing figures: *N. Y. Times* – 140; *Pathfinder* – 40; *Graphic* – 130; *Liberty* – 100; *Nation* – 130; *Harper's* – 100; *Smart Set* – 80. Even Clement Wood's *Modern Sexual Morality*, which is wholly argumentative and rather abstract, shows these results: *N. Y. Times* – 60; *Pathfinder* – 20; *Graphic* – 120; *Liberty* – 60; *Nation* – 120; *Smart Set* – 150; *Harper's*, not advertised.

Wickedness, or what people regard as wicked, even when it is only the history of wickedness, has undoubted attraction. It is the lure, naturally, of forbidden fruit, more often than a genuine interest in understanding the circumstances the better to know life thoroughly and enjoy it sanely. Still, though the interest is in forbidden fruit, the books that people buy in my University of Print will inevitably give them the facts, and thereby induce an interest in the facts. I am confident that there is no false coloring, no misleading evasion, in any books I print. That is why I consider the large interest in prostitution healthful rather than otherwise, for it is clear that the series of histories of prostitution, written especially for the Little Blue Books by Leo Markun, are among the best sellers nearly everywhere. Witness these figures:

Publication	Ancient Prostitution	Medieval Prostitution	Modern Prostitution
N. Y. Times	160	140	210
N. Y. Graphic	120	140	200
Nation	130	80	150
Smart Set	220	180	230
Total Copies Sold	**630**	**540**	**790**

These three books were not advertised in *Pathfinder*, *Nation*, or *Harper's*. The interest increases, understandably, as one nears modern times. And yet a book called *Sex Life in Greece and Rome*, though this may be due to a prevalent notion that Greece and Rome were immoral, sold like this: *N. Y. Times* – 160; *Pathfinder* – 50; *Graphic* – 130; *Liberty* – 60; *Nation* – 50; *Harper's* – 80; *Smart Set* – 210.

Even books about men and women, without stressing sex or love, create widespread interest and bring in hundreds of orders. In particular it is interesting to observe the figures for two books of quotations from great men and women writers, as follows:

232

A Comparison Of Advertising Mediums

Publication	What Great Men Learned About Women	What Great Women Learned About Men
N. Y. Times	60	70
Pathfinder	40	50
N. Y. Graphic	80	80
Liberty	60	30
Nation	70	50
Smart Set	140	130
Harper's	40	130
Total of Copies Sold	**490**	**560**

As usual, the women have it. This is substantiated by the success of a fairly new book called *What Frenchwomen Have Learned About Love*, which sold like this: *N. Y. Times* – 80; *Pathfinder* – 50; *Graphic* – 110; *Nation* – 50; *Liberty* – 70; *Harper's* – 140; *Smart Set* – 170.

I should point out here that the people *will* have sex in some form or other in their reading, and if they cannot get it as specific as they wish, they will take what they can get. The larger totals of some of the milder books in such magazines as *Harper's* prove this. If the readers are given a choice between a mild title and a sensational title, they will nearly always take the latter if they can't afford to buy both. If they can have only the mild title, they will take it rather than nothing. It is human nature.

Before passing to other subjects, I want to say that the largest lists of books were advertised in *Liberty*, *N. Y. Times*, and *Graphic*. I have been especially interested to notice that only one classification or group of titles in *Liberty* has a 100 percent sale – which is to say that not a title under this classification showed zero. This classification was PASSION. Even books that would not have sold if listed miscellaneously, sold extremely well when placed under this heading. These are the books so classified, with their sales figures:

Book Title	Sales Figure
A Nun's Desire and Other Poems	220
Mme. Tellier's Establishment. Maupassant	200
Passion in the Desert. Balzac	190
Amorous Tales of the Monks	180
Lustful King Enjoys Himself. Hugo	130
Quest for a Blonde Mistress	170
The Falcon, etc. Boccaccio	160
Sex Obsessions of Saints	150
Night in Whitechapel. Maupassant	140
Short Stories of French Life	140
Amateur Peasant Girl. Pushkin	130
A Bath, and so forth Emile Zola	130
Italian Tales of Passion	130
Unconventional Amour. Moore	120
Lost Phoebe Theodore Dreiser	110
Wages of Sin. W. D. Steele	100
Brazilian Love Stories. Lobato	90
Girl with 3 Husbands, etc	80
Policewoman's Daughter. Hecht	70
Jazz, etc. Ben Hecht	70
Polite Parisian Scandals	70
Hedda Gabler. Ibsen	70
Montes: Matador and Lover. Harris	60
Love's Heroism and Other Tales	50
Happy Hypocrite's Love-Life	50
Smart Epigrams. De Gourmont	40

All those over sixty are in the 100 best sellers for *Liberty*, which gives this classification outstanding importance. The heading PASSION is responsible, I know, because some of these titles, listed thus, do better than more sensational titles listed elsewhere.

For example, if Boccaccio's *The Falcon* were placed in competition with his *Illicit Love and Other Stories*, without any other description, the latter would do better. As it is, the former sold 160 against the latter's 130, which is truly amazing, for there is nothing suggesting love or sex in *The Falcon*. Similarly, Ibsen's *Doll's House* is zero, as against *Hedda Gabler's* 70, but the former is usually the better seller. Again, of Guy de Maupassant's books, *A Wife's Confession* is usually up for first honors, but in this advertisement it sold only 110; while *A French Prostitute's Sacrifice*, always a sensational seller, did only 140, as compared with 140 and 200 for the two Maupassant titles listed under PASSION. Likewise, Dreiser's *Lost Phoebe* just outdistances his *America and the Sex Impulse*, by 110 against 100, which is unheard of. It is the heading or classification that does it – such headings are an important part of my advertising.

It is significant, too, that the best seller under the listing PASSION is a book of poems – entirely because the title is the most sensational. Even poetry, generally a difficult form of reading to sell, will be clamored for if it is linked up with sex or love or their manifestations.

Incidentally, the classifications FAMOUS LOVERS and WOMEN do less well, on the whole, than might be expected. Casanova, for example, does not arouse interest unless his amorous reputation is known. *Casanova: History's Greatest Lover* shows these revealing figures; as compared with other famous lovers, better or less known, as the case may be:

Publication	Casanova	Cleopatra	Catherine the Great	Madame du Barry	Abelard & Heloise
N. Y. Times	60	60	50	80	10
Pathfinder	10	80	10	60	0
N. Y. Graphic	40	150	100	70	20
Liberty	20	30	30	50	0
Nation	150	60	60	50	40
Harper's	N/A	90	80	90	100
Smart Set	N/A	N/A	N/A	150	N/A

Casanova and Abelard with his Heloise sell best among the more educated readers of the *Nation* and *Harper's*. The women, once more, do best of all. The omission of most of these FAMOUS LOVERS titles from the *Smart Set*, I should explain, was not due to censorship, but to lack of space – only one page was used in this magazine.

Even in matters of health the sex interest dominates, for instead of general rules of health, the people prefer to buy a book that tells them how to take care of their skin and hair – in other words, they put the emphasis on external appearance. Sex rejuvenation, of course, and sex physiology, with books about venereal diseases, also take the lead. These are authentic medical books, written by recognized physicians, under the general supervision of Dr. Morris Fishbein of the American Medical Association. This is the way these books compare:

Publication	General Health Rules	Care of Skin and Hair	Sexual Rejuvination	Venereal Diseases	Syphilis
N. Y. Times	60	80	130	80	30
Pathfinder	50	70	60	50	20
N. Y. Graphic	60	N/A	110	180	100
Liberty	20	50	90	70	30
Nation	10	70	N/A	110	80
Harper's	30	N/A	N/A	N/A	N/A
Smart Set	N/A	N/A	90	90	70

Interest in other phases of health and other diseases is not as universal, as is shown by these figures from the periodicals in which the books were advertised:

Publication	Cancer	Diabetes	Tuberculosis	Teeth	Medicine Patent
N. Y. Times	40	20	20	20	0
Pathfinder	40	30	30	40	0
Liberty	0	10	10	0	10
Nation	0	0	10	10	10
Total Copies Sold	80	60	70	70	20

This interest in sex will be found to run through all other subjects, for even when we come to humor and jokes, there are jokes about lovers, kissing, married life, and so forth. The general collections of jokes have these figures.

Publication	Kissing Jokes	Married Life Jokes	Lover Jokes	Ford Jokes	Drunk Jokes	College Jokes
N.Y. Times	50	30	40	30	30	70
Pathfinder	60	60	40	20	20	20
N. Y. Graphic	130	110	90	20	40	40
Liberty	40	40	50	10	20	30
Nation	50	50	30	10	30	40
Harper's	20	70	40	10	0	40
Smart Set	90	90	100	90	30	20
Total Copies Sold	440	450	390	190	170	260

When it comes to nationalities and humor, the Irish have it. Proverbial Irish wit has made itself famous around the world, and here is the indisputable evidence:

Publication	Irish Jokes	Black Jokes	American Jokes	Jewish Jokes	Scottish Jokes	Yankee Jokes	Rube Jokes	Hobo Jokes	Totals
N.Y. Times	100	60	70	170	100	60	20	70	650
Pathfinder	150	60	60	60	60	30	20	10	450
N. Y. Graphic	50	30	90	70	40	70	20	40	410
Liberty	30	10	20	30	60	20	0	20	190
Nation	20	50	30	n/a	30	20	10	70	230
Harper's	100	50	30	50	90	30	20	10	380
Smart Set	90	90	40	60	100	20	20	30	420
Total Copies Sold	540	320	340	440	480	250	110	250	

It is amusing to notice the popularity of Jewish jokes among the readers of the *N. Y. Times*, a popularity that extends somewhat to the readers of the *N. Y. Graphic*, as well. But the Irish win the vote, beyond any question, and the Jews and the Scots come next. Though the last two columns are not nationalities, I listed them for comparison. There is comparatively little interest, it appears, in rube jokes – the metropolitan readers of *Liberty*, in fact, evince no interest whatever, and *Pathfinder*, going to small towns and rural districts, shows as much interest as any. One fact, not in the table, is that Best German Humor is among the 100 best sellers in the *Nation*. What this means, however, I cannot say.

Suppose we next look to the jokes about the professions, and see which of our professional classes provides the most fun for the masses:

Publication	Jokes About Doctors	Jokes About Lawyers	Jokes About Preachers	Total of Copies Sold
N.Y. Times	70	60	50	180
Pathfinder	80	60	30	170
N. Y. Graphic	90	60	30	180
Liberty	20	0	10	30
Nation	50	90	30	170
Harper's	20	50	40	110
Smart Set	30	40	50	120
Total Copies Sold	360	360	240	

The conclusion to be drawn, it seems, is that people like to laugh at themselves, or at their competitors, for it is assumable that lawyers are found largely among readers of the *Nation* and *Harper's*, although it may not be true that doctors particularly favor the *Graphic*. A craving for humor is not strong among readers of *Liberty*, as is shown by both this and the foregoing table. A liking for jokes, as a matter of fact, seems to be most compelling among readers of the *N. Y. Times*.

Even tastes for humor vary widely, at times, however. Besides the collections of jokes already listed, of which those seventy or over are among the 100 best sellers in the *N. Y. Times,* the 100 best sellers for this paper also include the *Popular Jokebook* (80), *Humor of Lincoln* (80), and *Best Jokes of 1926* (90). *Pathfinder* has among its 100 best sellers, in addition to those sixty or over in the preceding tables, *Toasts for All Occasions* (140), *Best Jokes of 1926* (100), *Popular Jokebook* (70), *Funny Ghost Stories* (80), and Mark Twain's *Answers to Correspondents* (120). The *N. Y. Graphic,* besides those eighty or over in the preceding tabulations, includes among its 100 best sellers *Humorous Anecdotes* (80), *Broadway Wisecracks* (90). *Liberty* has only the following in its 100 best sellers that can be classed as evidence of a sense of humor: *Best Jokes of 1926* (60), *Scotch Jokes* (60), *Funny Ghost Stories* (60), *Toasts for All Occasions* (100), and Mark Twain's *English As She Is Spoke* (70). Readers of *Harper's* show a wider choice, for besides those already mentioned as eighty or over, they picked out these: Mark Twain's *English As She Is Spoke* (100), *Toasts for All Occasions* (120), Stephen Leacock's *Ridiculous Stories* (120) and also his *Funny Dramatics* (100), and the *Humor of Lincoln* (90) – all of which must be included in the 100 best sellers for the *Harper's.* Readers of the *Smart Set* insist that *Masterpieces of American Wit* (100) be among their 100 best sellers, together with *Popular Jokebook* (130), *Toasts for All Occasions* (180), Mark Twain's *Answers to Correspondents* (130), and *Best Jokes of 1926* (140), with any in the preceding tables that show a figure of ninety or over.

Interest in self-improvement and self-education manifests itself chiefly in a strong desire to better one's English – to speak well, pronounce correctly, spell according to the dictionary, and so on. The books under the classification Better English are all good sellers. Best of all are those on conversation and improving vocabulary. Here are the figures so you may compare them:

Publication	How To Improve Conversation	How To Improve Vocabulary	Spelling Self Taught	Grammer Self Taught	Punctuation Self Taught
N.Y. Times	200	190	110	200	160
Pathfinder	150	90	60	120	100
N. Y. Graphic	140	140	60	80	60
Liberty	180	100	30	60	70
Nation	90	40	20	40	60
Harper's	160	120	80	130	120
Smart Set	220	160	90	100	90
Total Copies Sold	1140	840	450	730	660

Publication	Rhetoric Self Taught	Composition Self Taught	Book of Useful Phrases	Most Essential English Words	Common Faults in English
N.Y. Times	110	110	160	150	150
Pathfinder	0	10	80	30	90
N. Y. Graphic	40	60	110	110	70
Liberty	50	60	90	60	120
Nation	10	10	60	40	50
Harper's	60	50	110	80	110
Smart Set	80	50	110	110	140
Totals	350	350	720	580	730

240

A Comparison Of Advertising Mediums

Publication	American Slang Dictionary	Book of Synonyms	Words Often Mispronounced	How To Pronounce Proper Names	How To Write Letters
N.Y. Times	140	100	170	110	140
Pathfinder	50	60	40	40	50
N.Y. Graphic	110	50	100	70	260
Liberty	120	90	90	20	90
Nation	50	50	40	10	10
Harper's	70	150	120	120	50
Smart Set	160	140	70	50	150
Totals	610	640	630	420	750

From these figures it is clear that there is a feverish interest in our mother tongue throughout the reading range of these seven publications. Readers of the *Nation* are least interested, first of all, I daresay because many are well educated. Indeed, only one of the Better English books is numbered among the *Nation*'s 100 best sellers, and that is *How to Improve Your Conversation*. The *Pathfinder* also shows low figures, but this is partly because the selections of *Pathfinder* readers are spread over the widest variety of titles. Those sixty or over are among the 100 best sellers for *Pathfinder*, and these are also in this popular 100: *Hints on Public Speaking* – 90, and *Hints on Writing Short Stories* – 200.

The popularity of the *Book of Synonyms* is really astonishing – this book has always been one of the best sellers in the series. It is hard to explain, unless people associate it with improving their vocabulary, for there is certainly a universal passion for improving vocabularies if the sales of Little Blue Books are any indication. The interest in the *Dictionary of American Slang* is probably as much curiosity as any desire for self-improvement, but the book is listed under Better English, which proves the attractiveness of this classification.

An interesting variation is shown by *Smart Set* readers, for among the

241

100 best sellers for this magazine is *Hints on Writing Poetry*, which sold 100 copies in 1,000 orders. Of the books listed in the preceding tabulations, those selling ninety or over are among the *Smart Set*'s 100 best sellers. Also among the favored 100 are *Foreign Words and Phrases* – 110, *How to Talk and Debate* – 100, *The Romance of Words* – 90, and *Hints on Public Speaking* – 90. But the interest in writing poetry is the most remarkable, for this is the only magazine where this book sold at all well. It is probably due to the younger element in this magazine's readers; the next nearest periodicals for this book are the *N. Y. Times* and the *Graphic*, the readers of both of these buying thirty copies in each thousand orders.

Readers of the *N. Y. Graphic*, on the other hand, showed the most interest in *How to Write Business Letters*, selling 120 in every thousand orders. All books running eighty or over are in the *Graphic*'s 100 best sellers. This also includes *How to Talk and Debate* (180), and *How to Argue Logically* (90). Readers of this tabloid are evidently desirous of improving their ability to aid the progress of business, for the next nearest competitor on this book is the *N. Y. Times* at ninety. The *Times*, however, backs up its interest with *How to Make Money in Wall Street* among its 100 best sellers at eighty – a book that sold only thirty to every thousand *Graphic* readers, forty to every thousand readers of the *Nation*, and only twenty to every thousand *Liberty* readers who ordered Little Blue Books.

Of related interest is the series of Little Blue Books teaching foreign languages, together with pocket foreign-language dictionaries, easy readings, and so forth *French Self Taught* (80) is among the 100 *Times*' best sellers and, also *Liberty*'s 100 best (70), but *Spanish Self Taught* (90) is among the 100 best for *Pathfinder*. These are the only two periodicals that showed a foreign-language book among the 100 best sellers. The general result is as follows:

A Comparison Of Advertising Mediums

Publication	German	French	Spanish	Italian	Latin
N.Y. Times	30	80	10	40	70
Pathfinder	40	60	90	60	10
Liberty	10	70	50	10	20
Nation	30	30	20	20	20
Total of Copies Sold	110	240	170	130	120

General books of self-improvement and education are in demand also. John Cowper Powys' essay, *The Secret of Self-Development*, is among the 100 best sellers of *Harper's* (80), and the *N. Y. Graphic* (90). Thomas Huxley's *How to Get a Liberal Education* is likewise a best seller in the *Graphic*, at seventy in each thousand orders; it is also a best seller in the *Pathfinder* at sixty. The *Graphic*, however, is the only publication where *How to Work Your Way Through College* sells at all, where it is bought at the rate of forty copies in every thousand orders. These tabloid readers are far from hopeless, my friends! *Graphic* readers, indeed, buy *How to Conquer Stupidity* at the rate of eighty per thousand orders, pulling the book among the 100 best sellers for this paper. In this popular 100 for the *Graphic* also are these: *Is Life Worth Living?* – 100, *Facts You Should Know About Will Power* – 120, *How to Improve Memory* – 120, and *The Conquest of Fear* – 120. I wonder what this will signify to those who are aghast at the state of American culture. These readers are trying hard, at any rule, to better themselves.

As a matter of fact, readers of the *Graphic* buy twenty-two percent self-educational books when given their choice. This is the most of any of the seven publications we are discussing, except the *N. Y. Times* and *Pathfinder*, each of which is thirty-one percent. Numbered among the *Graphic's* 100 best sellers will also be found a book of philosophy, *Story of Nietzsche's Philosophy*, by Will Durant (130); a book of psychology, *Mental Differences Between Men and Women* (110); two books of poetry, *Rubaiyat of Omar Khayyem* (90) and *Dante's Inferno* (80). These people are even seeking to free themselves from religious bigotry and superstition, for their 100 most popular titles include Thomas Paine's *Age of Reason* (80), *Self-Contradic-*

tions of the Bible (80), Joseph McCabe's *Degradation of Woman* (100), and Ingersoll's *Reasons for Doubting the Inspiration of the Bible* (110).

No doubt many righteous people will be horrified at the sale of these heretical books. But the facts are that the readers want to get at the facts, and if they are given a chance to buy the books they will order and read them. It is true that more books on religious controversy are sold to readers of the *Nation* than to any other group, but this is to be expected. What is more interesting is that readers of the conventional publications are also buying such books, and buying them in appreciable quantities. An undercurrent of freethought and skepticism is, judging from my sales figures for Little Blue Books, running through the country among people of all classes. Look at these figures:

Publication	Bible Contradictions	Age of Reason	Reasons for Doubting Bible	Why I Am An Infidel	Totals
N.Y. Times	30	10	40	40	**120**
Pathfinder	0	20	50	10	**80**
N. Y. Graphic	80	80	110	80	**350**
Liberty	40	50	60	40	**190**
Nation	100	60	150	130	**440**
Harper's	110	140	80	130	**460**
Total Copies Sold	**360**	**360**	**490**	**430**	**1640**

When I see figures like these I am for the people who read the *Graphic*. They show more gusto and progressiveness than the sober readers of the *N. Y. Times*, for while the *Times*' readers are afraid to face honest doubts, readers of the *Graphic* courageously try to find out the facts – there you have it, 350 out of every thousand *Graphic* readers buying these four skeptical books as against only 120 out of every thousand of the *N. Y. Times*. Luther Burbank's *Why I Am an Infidel*, by the way, is one of my very best sellers – a fact that I like to think about and dream over, for to me it tells much of the future of human thought and progress. It makes the pessimism of Maynard Shipley's *War on Modern Science*, for example, a little easier to bear. Skeptical books were, I am sorry to say, omitted from the *Smart Set* for lack of space, but I feel sure that *Smart Set*'s younger readers would have bought them avidly.

We can pass easily from freethought to the great thinkers of the world, the philosophers about whom Will Durant wrote in his best-selling *Story of Philosophy* – which also sells well in Little Blue Book form. What do the sales figures for the little Blue Books have to say about the popularity of philosophy in America? Here are some figures for some of the world's outstanding thinkers, as computed from the sales totals of the Little Blue Books about them:

Publication	Nietzsche	Schopenhauer	Plato	Voltaire	Spinoza	Aristotle
N.Y. Times	70	50	60	60	70	50
Pathfinder	0	0	20	30	0	0
N. Y. Graphic	130	70	40	N/A	50	70
Liberty	80	10	40	10	20	20
Nation	80	120	20	80	90	80
Harper's	230	190	170	N/A	220	200
Total Copies Sold	**590**	**440**	**350**	**180**	**450**	**420**

Publication	Bergson	Emerson	Bacon	Spencer	Kant
N.Y. Times	50	20	20	20	90
Pathfinder	10	50	0	0	0
N.Y. Graphic	50	N/A	10	70	70
Liberty	10	0	20	0	20
Nation	80	0	30	30	90
Total Copies Sold	390	70	240	280	490

The moral of all the above is that if you want to sell philosophy advertise it in *Harper's*. Your next best bet would be the *Nation* and, strange though it may seem, the next is the *N. Y. Graphic*, a tabloid. For, considering that two of these philosophical titles were omitted, the *Graphic* beats the *Times* though both total 560 above. Nietzsche attracts the most readers, but Schopenhauer follows close after him, and the interest in other philosophers is much larger than one might think. Even readers of the *Pathfinder* are not hopeless, though they are handicapped by a lack of classical education, for among *Pathfinder's* 100 best sellers is *Chinese Philosophy of Life* to the tune of 100 copies in every thousand orders.

To digress for a moment to a few individual titles, there is one that is on the list of best sellers for all of these publications except the *Nation*. This is *Party Games for Grown-Ups*, with these figures: *N. Y. Times* – 80, *Pathfinder* – 200, *N. Y. Graphic* – 100, *Liberty* – 90, *Nation* – 40, *Harper's* – 110, *Smart Set* – 100. The consistent popularity of this book speaks well for the good disposition of humanity at large for there is evidently a universal desire for passing away the time happily in all kinds of good fun.

Another consistent best seller is Esther Floyd's *Hints on Etiquette*, which has these figures: *N. Y. Times* – 110, *Pathfinder* – 40, *N. Y. Graphic* – 80, *Liberty* – 80, *Nation* – 70, *Harper's* – 50, *Smart Set* – 50. It seems that the rural readers of *Pathfinder* have not so much need for etiquette, while perhaps the readers of *Harper's* already feel proficient in its conventions, and the youngsters of the *Smart Set* are not yet ready for it. I offer these guesses merely to explain the lower figures for these publications; the book is a good seller in all, nevertheless.

I am especially interested in the figures for *Facts You Should Know About the Classics*, because this is a new title replacing Albert Mordell's book, *Dante and Other Waning Classics*, which was a failure. The change in title made a good seller out of a bad one, so I had Joseph McCabe write a new book to fit the new title. This title brought these results: *N. Y. Times* – 70, *Pathfinder* – 40, *N. Y. Graphic* – 10, *Liberty* – 30, *Nation* – 60, *Harper's* 130; *Smart Set*, omitted. Apparently classics do not seem practical to readers of the *Graphic*, but they appeal strongly to readers of *Harper's*.

The greatest interest in miscellaneous fiction, particularly of the detective and adventure sort, is shown by readers of *Pathfinder*. This must be because time passes slowly in rural regions, and good reading is perhaps difficult to obtain. At any rate, the following belong in *Pathfinder's* list of 100 best sellers, with the figures noted:

Book Title	Copies Sold
Sherlock Holmes Tales. Conan Doyle (70 each of 4 different titles of Holmes stories)	280
A Bath, etc. Emile Zola	140
One of Cleopatra's Nights. Gautier	130
Voyage to the Moon. Jules Verne	110
Adventure Stories. Jack London	110
Girl with Three Husbands, etc	100
Quest for a Blonde Mistress	100
Mark of the Beast. Kipling	90
Tales of Far North. Jack London	90
Five Weeks in Balloon, Jules Verne	90
Tales of Terror and Wonder	90
Adventures of Kit Carson	90
A Wife's Confession. Maupassant	90
Book of Real Adventurese	80
Mysteries of Egypt's Pyramid	80

Book Title	Copies Sold
Gruesome Tales. E. A. Poe	80
On the Bum: Tramp Life Sketches	80
Carmen: Adventure Story. Merimee	80
Great Sea Stories	70
Battles of Seamen. Capt. Marryat	70
Great Pirates and Their Deeds	70
Great Detective Stories	70
Dr. Jekyll and Mr. Hyde. Stevenson	60
Great Ghost Stories	60

Consistent with this interest in adventure, *Camping, Woodcraft, Wildcraft* (70) is also among *Pathfinder*'s 100 Best, and likewise *How to Know the Songbirds* (100).

Before passing on to some of the peculiar choices of other publications, I should point out that *Pathfinder*'s 100 best sellers also include the following: *How to Tie Knots* – 100, *How to Make Candy* – 110, *Familiar Quotations* – 110, *500 Riddles* – 110, *How to Think Logically* – 90, *Popular Recitations* – 110, *Lives of U. S. Presidents* – 100, *Puzzles and Brainteasers* – 120, *Speeches of Lincoln* – 80, *Sailor Shanties and Cowboy Songs* – 80, *Interior Decoration for Small Homes* – 80, *Dictionary of Authors* – 80, *Amateur Magic Tricks* – 70, *How to Play Checkers* – 70, and so forth. You can, if you consider these judicially, discern a rural inclination all through – some of these are books that people are likely to buy in the outlying country districts.

Turning to the younger readers of the *Smart Set*, and the 100 best sellers they have selected, we find them also interested in *How to Make Candy*, to the extent of 200 copies in every thousand orders. They picked out from Wilbur Daniel Steele's trio, *A Devil of a Fellow* – 100, and they expressed a strong wish to read Kipling's *Without Benefit of Clergy* – 130. Their interest also centered itself in *The Truth About N. Y.'s Chinatown* – 120, *Beginning Married Life Right* – 100, *The Charming Hostess* – 90, *How to Play Card Games* – 90, and *Genetics for Beginners* – 90, all of which is more hopeful than otherwise.

A Comparison Of Advertising Mediums

I have already had a great deal to say about the readers of *Liberty*. As final clean-up data at hand, I can add that they picked out, among their 100 Best, Jack London's *Son of a Wolf* – 80, Fielding's *Puzzle of Personality* – 70, Kipling's *Gunga Din* – 70, both *Crossword Puzzle Books* – 70 each, *Handbook of Commercial Law* – 70, *Mathematical Oddities* – 60, and so forth. *Liberty* is the only medium in which the crossword puzzles were so popular as to be among the 100 best sellers. This is perhaps due to the fact that *Liberty* has run, for a long time, a weekly puzzle as part of its editorial content.

Of the *N. Y. Times* much can be said. In general, it has always been an excellent medium through which to sell Little Blue Books. In addition to titles already mentioned elsewhere in this chapter, however, the following of the 100 best sellers are significant: *Mystery of the Man in the Iron Mask* – 100, *Mary, Queen of Scots* – 100, *Louis XVI and His Corrupt Court* – 90, *Shelley and His Loves* – 90, *Familiar Quotations* – 100, *Facts About Fortune-Telling* – 90, Ibsen's *Doll House* – 80, *Facts About Architecture* – 80, *Memories of Sarah Bernhardt* – 80, *Memoirs of Madame de Stael* – 80, Dante's *Inferno* – 70, and so on.

Characteristic of what has been said about the readers of the *Nation* are the following additional citations from the 100 best sellers: Maeterlinck's *Pelleas and Melisande* – 90, Bertrand Russell's *What Can a Free Man Worship?* – 200, Frank Harris' *Daughter of Eve* – 100, Joseph McCabe's *Phallicism in Religion* – 100, Bierce's *Debunking Tales* – 100, McCabe's *Did Jesus Ever Live?* – 130, Harris' *A Mad Love* – 90, *Luther Burbank's Funeral Oration*, by Judge Lindsey – 80, Clarence Darrow's *Voltaire Lecture* – 80, *Behaviorism, Newest Psychology* – 100, Darrow's *Debate on Capital Punishment* – 80, *Astronomy for Beginners* – 80, McCabe's *World's Great Religions* – 80, Dumas' *Crimes of the Borgias* – 70, Upton Sinclair's *Naturewoman* – 70, Darrow's *Is Mankind Progressing?* – 70, McCabe's *Horrors of the Inquisition* – 70, McCabe's *Seven Infidel U. S. Presidents* – 70, McCabe's *The Dark Ages* – 60, and so forth. The strong interest in Behaviorism may be due in part to the recent series emphasizing it that ran for a time in the *Nation*. Special considerations like this, when known, sometimes explain what might otherwise be mystifying preferences shown by readers of different periodicals.

Of the *N. Y. Graphic* I have probably said sufficient. However, I must take a sentence to say that *How to Teach Yourself to Swim* is in the *Graphic's* list of 100 best sellers, with 110 sold in every thousand orders. It is not in any other list of best sellers.

Coming finally to *Harper's*, I notice a strong interest in psychology, more consistently displayed than in any of the other publications I have here discussed. These titles, for example, are among the 100 best sellers: *Psycho-Analysis Explained* – 120, *How to Psycho-Analyze Yourself* – 120, *The Psychology of Leadership* – 100, *Behaviorism* – 120, *Psychology of Character Building* – 100, *Sex Symbolism* – 90, *Psychology for Beginners* – 80, and so forth. Evidently psychology and philosophy, before mentioned, are excellent subjects to advertise in *Harper's*.

Harper's is the only one of these seven publications, too, where books giving the facts about palmistry (160), astrology (100), and fortune-telling (70) are excellent sellers. There is a strong interest in entertainment of all kinds, it seems, for *Curiosities of Mathematics* (160) and *Mathematical Oddities*, (100), are both best sellers. Others on the favored list of 100 are: Dante's *Inferno* – 140, *Cellini, Swordsman, Lover, Sinner* – 100, Hecht's *Tales of Chicago Streets* – 120, Bierce's *Devil's Dictionary* – 120, McCabe's *Did Jesus Ever Live?* – 100, *Marriage and Morals in Soviet Russia* – 90, *Love Letters of a Parisian Actress* – 90, *Memoirs of Madame de Stael* – 90, H. G. Wells' *Stolen Bacillus and Other Stories* – 90, McCabe's *Phallicism in Religion* – 90, *Speeches of Lincoln* – 80, Kipling's *Vampire* – 80, Kipling's *Mulvaney Stories* – 80, and so forth.

I have taken particular pains in these last wholesale listings of best sellers to select titles that are peculiar to the magazine cited – by which I mean titles that are not best sellers (limited to 100 for each publication) in the other six. I thus indicate partially some of the peculiarities, some of the special choices made by different groups of readers.

In summing up, I do not wish anyone to emphasize too much these differences – for these figures are necessarily limited. Though a book is not among the 100 best sellers, it may sell well enough to pay to advertise it in a given publication. In general, when the choice is spread over a large group, it is possible to advertise a list of 500 good sellers in all seven of these publications, without any change of emphasis for any one of them apart from the others, and get substantially the same results. It is true, however, that in a larger assortment, readers of *Pathfinder* would be more interested in detective and adventure books than in philosophy, while readers of *Harper's* would like to have more philosophy and psychology. Readers of the *Nation* would like more controversial subjects, particularly books giving the facts about religion. And so on. All of them, I repeat, want books dealing in some way with sex, or love, or marriage. That is perhaps the only general conclusion that can be drawn from the statistics I have here presented. But I add to it a growing interest in skepticism and free thought – otherwise how is it possible to explain the success of the Little Blue Books, which lean strongly toward rationalism, and yet have sold over 100,000,000 copies in the past nine years?

Three things – three main subject classifications – I would name as the trio that will encompass most of the interest displayed by the readers of these seven publications, if taken *en masse*. They want Sex, which includes love, marriage, passion, men, women, birth control, and so forth, Self-education and Self-improvement, which includes bettering their English, educating themselves in particular subjects, philosophy, psychology, and so forth, and Free-thought or Skepticism, which means releasing themselves from the fetters of superstition, religious bigotry, and theological dogmatism. Perhaps, however, I should put on a par with Free-thought the widespread desire for fun and laughter – which includes jokes, games, sports, and so forth But if I increase the trio to these four – Sex, Self-improvement, Free-thought, and Entertainment – I am sure that I cover ninety percent of the reading interests of America.

CHAPTER XVII
THE PASSING OF
THE SALES POLICY

Why the Little Blue Books No Longer Need Date-Line Sales

For a little over eight years the Little Blue Books were in an experimental state. Then, for the first time, a clear way began to appear toward something more dependable, toward something established. By experimental I mean that the Little Blue Books, for at least eight years, were fighting their way toward real commercial success. The goal was not quite reached, perhaps, during 1927 – a peak year with a total distribution of 21,000,000 books – but as 1928 opens I can assert with great confidence that the experimental period during which *date-line sales* were a necessity has passed.

No date-line advertising copy – by which I mean advertising that gives a definite closing-date, before which all orders must be mailed in order to get the benefit of the sale – has been used in Little Blue Book sales promotion for almost a year. It is true that *closing out* copy has been used, especially during the early winter months of 1927-1928, but I explain this a little later. This was not sales copy in the usual sense, but a statement of policy – it was thought expedient to close out the Little Blue Books to make room for a new series. Results indicated that the Little Blue Books had not yet reached a saturation point. The public is not weary of the five-cent pocket series, so it is going on – with new advertising that offers only the pick of the list, without a date-line, and without any *hurry-up* sales feature.

To tell the story from the beginning I must go hack to 1919, when the Little Blue Books were in embryo. Or perhaps I should not use that figure, for some of the books were in existence in 1919 – books that were the nucleus of the series that was to be. Perhaps I should say that in 1919 the Little Blue Books were like a very young infant, an infant with promise of robust health, an infant with husky lungs and a loud voice betokening strong adolescence and sturdy manhood. Even now the child is only nine years old – yet it is ready to stand firmly on its own legs, without any special pleading or sensational argument to insure its support.

I ask my readers to bear in mind continually that the Little Blue Books are only nine years old, that even now the series is beginning only its tenth year. This extreme youth throws a helpful light on much of the history of the Little Blue Books. This youth is the real explanation of the experimental eight years or so during which various advertising expedients were genuinely imperative.

In 1919 the Little Blue Books sold for twenty-five cents apiece, then at five for a dollar, and later, as an experiment, they were offered at ten cents each. Each price reduction meant, in effect, that the total distribution must leap up in inverse ratio: if the price were halved, the sales must more than double, and so on. Briefly, this is because the selling expense must be reduced by a larger volume of sales from the greater effectiveness of the new selling point of a lower price. At the same time the initial expense of putting a new title into the list must be diffused over a wider distribution of the books – though the manufacturing cost per book would remain the same until production could be increased to a point where newer and more au¬tomatic machinery could be installed.

This sounds involved. Perhaps I can make it clearer by using a small store as an example. Suppose this store has two clerks, and they are idle more than half the day. Though the store may be paying expenses, and netting a fair percentage on the investment, and though both clerks may be needed to handle the routine, there is a possibility that the store can increase its business, and its profits, by a price reduction. Suppose that the prices are cut twenty-five percent. This is a real inducement for customers to come and buy. If the increased business swells the volume so that the clerks are kept busy, and makes the turnover or disposal of stock twice as rapid as before, the store can be content with a smaller margin of profit on the larger volume of business because the selling expense per dollar has really been reduced. Two clerks now handle twice as much business as they did when they were idle much of the time. The customers get the benefit of the increase in sales, and, reacting to the price reduction, feel more disposed to buy because they are getting more for their money.

Clerks are machinery, and vice versa. It is better for any plant to sell its capacity output at a low price per unit, than to sell only half of its capacity at two or three times that price per unit.

This is, in summary, what has happened to the Little Blue Books. It has been one experiment after another. I have always had to find out if it was possible to increase the distribution sufficiently to justify a reduction in the price. If the eight years from 1919 to 1926 inclusive have seemed to some readers a chaotic succession of last-minute sales, this is because eight years after all are not a very long time.

It was in 1922 that the first five-cent sale was advertised – when the series contained 300 titles. These Little Blue Books, to speak in general terms, cost so much apiece to produce, and at this time they were selling regularly for ten cents each. Of each dime received for each book a large part bad to go to pay the advertising or selling expense – which is the expense of informing the prospective buyer that Little Blue Books are available at such and such a price and placing before him a list of the titles so that he can make his choice. When the books sold for ten cents apiece I was ready to spend five cents of each dime received for them to advertise and sell them.

My problem was just this: Could I attract more buyers at a five-cent price – enough more to enable me to spend only two and a half cents to sell each book, and at the same time enough more to tax my plant's output to capacity and keep the manufacturing cost down? I thought I could. I was ready to try the experiment anyway.

If any of my readers have the impression that Little Blue Books – or any other product – will sell just by being advertised, it is time that they abandoned such a fantastic notion. This point can be reached only after constant repetition of persuasive advertising. A reputation must be built up. A product of wide appeal must be evolved. A sound economic ratio between the selling price and the cost of producing and selling must be reached. All these things require testing – it is inevitably a constant laboratory process of trial and error.

I have pointed out elsewhere that at first the ten-cent price – and then the five-cent price – was so sensational in itself that people bought the books, many books that later became poor sellers, just to get them at that price. From this, slowly but surely, I was to learn what the readers really want – and how to give it to them. The list of 1,260 Little Blue Books now, in 1928, being advertised without date-line persuasion, is the result of this evolution – it has taken almost ten years to bring into existence a series of such wide appeal, and with such a thoroughly established reputation, that the books will sell spontaneously on the mere announcement and printing of the list.

Advertising, to get back to my story, takes various forms – from actual display space in newspapers and magazines to all kinds of catalogues, circulars, letters, and so on – but advertising of some kind is always necessary to place any product before the modern public and find the right market for it. Or even to find out whether the product has a market, and a big enough one to justify its manufacture. This advertising must, furthermore, attract attention – it must get attention and then focus this attention on the merits of the product. If the product is a new one, without a reputation, the attention must be secured by something besides the mere announcement of the product.

I had a ten-cent book to sell, and I wanted to sell the same book for five cents. The more people who knew of the Little Blue Books, the more sensational would any price relating to them become. I could attract attention by the nickel price; the next thing I had to do was to concentrate this attention on the books, and compel immediate action. I was looking ahead, even as far back as 1922, to the day when a Little Blue Book could be sold for five cents post-paid to any address in the world. But to announce this too early would have meant disaster. I could not simply mark down the price and sit back to wait for the public to grab the books for a nickel apiece. For, in the first place, the public would not do it; in the second place, the public would not do it enough.

There is a vast difference in the appeal of a choice of 500 titles, and a choice of 1,260 titles. Ten people could examine a list of 500 titles, and perhaps only five or six will find something to interest them enough to make them spend their money. But the same ten people can examine a list of 1,260 titles, and perhaps as many as eight will find some books to interest them.

But to increase 500 titles to 1,260 is a task. I know, now that it is done, that it could not have been accomplished in the nine years just past without what some people like to call *sensational* advertising. I had my choice of doing it in nine or ten years, or doing it in twenty-five or thirty years. I chose the shorter time.

Incidentally, by 1,260 titles I do not mean just any titles that happen to come along. I mean 1,260 really popular titles. In the nine years of publishing Little Blue Books, nearly 2,000 titles have been in print at some time or other, if you add in all the books that were in print and later were withdrawn to be replaced by other books.

A buyer is phlegmatic when faced with a product that he does not recognize as something he needs. If he sees no reason to grab it, he will take his good time about making a purchase – if he makes one at all. If, in 1922, I had calmly advertised that after the first of February the Little Blue Books would be only five cents each, people would have read the announcement and most of them would have made a mental resolution to buy some one day soon. But how soon? And how many would remember to do it?

Instead of that, I announced a sale – an experimental sale to make a test of the five-cent price. Until a certain date – say March 31st – people could buy the Little Blue Books for five cents each, half price. After midnight of March 31st, the price would go back to ten cents, the usual price.

In this way I made certain that everyone really wanting to buy Little Blue Books for a nickel instead of a dime each would do so by the 31st of March. I also made sure just how many people would respond to each advertisement of the sale, and how soon they would respond – for sales advertising is substantially dead after the date-limit of the sale is passed.

By announcing a sale, with a definite date-limit, I was in effect holding a caucus. I was polling votes for and against the five-cent price for Little Blue Books. All votes had to be in by March 31st. The votes received were affirmative ones; the expense of polling the votes could be considered as standing for negative ones. It was thus a simple matter to figure the manufacturing cost of the books sold during the sale, plus the expense of handling and filling orders, plus the expense of selling whatever books were sold through the sales advertising.

The first five-cent sale of the Little Blue Books did not justify making the nickel a permanent basis for selling the books. On the expiration date the price did indeed go back to ten cents apiece, and in several subsequent sales, when the price was again advertised at five cents, when the volume of sales totals due to the date-line advertising was past, the price reverted of necessity to ten cents for each book.

By this sales policy and date-line advertising through eight experimental years, I galvanized the book-buyer into immediate action. I said to him, in effect: "Here is a bargain—until a certain date you can have it for five cents. After that date the price will be ten cents." He has had to act by the date limit I set, or he has lost the opportunity to act at all.

No, some cynic is saying, he has not lost the opportunity forever – but only until the next sale comes around. My answer to that is that he did not have any assurance that there would ever be another sale. His decision to buy the books during a given sale must always be arrived at from the facts before him. He has an opportunity to buy books for a nickel each until May 30th. Perhaps there will be another opportunity six months later, but this is only speculation. Meanwhile, his attention sharply arrested by the sales copy, he pauses to look over the books. He finds some, probably, that he would like to have. If he orders them before May 30th, they will cost five cents each. If he tarries until after that date, he is told in very clear language that they will cost him twice as much. If he wants the books and has the money to buy them, the chances are much in favor of his sending his order before the closing date.

The five-cent price remained uncertain for nearly eight years. During a date-line sale the five-cent price would be justified, but as soon as business

258

dwindled after the sale – as it always must, unless other advertising is sufficiently compelling to carry on the volume – the five-cent price would be expensive to maintain. Because I knew that somewhere there was the right ratio between selling price, cost of manufacturing and selling, and number of titles for choice – and that it was my job to discover this ratio – I even tried a few sales with the price as low as four cents, and once as low as three cents. The increased business on these two lower prices, however, was not enough to indicate that they are feasible.

As a matter of fact, at one time – it was in the early summer of 1925 – I came near to facing failure. The distribution for the year, to the first of May, was not enough to warrant continuing the Little Blue Books at five cents each. To go back to a higher price at that time, when I thought the permanent five-cent unit price was in sight, would have meant ruin. My only course was to go ahead – which meant to find out for certain if the Little Blue Books were doomed. If the five-cent price were not swiftly vindicated I would have to quit.

I know that many readers have not forgotten that I threatened to quit at that time. I said to them, through my advertising: "I shall stop publishing the Little Blue Books – unless you send me enough orders to prove to me that the books are still wanted. You have until June 30th to mail your order. Let me know your answer on or before that date." These were not the words I used, but they are the gist of my announcement.

This sale was sincere enough. I either had to sell the books – or stop making them. I gave the public its choice – if the orders during the sale had not passed beyond a certain deadline, I would have kept my word and quit. Even as it was, I kept my word, for I found out that the orders passed far beyond the deadline, and that the clamor was for the Little Blue Books to go on. This sale, indeed, put 1925 over with a distribution a little better than the previous year – I am proud that each year has been a little better than the last.

The sales headlines were true, and they did the work. People read these Little Blue Book advertisements and checked off the books they wanted – because they wanted to get them before they were all gone. These same people mailed their orders before the closing date, because they did not want to be left out. This was encouraging – for it showed that the time would yet come when the Little Blue Books could attract enough attention without *hurry-up* slogans and date-lines to keep on with mass production and a five-cent price.

The next sale was in the winter of 1925-1926, closing February 28th, 1926. It was during 1925 that investigations showed that any classic, just because it was offered in a five-cent edition, would not sell in large quantities. I have described in the chapter entitled "The Hospital," and further in that called "The Morgue," how failing Little Blue Books were either saved or killed. But I did not like to withdraw those classics without giving Little Blue Book readers a chance to express an opinion on the change of policy – via orders for books they really wanted.

The reason for this sale was the change of policy implied in withdrawing certain books and replacing them with more popular titles. I did not advertise exactly which books were to be withdrawn – for I did not know myself. I knew that certain titles would have to go if the sale did not improve their showing, but even I had to wait for the results of the sale before I could be sure.

The attention of the public was drawn to the advertising of this sale as though by a magnet. Date-line copy is sound sales psychology, beyond any possible doubt. If you have until February 28th to act, you will act before then if you really want to benefit by it. The entire list of Little Blue Books was printed during this sale, and it was announced that after February 28th many of them would be withdrawn, never to be reprinted. The avalanche of orders showed that people did not want Little Blue Books to be withdrawn, but –

This *But* is a big one. The public proved to my satisfaction that Little Blue Books were wanted, but the public, in making its selection from the complete list of books, proved also that it wanted what had already been shown to be the most popular books. Most of the titles that had failed during 1925 continued to lag behind in the sale. When given their choice, the people bought the books that my experience had taught me were of widest appeal.

I have withdrawn those books, as I said I would. This is shown by even

260

a cursory comparison of my listings in January, 1926, with my new listings for January, 1928. The differences are wide and often drastic. More than 200 books have been withdrawn or in some way popularized during the two-year interval. More than 400 books have been altered at least in the title or the listing in the catalogue.

This 1925-1926 sale proved conclusively that a sale justified by necessary revision or alteration of policy would make that policy even more desirable by confirming it. Though the people responded to the date-line sales advertising because they wanted to get the books that appealed to them *before any books whatever were withdrawn*, less than five percent of the people ordered any of the books actually slated to be killed (unless the new sales copy improved their showing). The sale told me what I wanted to know and I went ahead on that information. I should add, also, that by *popularizing* the series of Little Blue Books I have never meant lowering their standard or in any way vulgarizing the list.

Even during the eight experimental years, I gave copy other than date-line sales copy a chance. I kept testing out straight advertising, copy without any sales feature as persuasion, but until the latter part of 1927 it never paid out. Until that time only imperative headlines, *hurry-up* copy, was sufficiently forceful to goad buyers into immediate action and keep the yearly turnover of the Little Blue Books enough to justify their production for a nickel apiece. I say again that sales copy of this kind, insisting that the books had to be bought by a given date or not at all, is all that made possible 1,260 different titles in only nine years.

During the spring and summer of 1927 small (less than full page) advertisements were used, listing books of certain classifications only, making special drives on their particular appeal. I shall discuss in another place the success of this form of sales promotion for the Little Blue Books. What I wish to point out here is that no sales copy – no date-line – was used.

Then, when it became necessary to plan the advertising policy for the fall of 1927 and the winter of 1927-1928 a serious situation was revealed. Sales had dropped alarmingly during the late spring, compared with what the year should show if the Little Blue Books were to keep up the pace necessary to keep them alive. Something must be behind it – was I facing

261

failure again?

The situation in the automobile market was a keynote to popular feeling. I thought that the people might also be weary of a standardized five-cent book, as they appeared to be of Henry Ford's Model T. It seemed that a more expensive book might be wanted – which is to say a *better looking* book, for the contents are as excellent as they can be now – and I thought that the time might have come for abandoning the Little Blue Books entirely in favor of a more expensive series.

The advertising policy was determined by these conditions. I embodied these general conclusions in the fall and winter advertising campaign. I had somewhat over six million books in my warehouse; those in the process of manufacture would bring this to over seven million. If I really had to start another series, I must first sell these books. Why not test the public's feelings in the matter? Why not ask people if they wanted these books?

So the advertising said that the Little Blue Books would be discontinued for a bigger and better looking series of more expensive books. But here is the important fact about this advertising – it carried no date-line whatever. I said the Little Blue Books would be discontinued when they were sold out, but I did not give any date. I even *guaranteed* to fill every order received from this advertising. The readers were not persuaded by any dictatorial headlines as they had been in the past – but they were given their choice of the most popular Little Blue Books, while they might last

The first returns from the early fall advertising were very encouraging. I began to suspect that the standardized five-cent book had not yet outlived its popularity. Later returns confirmed this – the response, finally, saved the Little Blue Books. Thousands of letters, besides the orders, poured in from all over the country and even from foreign lands protesting against the cessation of the series. "Start a new series," the usual recommendation was, "but let the Little Blue Books go on."

The significance of this latest advertising campaign is far-reaching. It means that the Little Blue Books have at last reached that happy ratio between selling price, manufacturing and selling cost, and scope of choice, which makes them alluring without date-lines and without any *hurry-up* sales feature.

The Passing Of The Sales Policy

In fact, the 1928 campaign began with straight copy – a complete list of 1,260 books, a catalogue printed on a full-sized newspaper page – and this copy is more than holding its own against the previous record of date-line sales copy. Here are the figures for the Chicago *Tribune* in which a full page, listing all the books, appeared Tuesday morning, January 10, 1928:

First Day returns from Jan. 10, 1928, no sales feature, $320. First Day returns from next best previous insertion, with date-line sales feature, $265.

In keyed advertising such as I use for selling the Little Blue Books, it can always be assumed that the first day's returns will indicate the general outcome of the entire run of returns from that advertisement. The preceding figures show that this 1928 page will surpass the result of any previous advertisement in the same paper.

This late 1927 campaign, indeed, was so successful that I quickly made the decision to go on with the Little Blue Books, and those titles selling out quickest were rushed to the presses again to fill the rush of orders. No one was disappointed. Now the first part of 1928 is busy largely with the preparation of new catalogues, of this new advertising copy without a date-line and without any sales feature – advertising that has shown itself to be the right kind at last. In the tenth year of the Little Blue Books they have reached their goal – more than 1,200 titles at five cents each postpaid to any address in the world.

I realize that my past policy of selling Little Blue Books through date-line sales was considered by many to be objectionable. I am sure, though, that those people did not grasp the experimental nature of the series during that time. They forgot that the books had been in existence only five or six or seven years. They did not remember, in fact, that the series came into existence *after* the close of the World War. Surely so far-reaching an enterprise could have been considered experimental even for ten years, instead of slightly more than eight.

Another reason why my sales perhaps seemed to some people so constant is that, in number of agate lines (in which advertising is measured), according to actual figures, I do more national advertising every year than

263

any other book publisher — and my product sells for the least per unit. These two facts explain much.

I can plead plenty of justification. I have already shown that the advertising has never been deceptive, and that it always represented the actual situation. I threatened to withdraw classical Little Blue Books because people did not want them; the people proved they did not want them and I withdrew them. I announced, as a change of policy, that the Little Blue Books would be discontinued to make way for another series; I was told, by the results, that the Little Blue Books were still wanted, and so they are continuing.

The answer to my announcement of this change of policy is even more convincing because the announcement carried no date-line. This told me at once that the time had really come to try *straight* advertising, on the appeal of the books themselves, at the established price of five cents each postpaid anywhere in the world. I am as glad as anyone that 1928 opens without a sales feature in Little Blue Book advertising. The goal has been reached, and it is curious to note that it comes almost simultaneously with the sales total of 100,000,000 books in nine years.

In conclusion, I am not the only publisher who has used sales advertising with a date-line. I am willing to admit that I have used more of it, because my annual advertising runs into a larger figure. I use more mediums, that is. For example, the Little Blue Books have regularly used full page space in newspapers throughout the country. I am the only publisher, indeed, who uses the tabloid newspapers to sell any books whatever of an educational and, avowedly high literary standard. The success of the Little Blue Books in the tabloids is a triumph in itself.

I am sorry if the date-line sales have displeased some of the readers of Little Blue Books. I had to risk displeasing the few in order to reach the many — and thereby keep the Little Blue Books moving ever ahead toward the ultimate goal. That goal seems now to have been reached. I am grateful to the thousands of readers who have made it possible — and I hope that in this chapter I have given a clear exposition of why the sales were also necessary to reach this goal.

The Passing Of The Sales Policy

CPSIA information can be obtained
at www.ICGtesting.com
Printed in the USA
BVHW072138271220
596441BV00005B/302